COMPLETE
FRENCH GRAMMAR
REVIEW

Renée White, M.A.

Greenhill School

Dallas, Texas

Consultant in AP French for the College Board

BARRON'S

Special thanks to my husband for his love and encouragement,
and to my children and grandchildren for having faith in me.

To the memory of Alan.

About the Author

A native French speaker, Renée White holds an M.A. in French Literature from Southern Methodist University. She started the AP French Program, and coordinates international studies, at the Greenhill School in Dallas, Texas. Currently an AP French consultant for The College Board, Ms. White has also been a member of their advisory board for the Southwest Region. A lead consultant for several AP Summer Institutes in the United States, she also conducts workshops on teaching French, both nationally and internationally. Ms. White also authored the Barron's book *How to Prepare for the SAT II French*. Her numerous awards include The College Board's AP Recognition Award, the French Ministry of Education's induction into the order of Chevalier des Palmes Académiques, the National Award for Excellence in Teaching from the American Association of Teachers of French, and the French Teacher of the Year by the Texas Foreign Language Association.

© Copyright 2007 by Barron's Educational Series, Inc.

All inquiries should be addressed to:
Barron's Educational Series, Inc.
250 Wireless Boulevard
Hauppauge, NY 11788
www.barronseduc.com

Library of Congress Control Card 2006026223

ISBN-13: 978-0-7641-3445-6
ISBN-10: 0-7641-3445-0

Library of Congress Cataloging-in-Publication Data
White, Renée, 1938–
    Complete French grammar review / by Renée White.
        p. cm. — (Barron's educational series)
    English and French.
    Includes index.
    ISBN-13: 978-0-7641-3445-6
    ISBN-10: 0-7641-3445-0
        1. French language—Grammar. 2. French language—Self-instruction.
    3. French language—Textbooks for foreign speakers—English. I. Title.

PC2112.5.W45   2007
448.2′421—dc22   2006026223

Printed in the United States of America
9 8 7

Contents

PART IV: *Appendices* 301

Introduction

As a child, I used to think grammar was dull. However, I soon realized that, because of its crucial role in the learning of a language, its mastery was necessary if I wanted to become proficient. Grammar doesn't have to be boring! I have learned from my many years of teaching French that explanations that are not ambiguous, the existence of a large number of examples, fun exercises, and a personal touch can make a world of difference.

Designed for intermediate and advanced levels of French, this book offers a wide range of exercises, including some that are oral. As a result, the students may practice what they have learned by writing or speaking. They can record their answers and also apply their newly acquired knowledge to conversations with a classmate. The directions for all exercises are in French. This aims at building confidence and further enhancing proficiency. Answers to frequently asked questions are also included. In addition, cultural notes provide information on France and other French-speaking countries. On a lighter note, at the end of each chapter, there are crossword or word search puzzles that reinforce what has been studied.

At the back of the book, more idiomatic expressions as well as some slang are introduced. These are taken from "everyday" French so that students can feel more comfortable in a French-speaking environment. Some common proverbs follow, together with their English equivalents. Proverbs not only give a cultural dimension to a language, but they are also fun to study.

Some synonyms and antonyms are provided that will help enrich the students' knowledge of vocabulary. These are followed by a list of cognates, some of which are slightly different from their English counterparts but are still recognizable. Cognates make for better understanding of a foreign language. A list of false cognates follows—it is crucial to be familiar with some of them in order to avoid common language traps!

Also included is a list of verbs and their conjugations.

At the back of the book, you will find a list of frequently used vocabulary that can be used for reference, answers to all of the exercises, as well as solutions for all the crossword and word search puzzles.

PART I:
Reviewing and Practicing the Basics

1

French Pronunciation and Spelling

Vowels
Les voyelles

Vowels are sounds that are pronounced without using the lips or the tongue. In English there are five vowels (**a**, **e**, **i**, **o**, **u**), whereas in French there are six vowels:

A E I O U Y

The French **y** is pronounced like **i** and, therefore, is also considered a vowel.

3

Vowels	Pronunciation	Examples
a	Similar to the "a" sound in *father* or *ah!*	**malade**/*ill* **sale**/*dirty*
e*	Similar to the "u" sound in *fur*.	**petit**/*small* **venir**/*to come*
i	Similar to the "i" sound in *machine*.	**mille**/*one thousand* **vite**/*quickly*
o	Similar to the "o" sound in *sorry*.	**fort**/*strong* **dehors**/*outside*
u	There is no similar sound in English. The French "u" sound is obtained by clenching the teeth, saying "ee" then pursing the lips while continuing to say "ee." This sound will change into the French "u" sound.	**pur**/*pure* **jupe**/*skirt*
y**	Similar to the English "y" in *yogurt*.	**lycée**/*high school* **gymnaste**/*gymnast*

*When the vowel **e** (without an accent) is placed at the end of a word, it is usually not pronounced. It is called a *mute e* or **e muet**.
The letter **y is called **i grec** or *Greek i* because it was used in Latin to represent the Greek letter *epsilon*.

When Vowels Follow Each Other

Vowels	Pronunciation	Examples
ai	"eh"	**mais**/*but*
au	"oh"	**faute**/*mistake*
ou	"oo"	**chou**/*cabbage*
eau	"o"	**beau**/*beautiful (handsome)*
eu	"u" (as in *fur*)	**peu**/*little (quantity)*
oi	"wah"	**moi**/*me*
oeu	"euh" (as in *nerve*)	**oeuf**/*egg*
oei	"euh-i" (pronounced as in *foil* but replacing the "o" sound with "euh")	**oeil**/*eye*

VOWELS AND ACCENTS

French vowels are often topped with an accent (à, é, è, ï, ô, û).

The **accent aigu (é)** or acute accent is only used over the letter **e.** It is pronounced "ay," as in *hay* (**étudier**/*to study*).

The **accent grave (`)** or grave accent can be used on the letters **a, e, u.** When topped with an **accent grave (è)**, **e** is pronounced as the "ai" in *hair*. For the letters **a** and **u**, the accent grave helps to distinguish between two words that are alike but have different meanings: **à** (*at*) and **a** (*has*).

The **accent circonflexe (^)** or circumflex accent is used on **a, e, i,** and **u.** In most cases, it replaces the **s** that used to follow the vowel (**hôpital**/*hospital*). As for the accent grave, it is sometimes used to distinguish between two words that are alike but have different meanings: **du** (**de** + **le**/*some*) and **dû** (past participle of **devoir**).

The **tréma (¨)** is used over **e, i,** and **u** to indicate that the two vowels that are next to each other are pronounced individually: **Noël** (*Christmas*).

NOTE
Accents are not necessary over capital letters.

QUICK PRACTICE

I. Prononcez les mots suivants.

1. seau (bucket)
2. parle (speak)
3. peau (skin)
4. fou (crazy)
5. hôte (host)
6. note (note/grade)
7. mai (May)
8. poli (polite)
9. bureau (desk/office)
10. carré (square)

Consonants
Les consonnes

The consonants in French are the same as those in English except for the letter **y**.

B C D F G H J
K L M N P Q R
S T V W X Z

CONSONANTS	PRONUNCIATION	EXAMPLES
b	"beh"	**beau**/*beautiful* **banal**/*banal*
c (before **e**, **i**, **y**)	"say," similar to the letter **s** in English.	**cinéma**/*cinema* **cent**/*hundred*
c (before **a**, **o**, **u**)	Similar to the letter **k**.	**copie**/*copy* **café**/*coffee*
ç (before **a**, **o**, **u**)	The **cédille** (*cedilla*) under the **c** is used to change the **k** sound to an **s** sound.	**leçon**/*lesson* **ça**/*this* or *that* **reçu**/*receipt/received*
d	"day," similar to the **d** in English.	**début**/*beginning* **demain**/*tomorrow*
f	"eff," similar to the **f** in English.	**facile**/*easy* **parfait**/*perfect*
g (before **e**, **i**, **y**)	"zsay," similar to the letter **g** in *regime*. This is the soft **g**.	**genre**/*gender/type* **gymnaste**/*gymnast*
g (before **a**, **o**, **u** and before consonants)	Similar to **g** as in *great*. This is the hard **g**.	**gare**/*train station* **garçon**/*boy* **guerre**/*war* **grand**/*tall/big*
h	"awsh." There are two types of pronunciation. • **h muet** or *silent h*. Similar to the **h** in *hour*. Words beginning with a silent **h** are treated like words beginning with a vowel for liaisons. • **h aspiré** or *aspirate h*. The **h** is still not pronounced, but the words are treated like words beginning with a consonant for liaisons. (See section on **liaisons** in this chapter.)	<u>muet</u> **homme**/*man* (pronounced "**om**") **horrible**/*horrible* (pronounced "**orible**") **les hommes** ("**zom**") <u>aspiré</u> **homard**/*lobster* **honte**/*shame* **les homards**/("**omar**")

CONSONTANTS	PRONUNCIATION	EXAMPLES
j	"zsee," pronounced like the soft French g.	jeudi/*Thursday* jeune/*young*
k	"kah." Although it is similar to the letter k in English, it doesn't occur often in French.	kiosque/*kiosk* ski/*ski*
l	"el," similar to the letter l in English but, in the case of French, the tongue hits the upper teeth.	lundi/*Monday* parler/*to speak*
m	"em," similar to the m in English.	mer/*sea* mardi/*Tuesday*
n	"enn," similar to the n in English.	noir/*black* année/*year*
p	"peh," similar to the p in English.	paquet/*package* paire/*pair*
q	"ku," similar to the letter k. Like in English, it is usually followed by u.	qualité/*quality* quand/*when*
r	"err." The r sound in French is guttural. It is pronounced in the back of the throat, using the uvula, as if you were going to gargle.	rose/*pink/rose* rêve/*dream*
s	"ess," similar to the s in English when used at the beginning of a word. When used between two vowels, it is pronounced like a z. The s that indicates the plural of a noun is not pronounced unless the following word begins with a vowel, in which case it is pronounced as a z (**liaison**).	souple/*supple* salade/*salad* désir/*desire*
t	"teh," similar to the t in English (except the tongue goes on the upper teeth, unlike English where the tongue goes behind the upper teeth).	table/*table* timide/*shy*
v	"veh," similar to the v in English.	vache/*cow* avare/*stingy*
w	**double veh**. Pronounced like a v or like a w. Words that contain a w usually come from English, German, or Slavic languages.	wagon/*train car* (v) week-end/*week-end* (w)
x	"eex," pronounced as "gz" except in the numbers **six** and **dix** where it is pronounced as an s ("siss/diss").	xylophone/*xylophone* exiger/*to require*
z	"zed," similar to the z in English.	zèbre/*zebra* zero/*zero*

PRONUNCIATION OF NASAL SOUNDS

- **ain/aim**   Similar to the **an** sound in *hand* without pronouncing the **n**.

  pain /*bread*
  faim/*hunger*

- **an**   Similar to the nasal sound in *on* without pronouncing the **n**.

  écran/*screen*
  antenne/*antenna*

- **en**   Similar to **an**, but the mouth is rounded a little more.

  enfant/*child*
  cent/*one hundred*

- **in/im**   Similar to **ain**, but the mouth is rounded a little more.

  vin/*wine*
  important/*important*

- **on/om**   To make this sound, say first **an** then almost close the mouth to form a circle. It is similar to the nasal sound in *own*, without pronouncing the **n**.

  bon/*good*
  nom/*name*

- **un**   Similar to the nasal sound **euh**.

  un/*one/a*
  lundi/*Monday*

WHEN TWO CONSONANTS FOLLOW EACH OTHER

Consonants	Pronunciation	Examples
ch	Similar to the English **sh**.	**chocolat**/*chocolate* **chéri**/*darling*
sc	Before **e** and **i**, it is pronounced like an **s**. Before **a, o, u**, it is pronounced **sk**.	**scénario**/*scenario* (**s**) **scier**/*to saw* (**s**) **escaliers**/*stairs* (**sk**) **scorpion**/*scorpion* (**sk**) **sculpter**/*to sculpt* (**sk**)
gn	Similar to the "ny" sound in *canyon*.	**campagne**/*countryside* **signe**/*sign*
th	It is pronounced like a **t**.	**thé**/*tea* **thème**/*theme*
pn	Unlike English where, at the beginning of a word, only the **n** is pronounced, both the **p** and the **n** must be pronounced in French.	**pneu**/*tire* **pneumonie**/*pneumonia*

Consonants	Pronunciation	Examples
ps	Unlike English where, at the beginning of a word, only the **s** is pronounced, both the **p** and the **s** must be pronounced in French.	**psychiatre**/*psychiatrist* **pseudo**/*pseudo*

TIP

The combination of the letters t and i, followed by a vowel and then a consonant, as in nation, is pronounced "see-oh" ("nassion").

La révolution ("rayvolusee-oh")—*the revolution*

The combination of the letters q and u is pronounced like a k. As an example, qua in qualité (*quality*) is pronounced "ka".

Qui ("key")—*who*

The -ent present ending for the third person plural of a verb ending in -er in the infinitive, such as parler, aimer, etc. is not pronounced. It has the same role as a *mute e,* or e muet.

Ils parlent. ("parl")—*They speak.*

In verbs ending in -ger in the infinitive, the first person plural (nous) of the present indicative keeps the e before adding an -ons ending, in order to obtain the *soft g* sound. This also applies to the imperfect and passé simple conjugations before the letter a.

Nous mangeons. ("zsoh")—Je mangeais. ("zsay")/*We eat.—I was eating.*

The last consonant of a word is not pronounced in French.

le bruit ("brwee")—*the noise*
les élèves ("eh-lev")—*the pupils/students*

Exceptions: le tennis ("tennis" as in English, but the stress is on the second syllable)
donc ("donk")—*therefore, so*

QUICK PRACTICE

II. Lisez et prononcez les mots suivants. S'il le faut, servez-vous du dictionnaire.

1. hybride

2. brun

3. quantité

4. compagnon

5. théâtre

6. maison

7. gagner

8. psychologue

Liaisons
Liaisons

A **liaison** is the relation between two consecutive sounds. When a consonant that is normally silent at the end of a word is followed by a word beginning with a vowel or a mute **h**, this consonant is pronounced.

Le**s** enfants/*the children*	→	the **s** is pronounced like a **z**.
Deu**x** arbres/*two trees*	→	the **x** is pronounced like a **z**.
U**n** étudiant/*a student*	→	the **n** is linked to the word **étudiant**.
Quan**d** il parle/*When he speaks*	→	the **d** is pronounced like a **t**.
Ils von**t** aller/*They are going to go*	→	the **t** is linked to the verb **aller**.
Le**s** hommes/*the men*	→	the **s** is pronounced like a **z**.

NOTE
s, **x**, and **z** are always pronounced **z** in a liaison.

However, there is no liaison . . .

after **et**	→	**Lui et elle** ("lui ay elle")
after an aspirate **h**	→	**un héros** ("un ayro")
after an inverted question	→	**ont-ils étudié** ("oht-il aytudiay")
after a noun in the singular	→	**un enfant aimable** ("enfan aimable")
before the number **onze**	→	**ils ont onze ans** ("ilzoh onz an")
after **quand** before an inversion	→	**quand ont-ils lu** ("kah ont-ils")

QUICK PRACTICE

III. Lisez les phrases suivantes à haute voix (*aloud*)**. S'il le faut, servez-vous du dictionnaire.**

1. Les amis vont aller au théâtre.

2. Philippe et Annie font des achats.

3. Vont-ils apporter des fleurs?

4. L'enfant a des jouets.

5. Elles vendent onze livres.

6. Il y a des arbres dans le jardin.

7. Quand as-tu acheté la voiture?

8. Les huttes sont petites. (*aspirate h*)

9. Elle est en France.

10. Ils ont dix ans.

> **NOTE**
> When speaking French, the stress is always put on the last syllable.
>
> Compare: **American**
>   **Américain**

Homophones
Homophones

Homophones are words that sound exactly the same but are spelled differently and represent different things. Here are some examples.

French Word	Pronunciation	English Equivalent
autel	"o-tel"	*altar*
hôtel	"o-tel"	*hotel*
cent	"sah"	*hundred*
sans	"sah"	*without*
sang	"sah"	*blood*
sens-sens-sent	"sah"	1st, 2nd, 3rd persons singular of *to smell*

French Word	Pronunciation	English Equivalent
cour	"coor"	*courtyard/court*
cours	"coor"	*course*
court	"coor"	*short*
dans	"dah"	*in*
dent	"dah"	*tooth*
elle	"el"	*she*
elles	"el"	*they* (feminine)
aile	"el"	*wing*
foi	"fwah"	*faith*
foie	"fwah"	*liver*
fois	"fwah"	*time*
il	"il"	*he/it*
ils	"il"	*they* (masculine)
île	"il"	*island*
j'ai	"zsay"	*I have*
jet	"zsay"	*gush, spurt* (liquid)
geai	"zsay"	*jay* (bird)
jais	"zsay"	*jet* (black stone)
mais	"meh"	*but*
mai	"meh"	*May*
mes	"meh"	*my*
maire	"mair"	*mayor*
mer	"mair"	*sea*
mère	"mair"	*mother*
nom	"noh"	*name*
non	"noh"	*no*
pair	"pear"	*peer*
paire	"pear"	*pair*
père	"pear"	*father*
quand	"kah"	*when*
camp	"kah"	*camp*
Caen	"kah"	*Caen* (French city)
qui	"key"	*who*
quille	"key"	*bowling pin*

QUICK PRACTICE

IV. Mettez le mot qui manque. Choisissez dans la liste de droite:

1. Le dîner est prêt _____ je n'ai pas faim.
2. Je vais acheter une _____ de chaussures.
3. J'aime beaucoup le _____ de ce village.
4. C'est la première _____ que je mange du lapin.
5. Elle n'aime pas le _____ de mathématiques.

a. maire
b. cours
c. mais
d. fois
e. paire

LES HOMOPHONES

O	T	L	U	A	C	N	J	V	A	E	A	T	G	K
W	W	I	N	P	M	A	C	N	U	U	K	M	E	L
L	N	I	E	C	O	U	R	T	U	W	T	R	N	E
M	Z	L	F	S	K	S	J	X	X	R	E	E	Y	T
E	F	H	O	Z	N	W	I	C	B	M	U	D	L	O
K	L	J	I	D	Q	A	U	A	B	P	Q	U	H
Z	G	L	S	Z	H	T	S	L	J	L	L	W	N	H
I	D	A	I	Z	B	N	T	C	F	R	E	M	F	F
F	N	M	R	U	B	E	O	U	L	X	J	C	F	T
M	R	S	X	T	Q	C	K	E	P	M	M	V	Q	O
W	I	H	E	P	R	E	F	Z	G	A	O	Z	K	L
T	X	G	Z	T	X	O	N	R	Q	E	R	O	V	L
X	E	H	S	Y	I	Z	F	U	K	P	G	B	F	K
L	D	J	K	E	Q	L	G	B	E	L	K	E	D	B
J	B	N	Z	T	A	N	N	Y	H	P	W	Z	Z	K

AUTEL   JAIS   UN CAMP

CENT   JET   UNE FOIS

COURT   MER   UNE QUILLE

HOTEL   SANS

PART II:
Reviewing and
Practicing the Verbs

2

The Present Tense
of Regular Verbs

Que savez-vous déjà?
What Do You Know Already? (?)

What is the correct pronoun for the following conjugated verbs?

1. _____ finissez   6. _____ appellent

2. _____ achètes   7. _____ essaies

3. _____ espérons   8. _____ hésites

4. _____ voyagent   9. _____ choisit

5. _____ attend   10. _____ réussissez

In French, the present tense corresponds to three different forms in English:

Je parle. = I speak—I am speaking—I do speak

There are three conjugations for regular verbs, depending on the ending of the verb in the infinitive:

-**er** ending verbs such as   →   **parler** or verbs of the first group.
-**ir** ending verbs such as   →   **finir** or verbs of the second group.
-**re** ending verbs such as   →   **répondre** or verbs of the third group.

The present tense of regular verbs is formed by dropping the infinitive ending (-**er**, -**ir**, -**re**) and adding the present tense endings.

	PARLER	FINIR	RÉPONDRE
je	parle	finis	réponds
tu	parles	finis	réponds
il/elle/on*	parle	finit	répond
nous	parlons	finissons	répondons
vous	parlez	finissez	répondez
ils/elles	parlent	finissent	répondent

*The pronoun **on** means *we, you, they, people, one*. It is always conjugated in the third person singular.

OTHER REGULAR -ER VERBS

adorer	to adore/to love	mener	to lead
aimer*	to love	monter	to go up
allumer	to light	montrer	to show
amener*	to bring (people)	oublier	to forget
apporter*	to bring (things)	passer	to pass, spend time
appeler	to call	penser*	to think
arriver	to arrive	porter	to carry
chanter	to sing	préparer	to prepare
chercher*	to look for	présenter*	to present
continuer	to continue	quitter*	to leave (place/person)
danser	to dance	raconter	to tell (a story),
décider	to decide		to relate something
défier*	to challenge	regarder	to look at
demander*	to ask	regretter	to regret
deviner	to guess	rencontrer	to meet
dîner	to dine	renseigner	to inform
donner	to give	rentrer	to go back inside,
écouter	to listen to		to return to a place,
emmener*	to take along		to take back inside
emporter*	to take along	retourner	to return
entrer*	to enter	retrouver	to find, to meet (by
étudier	to study		appointment or date)
fermer	to close	saluer	to greet
garder	to keep	téléphoner*	to telephone
habiter*	to live (somewhere)	terminer	to finish
hésiter*	to hesitate	travailler	to work
hériter*	to inherit	trouver	to find
inviter	to invite	utiliser	to use
laisser*	to leave behind	voler*	to fly, to steal
manquer*	to miss	voter	to vote

*Most -er ending verbs are regular in French with the exception of the verb **aller**.

Verbs with Spelling Changes
Verbes avec changement d'orthographe

- **Verbs ending in -cer such as commencer (to begin)**

Je commence	**Nous commençons**
Tu commences	Vous commencez
Il/elle/on commence	Ils/elles commencent

Some other verbs: **annoncer** (*to announce*), **déplacer** (*to move or displace*), **placer** (*to place*), **prononcer** (*to pronounce*), **remplacer** (*to replace or substitute*).

- **Verbs ending in -ger such as manger (*to eat*)**

Je mange	**Nous mangeons**
Tu manges	Vous mangez
Il/elle/on mange	Ils/elles mangent

  Some other verbs: **changer** (*to change*), **corriger** (*to correct*), **déranger** (*to disturb*), **nager** (*to swim*), **voyager** (*to travel*).

- **Verbs ending in -yer such as essayer (*to try*)**

J'essaie	Nous essayons
Tu essaies	Vous essayez
Il/elle/on essaie	**Ils/elles essaient**

  Some other verbs: **envoyer** (*to send*), **employer** (*to employ*), **payer** (*to pay*), **nettoyer** (*to clean*).

- **Verbs ending in -eler such as appeler (*to call*)**

J'appelle	Nous appelons
Tu appelles	Vous appelez
Il/elle/on appelle	**Ils/elles appellent**

  Some other verbs: **épeler** (*to spell*), **rappeler** (*to call back, to remind*).

- **Verbs ending in -eter such as jeter (*to throw*)**

Je jette	Nous jetons
Tu jettes	Vous jetez
Il/elle/on jette	**Ils/elles jettent**

  Some other verbs: **projeter** (*to plan*), **rejeter** (*to reject*).

- **Verbs ending in -e + consonant + -er such as acheter (*to buy*)**

J'achète	Nous achetons
Tu achètes	Vous achetez
Il/elle/on achète	**Ils/elles achètent**

  Some other verbs: **lever** (*to lift or raise something*), **élever** (*to raise something to a certain level as in to raise one's voice, to erect, to raise a child*), **enlever** (*to remove*), **peser** (*to weigh*), **amener** (*to bring someone*), **emmener** (*to take along*).

- **Verbs ending in -é + consonant + -er such as espérer (*to hope*)**

J'espère	Nous espérons
Tu espères	Vous espérez
Il/elle/on espère	Ils/elles espèrent

  Some other verbs: **céder** (*to give up something to someone, to abandon*), **célébrer** (*to celebrate*), **préférer** (*to prefer*), **répéter** (*to repeat*).

TIP

aimer = *to love*, aimer bien = *to like*

> J'aime mes parents.—J'aime ce bracelet.—J'aime bien ce garçon.—
> J'aime ton sac.

amener = *to bring someone*

apporter = *to bring something*

> Elle apporte son album pour le montrer à ses amis.

chercher = *to look for something or someone*. It is important to note that the *for* is included; therefore, one doesn't say Je cherche pour mon livre but Je cherche mon livre. Chercher is also used idiomatically to say that one is picking up somebody from somewhere:

> Je vais chercher ma soeur à l'aéroport. *I am going to pick up my sister at the airport.*

défier = *to challenge*. When défier is followed by the preposition à + a noun, it means to challenge in a competition. Je défie mon copain à la course. When it is followed by the preposition de plus an infinitive, it implies that the person referred to will not be up to the challenge. Je te défie de prouver que j'ai tort.

demander = *to ask for something* (Demander quelque chose).

> Je demande l'heure.

demander à quelqu'un = *to ask someone*

> Je demande l'heure à mon amie.

emmener = *to take along someone*

emporter = *to take along something*

> Il emmène son frère à l'école.
> N'oublie pas d'emporter ton parapluie.

> **Other uses of** emporter: s'emporter = *to lose one's temper*
> à emporter = *to take out (as in take out food)*

entrer = before a noun, the verb entrer is followed by dans. Note that, in English, one would say *I enter the stadium* whereas in French, it is J'entre dans le stade.

habiter = *to live somewhere*. One can say: J'habite Paris, or J'habite à Paris, as well as J'habite un bel appartement or J'habite dans un bel appartement.

hésiter = *to hesitate*. It is followed by à before a verb and by entre when there is a choice between two things.

> Elle hésite à quitter sa famille.—Elle hésite entre ces deux voitures.

hériter = *to inherit*. It is used with the preposition de before the name of a person and can be used with or without de before the name of a thing.

> J'ai hérité de ma tante.
> J'ai hérité d'une maison.—J'ai hérité une maison.

habiter, hésiter, hériter **all begin with a mute** h **and must be pronounced** "abiter, ésiter, ériter."

laisser = *to leave something or someone behind*

> J'ai laissé mon livre sur la table.

TIP (continued)

manquer = *to miss.* When followed by the preposition à plus a person, it means *to be missed by.* When followed by de it means *to lack.*

J'ai manqué mon train. *I missed my train.*
Tu me manques. *I miss you.* (literally: *you are missed by me*)
Il manque de patience. *He is lacking in patience.*

penser = **this verb changes meaning depending on the preposition that follows:**

Je pense à mes amis. *I think about my friends.*
Que penses-tu de ce film? *What do you think about this movie?* (opinion)

présenter = *to present, to introduce, to show*

Je présente mon billet au contrôleur. *I show my ticket to the conductor.*
Je présente ma fiancée à mes amis. *I introduce my fiancée to my friends.*

quitter = *to leave a place or a person (or persons)*

J'ai quitté Paris il y a trois jours—Elle a quitté sa famille à l'âge de 18 ans.

téléphoner = *to telephone.* It is always followed by the prepositon à. In English you would say *I telephone my friends* but in French it is Je téléphone à mes amis.

tourner = *to turn.* In the expression tourner un film it means *to film a movie.*

voler = depending on the context, voler can mean either *to fly* or *to steal.* However, in French, when it means *to fly,* it cannot be used with a direct object.

I fly a plane. = Je pilote un avion.
The plane flies. = L'avion vole.
The bird flies. = L'oiseau vole.

OTHER REGULAR -IR VERBS

agir*	to act	nourrir	to feed
applaudir	to applaud	obéir	to obey
atterrir*	to land	pâlir	to turn pale
avertir	to warn	périr	to perish
chérir	to cherish	punir	to punish
choisir	to choose	réfléchir	to ponder/reflect
désobéir	to disobey	remplir	to fill
définir	to define	réunir	to (re)unite
établir	to establish	réussir*	to succeed
fournir*	to supply	rougir	to blush
guérir	to get well, cure	salir	to dirty
grossir	to gain weight	unir	to unite, join
maigrir	to lose weight	vieillir	to grow old

agir = *to act, to behave*. To act in a play is jouer.

> Il agit bien envers ses amis. *He behaves well toward his friends.*
> Il joue dans une comédie musicale. *He acts(performs) in a musical comedy.*

s'agir de means *to be about*. It is only used in the third person singular:
Il s'agit de.

> Il s'agit d'un film de guerre. *It is about a war movie.*
> De quoi s'agit-il? *What is it about?*

atterrir = *to land (a plane or by plane)*

> L' avion doit atterrir à 8 heures. *The plane must land at 8 o'clock.*
> (It does not apply to expressions such as *to land on one's feet*, which translates into retomber sur ses pieds.)

fournir = *to supply*, as in supplying a restaurant with groceries, or supplying information. To furnish an apartment is meubler un appartement.

réussir = *to succeed, achieve something, or pass a test*. Usually followed by the preposition à when referring to an exam.

> Elle réussit à tous ses examens. *She passes all her tests.*
> Son idée va certainement réussir. *His idea will certainly succeed.*
> *To take a test* = passer un examen

OTHER REGULAR -RE VERBS

attendre*	to wait for	pendre	to hang
confondre*	to confuse	prétendre*	to claim, to maintain
défendre*	to forbid/defend	rendre	to give back
dépendre*	to depend	répondre	to answer
descendre*	to go down	suspendre	to hang something
entendre*	to hear	tendre*	to stretch, to tighten up, to extend
étendre	to spread,hang/ stretch out		
		tondre	to mow, to crop (hair)
fondre*	to melt	vendre	to sell
interrompre*	to interrupt		

TIP

attendre = there is no preposition that follows this verb in French.

J'attends le train. *I wait for the train.*

confondre = *to confuse, to mix up*

Il m'a confondu avec mon cousin. *He took me for my cousin.*
to be confused is translated by ne pas comprendre
être confus(e) is translated by *to be embarrassed*

défendre = when meaning *to forbid*, it is followed by the prepositon à before a person and de before an infinitive.

Elle défend à Pierre de sortir sans son imper. *She forbids Pierre to go out without his raincoat.*

When meaning *to defend*, it is not followed by a preposition.

Elle défend son pays. *She defends her country.*

entendre = When used in the pronominal form, it means *to get along*

Jeanne et Claire s'entendent bien. *Jeanne and Claire get along well.*

dépendre = *to depend.* Before a noun, it is followed by the preposition de.

Nous dépendons de nos parents. *We depend on our parents.* Cela dépend des résultats de mon examen. *It depends on the results of my test.*

descendre = *to go down.* When used with a direct object, it means *to take down.*

Ils descendent tous les jours à 4 heures. *They go down every day at 4 o'clock.*
Elle descend la valise. *She takes the suitcase down.*

fondre = *to melt or to dissolve.* The idiomatic expression fondre en larmes literally translates into *melt into tears* (better translated by *burst into tears*).

interrompre = *to interrupt.* Although regular, this verb has a slight change in conjugation for the 3rd person singular: il interrompt.

prétendre = should not be confused with *to pretend*, which translates into faire semblant de.

Ils prétendent être bons en maths. *They claim to be good in math.*
Je prétends que ce n'est pas vrai. *I maintain that it isn't true.*

tendre = *to stretch out or extend, to tighten up.*

Elle me tend la main. *She extends her hand (holds out) to me.*
Il tend ses muscles. *He tightens his muscles.*

QUICK PRACTICE

I. Conjuguez les verbes entre parenthèses à la forme qui convient—attention aux accents!

1. Nous (réfléchir)_____ toujours avant de parler.

2. Vous (chanter) _____ très bien.

3. Je (payer) _____ dix euros à la vendeuse.

4. Nous (nager) _____ toujours en été.

5. La glace (fondre)_____ parce qu'il fait chaud.

6. Il (punir) _____ les élèves.

7. Elle (acheter) _____ la robe bleue.

8. Nous (espérer) _____ voir ce film.

9. Ils (rejeter) _____ ce concept.

10. Tu (appeler)_____ ton frère le dimanche.

II. Choisissez un des verbes de la liste et complétez les phrases qui suivent.

essayer	entrer	applaudir
quitter	manger	hésiter
rougir	maigrir	commencer
descendre	défier	laisser

1. Nous _____ toujours à midi.

2. Je _____ mon livre sur la table.

3. Ils _____ dans la salle de classe à 8h30.

4. Ils _____ Paris en décembre.

5. Elle _____ sa collègue de prouver sa théorie.

6. Nous _____ le ténor à la fin du concert.

7. Elle _____ quand on lui fait un compliment.

8. Tu _____ au rez-de-chaussée (*ground floor, first floor*).

9. Il _____ parce qu'il est malade.

10. Elle _____ d'ouvrir la porte mais c'est impossible.

11. Vous _____ entre ces deux solutions.

12. Nous _____ ce chapitre demain.

III. Répondez aux questions que vous pose votre amie Caroline:

Modèle: je finis toujours mes devoirs à 4 heures, et vous?
Nous finissons aussi nos devoirs à 4 heures.

1. Je prépare toujours le petit-déjeuner, et vous?

   Nous _____

2. J'aime les oranges, et vous?

   Nous _____

3. J'achète les livres d'aventure, et vous?

   Nous _____

4. Je choisis un film intéressant, et vous?

   Nous _____

5. Je réussis à l'examen de mathématiques, et vous?

   Nous _____

6. J'entends les enfants, et vous?

   Nous _____

7. Je mange un gateau, et vous?

   Nous _____

8. J'appelle mes amis, et vous?

   Nous _____

9. J'espère voyager, et vous?

   Nous _____

10. Je rougis beaucoup, et vous?

    Nous _____

Since, It Has Been . . . That
Depuis, Il y a . . . que, Voici . . . que, Voilà . . . que, Ça fait . . . que

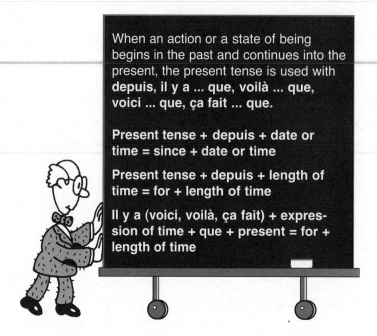

When an action or a state of being begins in the past and continues into the present, the present tense is used with **depuis, il y a ... que, voilà ... que, voici ... que, ça fait ... que.**

Present tense + depuis + date or time = since + date or time

Present tense + depuis + length of time = for + length of time

Il y a (voici, voilà, ça fait) + expression of time + que + present = for + length of time

Depuis combien de temps étudiez-vous le français?
How long have you been studying French?

J'étudie le français **depuis** trois ans.
Il y a trois ans **que** j'étudie le français.
Voici trois ans **que** j'étudie le français.
Voilà trois ans **que** j'étudie le français.
Ça fait trois ans **que** j'étudie le français.

The five preceding answers all mean *I have been studying French for three years.*

Depuis quand travaillez-vous ici?
Since when have you been working here?

Je travaille ici **depuis** le 20 janvier.
I have been working since January 20.

Only **depuis** can be used here because it refers to a *specific date*, not a length of time.

To Be . . . ing, To Be Used To
Entre en train de, Avoir l'habitude de

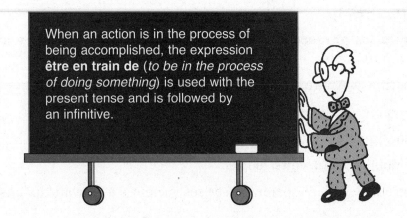

When an action is in the process of being accomplished, the expression **être en train de** (*to be in the process of doing something*) is used with the present tense and is followed by an infinitive.

Je suis en train de faire mes devoirs.
I am doing my homework.

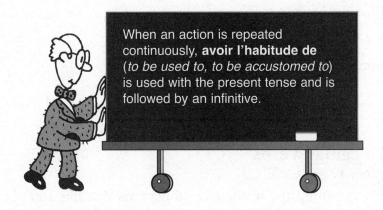

When an action is repeated continuously, **avoir l'habitude de** (*to be used to, to be accustomed to*) is used with the present tense and is followed by an infinitive.

J'ai l'habitude d'aller au cinéma une fois par semaine.
I am accustomed to going to the movies once a week.

OTHER EXPRESSIONS USED WITH THE PRESENT TENSE

En général (*generally*), **d'habitude** (*usually*), **chaque fois que** (*every time that*), **pendant que** (*while*), **tous les jours** (*every day*), **chaque jour** (*each day*), **en ce moment** (*at the present time*), **le lundi, le mardi, le mercredi**, etc. (*on Mondays, on Tuesdays, on Wednesdays, etc.*), **chaque semaine** (*every week*), **chaque mois** (*every month*), **chaque année** (*every year*).

En général, nous voyageons en été.
We generally travel in the summer.

Je téléphone à ma tante le mardi.
I call my aunt on Tuesdays.

QUICK PRACTICE

IV. Formez les phrases suivantes en ajoutant "depuis," "il y a . . . que," "voici . . . que," etc.

1. Catherine et André /travailler/en Europe/deux ans.

2. Ils/préparer/le dîner/midi.

3. Claude/projeter/ un voyage aux Etats-Unis/trois mois.

4. Paul/oublier/ses devoirs/hier.

5. Monsieur Berthier/espérer/passer ses vacances à Hawaii/dix ans.

V. Traduisez les phrases suivantes.

1. Usually, I take along the umbrella (*le parapluie*).

2. I have been studying for one hour.

3. She is looking for the book.

4. He travels every year.

5. They (f.) are accustomed to going out every day.

The Imperative of Regular Verbs
L'Impératif des verbes réguliers

The imperative is conjugated in the second persons singular and plural as well as in the first person plural. In the imperative, the verb is conjugated as in the present tense and the subject pronoun is omitted. The second person plural can either be the formal *you* or refer to several people.

parler	**finir**	**répondre**
parle	finis	réponds
parlons	finissons	répondons
parlez	finissez	répondez

EXCEPTION

For the imperative of **-er** verbs only, the second person singular does not take an **s**.

Finis tes devoirs!	*Finish your homework!*
Finissons nos devoirs!	*Let us finish our homework!*
Finissez vos devoirs!	*Finish your homework!*

THE NEGATIVE IMPERATIVE

The negative form **ne . . . pas** surrounds the imperative.

Ne parlez **pas!**　　　➔　　　*Don't talk!*

> **NOTE**
> **Ne traversez pas la rue!**
> *Don't cross the street!*

QUICK PRACTICE

VI. Monsieur Dupuis, le professeur de français, parle à un élève et à tous les élèves:

Modèle: sortir les livres
　　　　Sors les livres! Sortez les livres.

1. choisir un stylo

2. attendre un moment

3. réussir à l'examen

4. répondre aux questions

5. parler tout le temps (négatif)

6. hésiter tout le temps (négatif)

7. copier la réponse (négatif)

8. montrer la réponse (négatif)

9. commencer l'exercice

10. finir l'exercice

MOTS CROISÉS
Les present des verbes reguliers

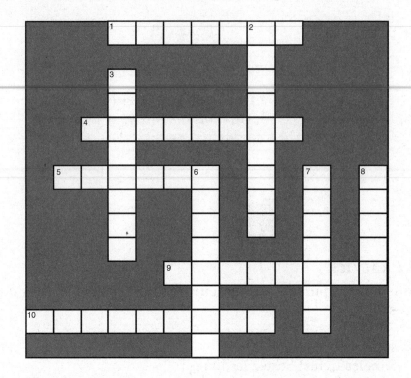

Across

1. Tu _____ (attendre)

4. Ils _____ (envoyer)

5. Il _____ (blesser)

9. Nous _____ (envoyer)

10. Elles _____ (finir)

Down

2. Ils _____ (dependre)

3. Nous _____ (manger)

6. Vous _____ (entendre)

7. Nous _____ (parler)

8. Je _____ (punir)

Culture Capsule 1

Le Français est

- La langue de la diplomatie dans une cinquantaine de pays.
- La langue principale des Jeux Olympiques. C'est en 1894 qu'un Français, le baron Pierre de Coubertin a lancé un appel à la Sorbonne pour le rétablissement des Jeux Olympiques. C'est lui qui a créé le Comité International Olympique. Depuis, ces évènements sportifs internationaux ont adopté la langue française comme langue principale.
- La langue officielle de l'Union Postale Universelle dont le siège se trouve en Suisse. Cette organisation compte aujourd'hui près de deux cents pays membres.
- L'une des langues officielles de l'OTAN et d'Interpol.
- La deuxième langue étrangère la plus enseignée dans les écoles de l'Union Européenne.
- Une langue universelle puisque l'on parle ou étudie le français langue seconde dans tous les continents. Il y a bien sûr les pays de langue française connus, tels que la Belgique, la Suisse (avec l'allemand), le Luxembourg, Monaco, l'Afrique du Nord, Madagascar, la Martinique, la Guadeloupe, Haïti, certains pays d'Afrique et la province du Québec au Canada. Mais ce qui est moins connu, c'est que, outre la langue locale, on parle aussi français en Nouvelle Calédonie, à Vanuatu (ancienne Nouvelles Hébrides), et au Royaume Uni: à Jersey et Guernesey.

VOCABULAIRE

une cinquantaine	around fifty
l'Union Postale Universelle	The Universal Postal Union
l'OTAN	NATO

3

The Present Tense
of Irregular Verbs

The most frequently used irregular verbs are **avoir** (*to have*), **être** (*to be*),
aller (*to go*), and **faire** (*to make, to do*).

avoir

j'ai	nous avons
tu as	vous avez
il/elle/on a	ils/elles ont

être

je suis	nous sommes
tu es	vous êtes
il/elle/on est	ils/elles sont

aller*

je vais	nous allons
tu vas	vous allez
il/elle/on va	ils/elles vont

faire

je fais	nous faisons
tu fais	vous faites
il/elle/on fait	ils/elles font

TIP

aller **also means** *to go well with*, **as in English, and** *to suit* (aller <u>à</u>).

Ce chemisier va bien avec le pantalon noir. *This blouse goes well with the black pants.* Le chapeau gris va bien à Colette. *The grey hat suits Colette.*

The special form s'en aller **means** *to leave* or *go away.*

Je m'en vais la semaine prochaine. *I am leaving next week.*

aller **is also used with expressions of health.**

Je vais bien. *I am well (fine).*

Irregular verbs can have different endings in the infinitive and do not necessarily all follow the same rules. The following verbs all have the same endings **s, s, t, ons, ez, ent**:

-**ir** ending verbs such as **sortir** (*to go out*)
-**re** ending verbs such as **vivre** (*to live*)
-**oir** ending verbs such as **voir** (*to see*)

IRREGULAR VERBS			
sortir		**vivre**	
je sor**s**	nous sort**ons**	je vi**s**	nous viv**ons**
tu sor**s**	vous sort**ez**	tu vi**s**	vous viv**ez**
il/elle/on sor**t**	ils/elles sort**ent**	il/elle/on vi**t**	ils/elles viv**ent**
voir			
je voi**s**	nous voy**ons**		
tu voi**s**	vous voy**ez**		
il/elle/on voi**t**	ils/elles voi**ent**		

When conjugating irregular verbs, it is important to memorize the first persons singular and plural, as well as the 3rd person plural since the root may change.

OTHER IRREGULAR -IR VERBS

dormir (*to sleep*)	je dors	nous dormons
mourir (*to die*)	je meurs	nous mourons (ils/elles meurent)
partir (*to leave*)*	je pars	nous partons
servir (*to serve*)*	je sers	nous servons
tenir (*to hold*)*	je tiens	nous tenons (ils/elles tiennent)
venir (*to come*)*	je viens	nous venons (ils/elles viennent)

If it is followed by the preposition à plus an infinitive, it means *to really want*.

Je tiens à voir ce film. *I really want to see this movie.*

If it is followed by the preposition de, it means *to take after*.

Ce garçon tient de son père. *This boy takes after his father.*

In the pronominal form se tenir means *to behave*.

Elle ne se tient pas bien en classe. *She doesn't behave in class.*

venir = when used with the preposition de, it means *to have just*.

Je viens de finir mes devoirs. *I have just finished by homework.*

OTHER IRREGULAR -RE VERBS

apprendre (to learn, study)	j'apprends	nous apprenons	ils apprennent
boire (to drink)	je bois	nous buvons	ils boivent
comprendre (to understand)	je comprends	nous comprenons	ils comprennent
conduire (to drive)	je conduis	nous conduisons	
connaître (to know)*	je connais	nous connaissons	
craindre (to fear)	je crains	nous craignons	ils craignent
croire (to believe)*	je crois	nous croyons	ils croient
dire (to say)*	je dis	nous disons	vous dites
écrire (to write)*	j'écris	nous écrivons	
lire (to read)	je lis	nous lisons	
mettre (to put)*	je mets	nous mettons	
peindre (to paint)	je peins	nous peignons	ils peignent
prendre (to take)	je prends	nous prenons	ils prennent
rire (to laugh)	je ris	nous rions	
suivre (to follow)*	je suis	nous suivons	

TIP

connaître = *to know someone or something, to know a place*. It is important not to confuse connaître and savoir. Savoir means *to know by heart*, as in to know a poem, to know a fact or to know about a fact, or to know how to do something.

Je connais son père. *I know her father.*
Je sais danser la valse. *I know how to dance the waltz.*

In the third person singular, there is a circumflex over the i (elle connaît).

croire = *to believe a person* (that this person is telling the truth).

Je crois ma voisine. *I believe my neighbor.*

When followed by the preposition à it means *to believe a thing*, or the fact that a person exists, is real.

Je crois à cette histoire. *I believe this story.*
Je crois aux anges gardiens. *I believe in guardian angels.*

To believe in God is translated by croire en Dieu.

dire = *to tell something*

Je dis la vérité. *I tell the truth.*

It is used with the preposition à before a person, and the preposition de before an infinitive.

Je dis à mon ami de venir chez moi. *I tell my friend to come to my house.*

écrire = before the name of a thing, there is no preposition. Before the name of a person, there is the preposition à.

Elle écrit une lettre à sa cousine. *She writes her cousin a letter.*

mettre = *to put*. When used pronominally and followed by the preposition à and an infinitive or a noun, it means *to begin to do something*.

Nous nous mettons à travailler/Nous nous mettons au travail. *We begin to work.*

The idiomatic expressions mettre la table and mettre le couvert mean *to set the table*.

suivre = *to follow*. In the expression suivre un cours it also means *to take a class*.

Il suit un cours d'allemand. *He takes a German class.*

OTHER IRREGULAR -OIR VERBS

apercevoir (*to notice, to see from afar*)	j'aperçois	nous apercevons	ils aperçoivent
devoir (*to have to, to owe*)*	je dois	nous devons	ils doivent
falloir (*to be necessary*)*	il faut		
pleuvoir (*to rain*)	il pleut		
pouvoir (*to be able to*)*	je peux	nous pouvons	ils peuvent
recevoir (*to receive*)	je reçois	nous recevons	ils reçoivent
savoir (*to know*)*	je sais	nous savons	ils savent
valoir (*to be worth*)*	je vaux, il vaut	nous valons	ils valent
vouloir (*to want*)*	je veux	nous voulons	ils veulent

TIP

devoir = When the meaning of the verb devoir is *to have to*, it is followed by an infinitive; otherwise the meaning is *to owe*.

Je dois étudier ce soir. *I must study this evening.*
Je dois vingt euros à mon ami. *I owe my friend twenty euros.*

falloir = This verb is used in the third person singular and is followed by an infinitive.

Il faut étudier avant l'examen. *It is necessary to study before the exam.*

pouvoir = As in English, it is used before an infinitive.

savoir = *to know how to do something, to know by heart, to know about something that happened*. It must not be confused with connaître (see note under -re verbs).

Elle sait danser. *She knows how to dance/she can dance.*
Je sais le poème par coeur. *I know the poem by heart.*
Je connais le poème. *I know the poem. (I have seen it, I have read it)*
Je sais qu'elle est à Paris. *I know that she is in Paris.*

valoir = it is also used in expressions such as il vaut mieux.

Il vaut mieux ouvrir la fenêtre. *It is better to open the window.*

The expression ça vaut la peine means *it is worth it.*

vouloir = as in English, it is followed by an infinitive.

Je veux lire ce livre. *I want to read this book.*

The polite form of je veux is je voudrais (*I would like*).

The Simple Negative
La négation simple

In the present tense, the simple negative (**la négation simple**) is formed by using **ne** before the verb and **pas** after the verb.

> **subject + ne + verb + pas**

Elle **ne** choisit **pas** la jupe noire. *She doesn't choose the black skirt.*

When two verbs follow each other, the second one is in the infinitive. In this case, the **ne** is placed before the first verb and the **pas** is placed between the conjugated verb and the infinitive.

Nous **ne** voulons **pas** sortir ce soir. *We don't want to go out this evening.*

When the verb conjugated begins with a vowel, the **ne** changes into **n'**.

Elle **n'**aime **pas** les légumes. *She doesn't like vegetables.*

The Simple Interrogative
La forme interrogative simple

The simple interrogative is formed by . . .

- **Using "est-ce que" before an affirmative sentence**

    (*affirmative*)   Tu achètes des fruits.
    (*interrogative*)   **Est-ce que** tu achètes des fruits?

- **Inverting the subject and the verb**

  Achètes-tu des fruits? *Are you buying fruits?*

- **When there is a subject noun, the noun is placed before the inverted question.**

  Guillaume est-il en classe? *Is Guillaume in class?*
  Le professeur sait-il que tu es malade? *Does the teacher know that you are ill?*

- **When a verb in the present tense ends in a vowel, and is followed by il or elle, a t is added between the verb and the pronoun:**

  Arrive-t-il avant ses amis? *Does he arrive before his friends?*

NOTE: *Except for the verbs avoir, être, and pouvoir, the inverted form cannot be used for the first person singular. In general, it is better to use the long form with est-ce que for the first person singular of all verbs.*

The Negative Interrogative
La forme negative interrogative

In the negative interrogative form, the negative **ne** is placed before the inverted question and the **pas** is placed after.

> **Ne + inverted question + pas + rest of the sentence**

Ne parlez-vous pas avec elle? *Aren't you speaking with her?*

For the long form, est-ce que is placed before the negative sentence.

Est-ce que vous ne parlez pas avec elle?

NOTE: *For an affirmative answer to a negative interrogative question, si is used instead of oui.*

Ne parlez-vous pas avec elle? Si, presque tous les jours! *Yes, almost every day.*

QUICK PRACTICE

I. Conjuguez les verbes entre parenthèses à la forme qui convient:

1. Nous (faire) _____ un gateau au chocolat.

2. Il (aller) _____ au cinéma avec ses amis.

3. Elles (voir) _____ les voisins. (négatif)

4. Tu (connaître) _____ le directeur.

5. Ils (être) _____ à l'université.

6. Nous (peindre)_____ la salle à manger.

7. Est-ce que vous (suivre) _____ un cours de géologie?

8. Nous (aller) _____ à la montagne cette année. (négatif)

9. Vous (recevoir) _____ souvent des lettres de Corinne.

10. Nous (croire) _____ qu'il dit la vérité.

11. Ils (prendre) _____ leurs repas dans la cuisine.

12. Ce film (ennuyer) _____ maman.

13. Vous (faire)_____ vos devoirs avant le dîner.

14. Je (savoir) _____ nager. (négatif)

15. Tu (dormir) _____ beaucoup.

II. Mettez au pluriel.

Modèle: je fais—nous faisons

1. je peux _____

2. il fait _____

3. tu reçois _____

4. je crois _____

5. tu peins _____

6. tu pars _____

7. je tiens _____

8. il prend _____

9. je ris _____

10. j'écris _____

III. Refaites les phrases suivantes en employant l'inversion.

Modèle: Elle lit beaucoup.—Lit-elle beaucoup?

1. Stéphanie fait ses devoirs maintenant.

2. Ses parents voyagent beaucoup en hiver.

3. Il parle trois langues.

4. Vous êtes fatigué parce qu'il fait chaud.

5. Jacques veut lire ce livre cette semaine.

6. Ils croient la météo.

7. Ma soeur va à la plage.

8. Ils suivent un cours de maths.

9. Il vaut mieux finir les devoirs avant d'aller au cinéma.

10. Tu peux sortir maintenant.

IV. Posez les questions à la forme négative-interrogative.

Modèle: J'aime le chocolat.—N'aimes-tu pas le chocolat?

1. Il est en classe.

2. Nous voyons les enfants tous les jours.

3. Elle sort souvent pendant le week-end.

4. Je vais sortir ce soir.

5. Il donne ce cadeau à sa femme.

6. Ils partent pour New York.

7. Elle vient d'arriver.

8. Nous avons faim.

9. Ils font un chateau de sable (a sand castle).

10. Je reçois beaucoup de lettres.

V. Répondez aux questions suivantes, soit à la forme affirmative, soit à la forme négative.

Modèle: Aimez-vous les huîtres? *Do you like oysters?*
　　　　Oui, j'aime les huîtres.　ou　Non, je n'aime pas les huîtres.

1. Est-ce que vous pouvez lire ce passage?

2. Est-ce que vous écrivez à vos grands-parents?

3. Est-ce que vous dormez huit heures par nuit?

4. Est-ce que vous et vos amis commencez à apprendre le chinois?

5. Est-ce que vous employez le français tous les jours?

The Imperative of Irregular Verbs
L'impératif des verbes irréguliers

avoir	être	faire	savoir	vouloir
aie	sois	fais	sache	veuille
ayons	soyons	faisons	sachons	veuillons
ayez	soyez	faites	sachez	veuillez

Sois calme!	*Be calm!*
Soyons calmes!	*Let us be calm!*
Soyez calme(s)!	*Be calm!*

The verb **aller** follows the same rule as regular **-er** verbs.

Va	*go*
Allons	*let's go*
Allez	*go*
Vas-y	*go there/go ahead*
Allons-y	*let's go there /let's go ahead/ let's begin*
Allez-y	*go there / go ahead*

NEGATIVE IMPERATIVE

The negative form **ne . . . pas** surrounds the imperative:

N'écrivez **pas**! *Don't write!*   **Ne** dites **pas**! *Don't tell!*

QUICK PRACTICE

VI. Madame Leblanc dit à ses élèves . . .

Modèle: sortir les livres.—Sortez vos livres.

1. ouvrir les livres

2. lire attentivement

3. sortir les cahiers

4. être attentifs

5. être distraits (négatif)

VII. Rémi parle à son collègue Thierry . . .

Modèle: Venir dîner chez nous demain.—Viens dîner chez nous demain.

1. être en retard (négatif)

2. aller chercher ta copine

3. quitter avant minuit (négatif)

4. conduire lentement parce qu'il va neiger

5. mettre un costume élégant (négatif)

VIII. Interaction—Demandez à un camarade ce qu'il fait pendant le week-end: il vous répond négativement (5 questions au choix).

Modèle: Est-ce que tu vas au cinéma?—Non, je ne vais pas au cinéma *(sortir avec les copains/ avec la famille/faire du sport/faire des achats/etc.)*.

MOTS CROISÉS
Le présent des verbes irréguliers

Across
1. Ils _____ (craindre)
3. Ils _____ (sortir)
4. Je _____ (vouloir)
5. Je _____ (vois)
6. Elle _____ (mettre)
8. Nous _____ (aller)
10. Elles _____ (prendre)
11. Je _____ (savoir)

Down
1. Nous _____ (conduire)
2. Tu _____ (tenir)
5. Elles _____ (venir)
7. Nous _____ (boire)
9. Vous _____ (dire)

Culture Capsule 2

La liberté de la presse française date de 1789, année de la Révolution Française. Jusque là, la presse subit une très stricte censure. Cela fait que la plupart des intellectuels et libres penseurs se servent de livres ou pamphlets pour diffuser leurs idées. La Déclaration des Droits de l'Homme et du Citoyen soutient que tout citoyen peut écrire librement. De 1788 à 1792 on passe d'une douzaine de journaux à plus de 200 pour toute la France. Les journaux les plus célèbres de l'époque sont les journaux révolutionnaires, tels que "Le Patriote français", "L'Ami du peuple", et le journal hebdomadaire de Robespierre, "Défenseur de la Constitution". Parmi les journaux contre-révolutionnaires, on cite "Le journal politique national" et le "Journal général".

Cependant à partir de 1792, le gouvernement reprend contrôle de la presse et ce n'est qu'après la loi du 29 juillet 1881 que la liberté de la presse est garantie.

Aujourd'hui, il existe des journaux nationaux tels que "Le Monde", "Le Figaro", "Libération", et "L'Humanité" et des journaux régionaux tels que "Ouest France", "La Voix du Nord", "La Dépêche", et "La Provence". N'oublions pas les magazines tels que "Elle", " Marie-Claire", "Paris Match", "L'Express".

Comparée à la presse anglophone qui se sent obligée de ne préciser que les faits avant de les commenter, la presse française estime que l'interprétation joue un rôle tout aussi important. Aujourd'hui, en lisant un quotidien français, il n'est pas surprenant de voir dans les titres un bon jeu de mots faisant appel au sens de l'humour du lecteur.

VOCABULAIRE

une douzaine	*(about) a dozen*
Les journaux	*the newspapers*
hebdomadaire	*weekly*
un quotidien	*a daily newspaper*
un jeu de mots	*a play on words*

4

The Imperfect

Que savez-vous déjà?
What Do You Know Already?

Can you fill in the blanks with the correct form of the imperfect tense of the verb indicated in parentheses?

1. Ils (parler)_____ beaucoup.

2. Nous (écrire) _____ une lettre.

3. Elle (aller) _____ à l'école.

4. Il (être) _____ en classe.

5. Vous (écouter) _____ la radio.

6. Je (manger) _____ une omelette.

7. Tu (avoir) _____ une bonne idée.

8. Ils (aimer)_____ les vacances à la montagne.

9. Vous (rire) _____ souvent.

10. Je (boire)_____ du café.

The imperfect tense in French, or the **imparfait**, is used to express, in the past:

- a state of being
- a repetitive, continual, or habitual action
- a feeling or an emotion
- a description or condition in the past
- an action that is interrupted by another action

It is formed by taking the first person plural of the present tense of the verb and replacing the **-ons** ending by the following endings:

ais	ions
ais	iez
ait	aient

Parler (*nous parl**ons***)		
Je parl**ais**	Nous parl**ions**
Tu parl**ais**	Vous parl**iez**
Il parl**ait**	Ils parl**aient**
Elle parl**ait**	Elles parl**aient**

Finir (*nous finiss**ons***)		
Je finiss**ais**	Nous finiss**ions**
Tu finiss**ais**	Vous finiss**iez**
Il finiss**ait**	Ils finiss**aient**
Elle finiss**ait**	Elles finiss**aient**

Attendre (*nous attend**ons***)		
J'attend**ais**	Nous attend**ions**
Tu attend**ais**	Vous attend**iez**
Il attend**ait**	Ils attend**aient**
Elle attend**ait**	Elles attend**aient**

TIP

Verbs that end in -ier in the infinitive (such as étudier—*to study*) **have two i's for the** nous **and** vous **forms of the imperfect:**

Présent	nous étud**ions**	vous étud**iez**
Imparfait	nous étud**iions**	vous étud**iiez**

Some of the other verbs in which the nous **and** vous **forms keep the i or y before the imperfect endings are:**

Croire (*to believe*)	nous croyions	vous croyiez
Essayer (*to try*)	nous essayions	vous essayiez
Essuyer (*to wipe*)	nous essuyions	vous essuyiez
Rire (*to laugh*)	nous riions	vous riiez

On (*one, we, you, they*) **is always followed by the verb conjugated in the third person singular:** on parlait = *one spoke, we spoke, you spoke, they spoke.*

The imperfect of irregular verbs is also formed by taking the first person plural of the present of the verb, dropping the **-ons** ending, and adding the imperfect endings.

Aller (nous all**ons**)	J'all**ais**	Nous all**ions**
To go	Tu all**ais**	Vous all**iez**
	Il all**ait**	Ils all**aient**
	Elle all**ait**	Elles all**aient**

Boire (nous buv**ons**)	Je buv**ais**	Nous buv**ions**
To drink	Tu buv**ais**	Vous buv**iez**
	Il buv**ait**	Ils buv**aient**
	Elle buv**ait**	Elles buv**aient**

Devoir (nous dev**ons**)	Je dev**ais**	Nous dev**ions**
To have to—to owe	Tu dev**ais**	Vous dev**iez**
	Il dev**ait**	Ils dev**aient**
	Elle dev**ait**	Elles dev**aient**

Exceptions

The imperfect endings for the verb **être** are the same, <u>but they have a different stem</u>.

Etre (nous sommes)	J'ét**ais**	Nous ét**ions**
To be	Tu ét**ais**	Vous ét**iez**
	Il ét**ait**	Ils ét**aient**
	Elle ét**ait**	Elles ét**aient**

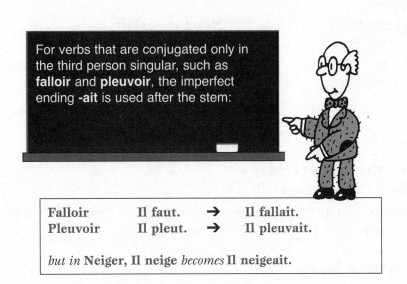

For verbs that are conjugated only in the third person singular, such as **falloir** and **pleuvoir**, the imperfect ending **-ait** is used after the stem:

| **Falloir** | Il faut. | → | Il fallait. |
| **Pleuvoir** | Il pleut. | → | Il pleuvait. |

but in **Neiger**, Il neige *becomes* Il neigeait.

Verbs with Spelling Changes
Verbes avec changement d'orthographie

> Verbs ending with **-cer** or **-ger** in the infinitive, such as **commencer** and **manger**, have the same endings in the imperfect. It is important to remember that, in the present tense, the first person plural of these verbs is conjugated as follows:
>
> Nous commençons   Nous mangeons

The **ç** and the **e** before the **-ons** endings are kept for all persons in the imperfect <u>except</u> for the **nous** and **vous** forms:

Commencer

Je commençais	**Nous commencions**
Tu commençais	**Vous commenciez**
Il(on) commençait	Ils commençaient
Elle commençait	Elles commençaient

Manger

Je mangeais	**Nous mangions**
Tu mangeais	**Vous mangiez**
Il(on) mangeait	Ils mangeaient
Elle mangeait	Elles mangeaient

When to Use the Imperfect
Quand utiliser l'imparfait

As mentioned at the beginning of this chapter, the imperfect is used to express, in the past:

- **a state of being**

  Ma soeur était malade.

- **a repetitive, continual, or habitual action**

  Tous les jours, je quittais la maison à 8 heures.

- **a feeling or an emotion**

  Ils étaient très inquiets.

- **a description**

  La plage était déserte.

- **an action that is interrupted by another action**

  J'étudiais quand papa est arrivé.

Whereas the **present tense** responds to the question:

What <u>is</u> going on? The door is closed. **La porte est fermée.**

The **imperfect** responds to the question:

What <u>was</u> going on? The door was closed. **La porte était fermée.**

The imperfect also translates:

- **was ...ing**

  I was studying. **J'étudiais.**

- **were ...ing**

  We were studying. **Nous étudiions.**

- **used to**

  When he was young, he used to play tennis.
  Quand il était jeune, il jouait au tennis.

- **would** (*when **would** means **used to***)

  ***When** I was in Paris, I **would** always take the metro.*
  (*I used to take the metro*—It is **not** a condition)
  Quand j'étais à Paris, je prenais toujours le métro.

  Compare with: ***If** I were in Paris, I would take the metro.*
  Si j'étais à Paris, je prendrais le métro.
  (*It is a condition, therefore the imperfect cannot be used with the verb* to take.)

Quite often, the imperfect is accompanied by expressions such as:

À l'époque (*at that time*)	*A l'époque, les femmes ne sortaient pas seules.*
Dans ce temps-là (*at that time*)	*Dans ce temps-là, nous étions des enfants.*
Autrefois (*in the past*)	*Autrefois, les hommes portaient des perruques.*
Parfois (*sometimes*)	*Nous allions parfois au cinéma.*
Quelquefois (*sometimes*)	*J'écoutais quelquefois la radio.*
De temps en temps (*from time to time*)	*Nous voyions nos amis de temps en temps.*
Souvent (*often*)	*Elle chantait souvent avec sa soeur.*
Toujours (*always*)	*Nous travaillions toujours ensemble.*
Jamais (*never*)	*Ils ne voyaient jamais leurs cousins.*
Chaque fois (*every time*)	*Chaque fois qu'il sortait, il prenait son anorak.*
Tandis que (*whereas*)	*Je lisais tandis que ma soeur jouait*
Pendant que (*while*)	*Je lisais pendant que ma soeur jouait.*
Lorsque (*when*)	*Lorsqu'il était jeune, Paul ne travaillait pas.*
Quand (*when*)	*Quand il était jeune, il faisait du ski.*

The following verbs are examples of verbs that are mostly used with the imperfect tense:

avoir, croire, espérer, être, savoir, vouloir

Elle espérait aller au Sénégal.
She was hoping to go to Senegal.

Je savais qu'il était malade.
I knew that he was ill.

Nous voulions aller au cinéma.
We wanted to go to the movies.

TIP
Si + the imperfect + ?
When si is followed by the imperfect tense and an interrogation mark, as in:

Si on allait au cinéma?

it doesn't imply a conditional sentence, but a *suggestion* or *advice*.

Si on allait au cinéma? *How about going to the movies?*
Si tu faisais tes devoirs? *How about doing your homework?*

Venir de in the imperfect + the infinitive
In the present tense, venir de **means** *to have just.*

Je viens de finir mes devoirs et je suis fatiguée.
I have just finished my homework and I am tired.

In the imperfect tense, venir de **means** *had just.*

Je venais de finir mes devoirs et j'étais fatiguée.
I had just finished my homework and I was tired.

Depuis + the Imperfect
Depuis + l'imparfait

When **depuis** is used with the present tense, it describes something that started at some time in the past and is continuing in the present.

> **Nous voyageons depuis deux semaines.**
> *We have been traveling for two weeks.*

When **depuis** is used with the imperfect tense, it describes something that began in the past and was interrupted by something. The sentence in the imperfect is usually followed by **quand** and the passé composé (see next chapter).

> **Nous voyagions depuis deux semaines quand nous avons rencontré ta cousine.**
> *We had been traveling for two weeks when we met your cousin.*

The question beginning with **depuis quand** (*since when*) requires an answer that gives a specific date or time, not a length of time.

> **Depuis quand était-il malade?**
> *Since when was he ill?*

> **Il était malade depuis le 3 juillet.**
> *He was ill since July 3rd.*

The question beginning with **depuis combien de temps** (*how long*) requires an answer that gives the length of time.

> **Depuis combien de temps était-il malade?**
> *How long had he been ill?*

> **Il était malade depuis dix jours.**
> *He had been ill for ten days.*

The expressions **ça faisait + expression of time + que** and **il y avait + expression of time + que** follow the same rule as **depuis**.

> **Il y avait deux semaines qu'ils voyageaient.**
> **Ça faisait deux semaines qu'ils voyageaient.**
> *They had been traveling for two weeks.*

QUICK PRACTICE

I. Madame Leclerc vient de rentrer de voyage. Elle parle à sa voisine de ses vacances:

A la Martinique, il (*faire*) un temps magnifique. Il (*pleuvoir*) de temps en temps, mais ça ne nous (*empêcher*) pas de profiter de la plage. Quelquefois, nous (*aller*) au grand marché. Mon mari, qui adore les fruits de mer, (*être*) ravi de trouver plusieurs restaurants dont ce(c') (*être*) la spécialité. Il ne (*vouloir*) manger que du poisson, des crabes, etc. Franchement, moi, je préfère goûter la cuisine locale, donc, nous en (*manger*) parfois. L'après-midi, après la plage, nous (*essayer*) d'aller voir des endroits célèbres, tels que la maison de Joséphine de Beauharnais, la première épouse de Napoléon 1er. Franchement, une semaine, ce n'est pas suffisant, et je n' (*avoir*) pas envie de rentrer en France!

II. Mettez les verbes entre parenthèses à l'imparfait:

1. Quand il (être) _____ jeune, il (avoir) _____ beaucoup de jouets.

2. Elle (nager) _____ très bien, mais aujourd'hui, elle ne nage plus.

3. Quand j'(aller)_____ à l'école, il (falloir) _____ que je porte un uniforme.

4. Tu (pleurer) _____ toujours lorsque ta mère ne te (permettre) _____ pas de regarder la télévision.

5. Chaque fois que quelqu'un (s'approcher) _____ de la porte, le chien (aboyer) _____ .

6. Il (pleuvoir) _____ beaucoup.

III. Traduction

1. She would never listen to her parents.

2. We used to study together.

3. He was dancing with Caroline whereas I was dancing with Josette.

4. We always started at 8 o'clock.

5. When I had the time, I would write letters.

6. She had just bought a car but it was too big.

7. How about going to the restaurant?

8. I was reading while she was writing a letter.

9. We knew that they were coming at 5 o'clock.

10. I didn't want to go out.

11. Since when was he driving?

12. He was driving since January.

IV. Demandez à un copain ou une copine ce qu'il/elle faisait en été quand il/elle était enfant. Servez-vous du vocabulaire ci-dessous.

Modèle: aller à la plage.

- Est-ce que tu allais à la plage?
- Oui, j'allais <u>souvent</u> à la plage. ou
- Oui, j'allais toujours à la plage. ou
- Non, je n'allais <u>jamais</u> à la plage.

1. Lire beaucoup d'histoires.

2. Regarder la télévision.

3. Faire des achats.

4. Faire du camping.

5. Faire du ski nautique.

6. Voyager dans un autre état.

7. Aller souvent au cinéma.

8. Pratiquer un sport.

9. Jouer avec des copains.

10. Aller à la piscine.

V. Travail oral à deux:

L'inspecteur Beauvois questionne le témoin d'un vol. Malheureusement il parle à voix très basse et nous ne pouvons entendre que les réponses. A partir de ces réponses, le deuxième étudiant (ou la deuxième étudiante) doit créer les questions en jouant le rôle de l'inspecteur.

- J'étais à la porte du magasin depuis vingt minutes.
- J'attendais mon mari (ma femme).
- J'attendais depuis cinq heures vingt-cinq.
- Quand j'ai vu cette femme prendre un sac et courir, il était six heures moins le quart.
- Je savais cela parce que l'horloge du magasin était en face de moi.

VI. Travail écrit:

Décrivez votre chambre quand vous étiez enfant.

Across

2. Nous _____ (boire)

4. Tu _____ (devoir)

7. Nous _____ (aller)

10. Il _____ (neiger)

11. Vous _____ (étudier)

Down

1. Never

3. Often

5. For or since

6. Il _____ (falloir)

8. Elles _____ (manger)

9. Vous _____ (etre)

Culture Capsule 3

Le mot "petit" en français, loin d'être péjoratif, indique plutôt une certaine affection envers la personne ou l'objet dont on parle. Ainsi, même si l'on a dix enfants, on dira, en parlant de sa famille "ma petite famille". On parle aussi de son "petit vin rouge", de son "petit chez soi", de manger un "petit gâteau", une "petite friandise" ... même si l'objet en question est loin d'être petit. On s'adresse souvent à une chère amie en l'appelant "ma petite (Josette, Corinne, Claire, etc.)". Souvent, quelqu'un qui n'est pas francophone sera surpris en entendant un francophone dire "Je suis à vous dans une petite minute" (*I'll be with you in a short minute*) ... soit exactement soixante secondes! Et si votre hôte vous dit "Vous voulez bien prendre un petit café avec moi?" cela n'indique pas toujours une toute petite tasse de café! Finalement, on dit souvent, en allant aux toilettes, que l'on va au "petit coin" (dans ce cas, il ne s'agit pas d'affection, mais de langage familier!).

VOCABULAIRE

envers	*toward*
chez soi	*one's home*
friandise	*delicacy*

5

The Compound Past Tense

Que savez-vous déjà?
What Do You Know Already?

Can you fill in the blanks with the correct form of the passé composé of the verb indicated in parentheses?

1. Elle (tomber) _____ dans le jardin.

2. Nous (voir) _____ un bon film.

3. Ils (finir) _____ les devoirs.

4. Je/J' (manger) _____ de la salade.

5. Qui (dire) _____ cela?

6. Ils (acheter) _____ une maison.

7. Elle (fermer) _____ la porte.

8. Vous (savoir)_____ la réponse.

9. Elles (venir) _____ la semaine passée.

10. Tu (comprendre) _____ la leçon.

The **passé composé** or compound past, unlike the **imparfait**, expresses an action that took place and ended at a certain moment in the past whereas the **imparfait** expresses a continuous, repetitive, habitual action or a description in the past.

> *I was running.* → **Je courais (imparfait).**
> *I ran.* → **J'ai couru (passé composé).**

As its name indicates, the **passé composé** is a compound tense. It is formed by using an auxiliary or helping verb in the present tense followed by the past participle of the verb being conjugated. The two auxiliary verbs used are **avoir** (*to have*) and **être** (*to be*).

FORMATION OF THE PAST PARTICIPLE OF REGULAR VERBS

-**er** ending verbs such as **parler** → parl**é** *(spoken)*
-**ir** ending verbs such as **finir** → fin**i** *(finished)*
-**re** ending verbs such as **répondre** → répon**du** *(answered)*

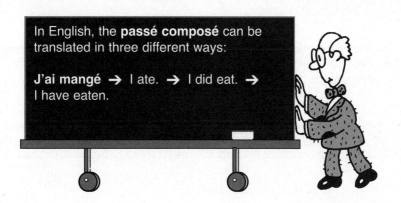

In English, the **passé composé** can be translated in three different ways:

J'ai mangé → I ate. → I did eat. → I have eaten.

Use of Avoir and Être
Faut-il utiliser avoir ou être?

Most verbs are conjugated using the verb **avoir** as an auxiliary verb. However, the following verbs require the verb **être**.

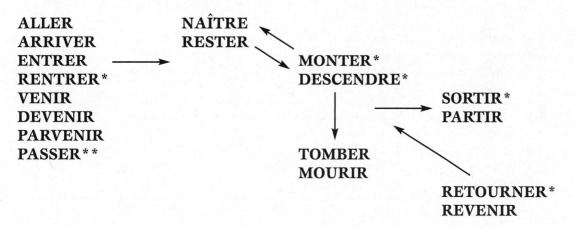

ALLER
ARRIVER
ENTRER
RENTRER*
VENIR
DEVENIR
PARVENIR
PASSER**

NAÎTRE
RESTER

MONTER*
DESCENDRE*

TOMBER
MOURIR

SORTIR*
PARTIR

RETOURNER*
REVENIR

*The verbs designated with an asterisk are those that can be used with **avoir** if they are followed by a direct object. For the verb **passer**, see the special note on the next page.

Il est sorti à huit heures. *He went out at eight o'clock.*
Il a sorti le chien. *He took the dog out.*

Elle est montée dans sa chambre. *She went up to her room.*
Elle a monté sa valise. *She took her suitcase up.*

Je suis retourné à l'école. *I returned to school.*
J'ai retourné la lettre à l'expéditeur. *I returned the letter to the sender.*

Il est rentré chez lui de bonne heure. *He came back home early.*
Il a rentré la voiture au garage. *He put the car back into the garage.*

> The verb **passer** can be used with either auxiliary **avoir** or **être** but the meaning will be different:
>
> **J'ai passé une semaine en Floride.** *I spent a week in Florida.*
> **J'ai passé un examen hier.** *I took an exam yesterday* (not *passed an exam*).
>
> **Je suis passé à la pharmacie.** *I went to the drugstore.*

In order to remember easily which verbs take **être** in the **passé composé**, it is useful to remember the code: Dr. and Mrs. P. Van der Trampp.

VERB	TRANSLATION	PAST PARTICIPLE
Descendre	*to go down*	descendu
Rentrer	*to go back, return (home)*	rentré
Monter	*to go up*	monté
Rester	*to stay or remain*	resté
Sortir	*to go out*	sorti
Partir	*to leave, depart*	parti
Venir	*to come*	venu
Aller	*to go*	allé
Naître	*to be born*	né
Devenir	*to become*	devenu
Entrer	*to go in, enter*	entré
Revenir	*to come back, return*	revenu
Tomber	*to fall*	tombé
Retourner	*to go back again, return*	retourné
Arriver	*to arrive*	arrivé
Mourir	*to die*	mort
Parvenir	*to be able to do something*	parvenu
Passer	*to go to, pass by*	passé

The verbs **rentrer**, **revenir**, and **retourner** have slightly different meanings:

- **Rentrer means to go back home**

    Il est rentré de vacances la semaine passée.
    He came back from vacation last week.

- **Revenir also means to come back as opposed to partir**

    Il est parti jeudi et il est revenu dimanche.
    He left on Thursday and came back on Sunday.

- Retourner means to go back again, to return to, to return or to turn over (something).

> Quand j'étais étudiant, j'ai passé un mois en France. J'y suis retourné cette année.
> *When I was a student, I spent one month in France. I went back again this year.*

> Elle a retourné le matelas.
> *She turned over the mattress.*

Past Participles of Irregular Verbs
Le participe passé des verbes irréguliers

avoir → eu		être → été	
j'ai eu	nous avons eu	j'ai été	nous avons été
tu as eu	vous avez eu	tu as été	vous avez été
il/elle/on a eu	ils/elles ont eu	il/elle/on a été	ils/elles ont été

VERBS ENDING IN -IR

Whereas, in the present tense, the **nous** and **vous** forms of regular -**ir** verbs end in **issons** and **issez**, irregular -**ir** verbs do not have **iss** before the ending. However, the past participle is also formed by taking off the -**ir** ending of the infinitive, and replacing it by **i**.

partir → parti	dormir → dormi	sortir → sorti
Je suis parti.	J'ai dormi.	Je suis sorti.

VERBS ENDING IN -RE

There are four different possible endings:

-re → -u					
attendre	**attendu**	connaître	**connu**	vivre	**vécu**
boire	**bu**	lire	**lu**	plaire	**plu**

-re → -is					
mettre	**mis**	permettre	**permis**	prendre	**pris**

-re → -it					
dire	**dit**	conduire	**conduit**	écrire	**écrit**

-re → -ri		
rire	**ri**	sourire	**souri**

Agreement of the Past Participle
L'accord du participe passé

When using the verb **être** as an auxiliary verb, the past participle agrees in gender and in number with the subject. For the feminine, an **e** is added to the ending of the past participle, and for the plural, an **s** is added to the ending.

Il est venu.	→	**Ils sont venus.**
Elle est venue.	→	**Elles sont venues.**

When using the verb **avoir** as an auxiliary verb, the past participle does not agree in gender or number with the subject.

Il a fini l'examen.	→	**Ils ont fini l'examen.**
Elle a fini l'examen.	→	**Elles ont fini l'examen.**

However, with the auxiliary verb **avoir**, if the direct object is placed <u>before</u> the verb, the past participle **will agree** with the direct object.

Il a ache<u>t</u>é la voiture bleue. →	**La voiture qu'il a achet<u>ée</u> était bleue.**
↓	↓
La voiture (*direct object*) comes **after** the verb **acheter.**	**La voiture** (*direct object*) comes **before** the verb **acheter.**

Interrogative and Negative Forms
Les formes interrogative et négative

- **When asking a question in the passé composé, if it is the long form, that is, using Est-ce que, there is no change in the order of words.**

> **Est-ce qu'il a vu** ce film?
>
> **Est-ce qu'elle est allée** à la plage?

- When asking a question in the passé composé using the inverted form, that is, putting the subject after the verb, the auxiliary verb comes first, followed by the subject, and then the past participle.

> **A-t-il vu** ce film?*
> **Avez-vous vu** ce film?
> **Est-elle allée** à la plage?

*In the interrogative form, when the inversion involves a vowel followed by another vowel (*a...il*) a *t* separates the two.*

These expressions are often used with the **passé composé**.

Hier	yesterday
Avant-hier	the day before yesterday
La semaine passée	last week
Récemment	recently
Il y a + period of time	period of time . . . ago
Le mois dernier	last month
L'année dernière	last year

QUICK PRACTICE

I. Caroline fait beaucoup de choses aujourd'hui. Quand sa copine Julie lui demande si elle fait la même chose tous les jours, elle lui répond affirmativement en commençant sa phrase par *hier*.

Modèle: Aujourd'hui, je fais mes devoirs.—Hier, j'ai fait mes devoirs.

1. Aujourd'hui, je vais à l'école avec mon petit frère.

2. Je déjeune à la cantine avec Thierry.

3. Je réponds aux questions du professeur.

4. Je mets mes livres sur mon pupitre.

5. Je rentre à la maison à 5 heures.

II. Refaites les phrases au passé composé.

1. Josette/sortir/la voiture/du garage.

2. Les élèves/entrer/dans la salle de classe.

3. Le mois dernier/nous/passer une semaine au bord de la mer.

4. La robe/elle/acheter/coûter cher.

5. Elles/rencontrer/des copains.

III. Racontez l'histoire de ces jeunes gens.

Hier, il (*pleuvoir*) toute la journée. Angélique et ses copains, Kevin et Daniel, (*décider*) d'aller au cinéma. Pour prendre des billets, il (*falloir*) attendre une demi-heure. Finalement, ils (*entrer*) dans la salle. Malheureusement, ils (*ne pas trouver*) trois places ensemble. Daniel (*devoir*) s'asseoir tout seul. A la fin du film, il (*ne pas pouvoir*) trouver ses copains. Il (*sortir*) et les (*attendre*) à la porte. Vingt minutes plus tard, il les (*retrouver*). Angélique et Kevin le cherchaient toujours!

Use of Adverbs
La place des adverbes

Most adverbs follow the past participle, except for the following, which are placed between the auxiliary verb and the past participle.

assez—beaucoup—bien—déjà—encore—jamais—mal—souvent—trop

Elle a assez dormi / elle a mal dormi / elle a bien dormi.

But
Elle a parlé intelligemment.

Some adverbs, such as **longtemps**, can be placed either before or after the past participle:

Il a longtemps attendu (*poetic*)
Il a attendu longtemps

To Leave
Laisser, Partir, Quitter

These verbs all mean *to leave*, with a slight difference in usage.

- **Laisser** = *to leave behind something or someone, to let + infinitive*

  J'ai laissé mon livre sur la table.
  I left my book on the table.

  Laisse-la seule, elle doit étudier.
  Leave her alone, she has to study.

  Laisse-moi regarder la télé, maman.
  Let me watch television, mom.

- **Partir** = *to leave a place (without necessarily naming the place), to leave from (**partir de**), to leave for (**partir à, en, au, aux**)**

  Il est parti à 9 heures.
  He left at 9 o'clock.

  Elle est partie aux Etats-Unis.
  She left for the United States (went to the United States).

  Ils sont partis en voyage.
  They left (went) on a trip.

- **Quitter** = *to take leave, to leave (a person or a place) for a very long time, to abandon*

  Il faut que je vous quitte parce que j'ai un rendez-vous.
  I must leave you because I have an appointment.

  Il a quitté son pays quand il avait vingt ans.
  He left his country when he was twenty.

  Elle a quitté son mari le mois dernier.
  She left her husband last month.

*Partir à is not always accepted by the purists, but is accepted in everyday language.

IV. Placez correctement l'adverbe dans les phrases suivantes:

Modèle: Il a voyagé *(déjà).*—Il a déjà voyagé.

1. Nous n'avons pas compris ce passage. *(bien)*

2. Ils sont sortis. *(rapidement)*

3. Elle a travaillé dans cette école. *(toujours)*

4. Le professeur a expliqué cette règle grammaticale. *(encore)*

5. Ils ont conduit. *(prudemment)*

V. Est-ce *laisser*, *partir*, ou *quitter*?

1. Ce matin, tu _____ ton chandail à la maison.

2. Il _____ sa profession.

3. Ils _____ en Italie le mois dernier.

4. Elle _____ sa famille lorsqu'elle avait 18 ans.

5. Le prof les _____ sortir avant la fin de l'heure.

6. Ne _____ pas vos chaussures devant la porte.

7. Elle _____ toujours de la maison vers 7h30.

8. Mon frère _____ toujours son travail vers 6h.

9. Le dimanche, elle _____ dormir ses enfants jusqu'à onze heures.

10. Je dois vous _____ parce que j'ai beaucoup de courses à faire.

Compound Past or Imperfect?
Passé composé ou imparfait?

To decide which of the two tenses to use, it is helpful to think about the following questions:

Imparfait	→	What was taking place?
Passé Composé	→	What interrupted that which was taking place?

Example: We were reading when the teacher arrived.

What was taking place?	→	*We were reading.*	→	**Imparfait**
What interrupted?	→	*The teacher arrived.*	→	**Passé Composé**

Therefore, the above sentence should be:

Nous lisions quand le professeur est arrivé.

NOTE

Most fairy tales as well as most dreams are told in the imparfait **and the** passé composé.

"Once upon a time, there **was** a beautiful princess whose name **was** Odile. One day, a handsome prince **arrived** to bring a message to the king. As soon as he **saw** Odile, the prince **fell in love** with her. He **wanted** to ask for her hand, but he **was** not rich and he **thought** that there was no hope. However, when Odile **saw** him, she too **fell in love** with him. She went to see her father and **told** him that she **hoped** the prince **wanted** to marry her because she **was** in love with him. The father **wanted** his daughter to marry a very rich prince, but because he **loved** her, he **agreed**."

"Il était une fois une belle princesse qui s'appelait Odile. Un jour, un beau prince est arrivé pour donner un message au roi. Aussitôt qu'il a vu Odile, le prince est tombé amoureux d'elle. Il voulait demander sa main, mais il n'était pas riche et il pensait qu'il n'y avait pas d'espoir. Cependant, quand Odile l'a vu, elle aussi est tombée amoureuse de lui. Elle est allée voir son père et lui a dit qu'elle espérait que le prince voulait l'épouser parce qu'elle était amoureuse de lui. Le père désirait que sa fille épouse un prince très riche, mais parce qu'il l'aimait, il a accepté".

QUICK PRACTICE

VI. Colette raconte à son copain Mathieu le rêve qu'elle a fait la nuit dernière, et il lui pose des questions:

Colette:	Je (se trouver) _____ dans un immense jardin.
Mathieu:	Est-ce que tu (être) _____ seule?
Colette:	Non, j'(être) _____ avec un groupe d'amis, mais c'est drôle, je (ne pas les connaître) _____ .
Mathieu:	Comment donc peux-tu dire qu'il (s'agir) _____ d'amis?
Colette:	Je ne sais pas, mais dans mon rêve, je (savoir) _____ qu'ils l'(être) _____ . Enfin, nous (jouer) _____ au ballon dans ce jardin, quand un homme bizarre (arriver) _____ . Il (être) _____ à cheval, et il (porter) _____ un masque.
Mathieu:	Comme Zorro?
Colette:	Non, pas tout-à-fait. Il (avoir) _____ des habits d'une autre époque, du dix-huitième siècle je crois. Et il (brandir) _____ une épée en or.
Mathieu:	En or? C'est passionnant ça!
Colette:	Soudain, il (me regarder) _____ et (jeter) _____ quelque chose vers moi. J'(être) _____ stupéfaite et je (ne pas pouvoir) _____ bouger.
Mathieu:	Cette chose, c'(être) _____ quoi?
Colette:	Ta chaîne en or!
Mathieu:	Ma chaîne? Celle que tu (m'offrir) _____ pour mon anniversaire?
Colette:	Exactement. Et puis il (me dire) _____ que tu (aller) _____ partir pour l'université.
Mathieu:	C'est extraordinaire ça! Justement, je viens de recevoir une lettre m'annonçant que j'(être) _____ accepté à l'université de Californie et que je vais faire partie de l'équipe d'escrime… l'épée en or, c'est incroyable! Tu as des pouvoirs surnaturels!
Colette:	*(riant)* Mais non! C'est ton père que je/j'(rencontrer) _____ ce matin et qui (me donner) _____ ces nouvelles!
Mathieu:	Alors, le rêve?
Colette:	C'(être) _____ une blague!

VII. **A VOTRE TOUR:** Avec un ou une camarade, crééz un dialogue dans lequel vous racontez un conte de fees (*a fairy tale*) ou un rêve (*a dream*).

VIII. **RÉDACTION:** Pendant les vacances de Noël, les Dufour sont partis faire du ski. Malheureusement, le premier jour, monsieur Dufour s'est cassé la jambe. A la suite de ce voyage, madame Dufour raconte à sa voisine ce qui est arrivé (*what happened*). Racontez ce qu'elle dit en vous servant du passé composé et de l'imparfait.

MOTS CROISÉS
Le passé composé

Across
6. Elles sont _____ (sortir)
8. J'ai _____ (avoir)
9. Ils sont _____ (passer)
10. To leave a person or a place
12. Ils sont _____ (devenir)
13. Recently

Down
1. Vous êtes _____ (descendre)
2. Nous _____ (voir—2 words)
3. Nous avons _____ (sourire)
4. Tu as _____ (répondre)
5. To leave something or someone behind
7. The day before yesterday (2 words)
8. Elle _____ (aller—2 words)
11. J'ai _____ (boire)

Culture Capsule 4

Les arrondissements de Paris datent de 1795. A cette époque, il y en avait douze, neuf sur la rive droite de la Seine et trois sur la rive gauche. En 1860, Napoléon III décida d'agrandir Paris en annexant quelques faubourgs. Cette annexion élargit la ville et donna naissance aux vingt arrondissements modernes. Le nom "arrondissement" vient du verbe "arrondir" (*to round*). En effet, ils sont attribués selon une spirale qui part du centre de la ville (quartier du Louvre) et tourne dans le sens des aiguilles d'une montre.

Il ne faut pas confondre "arrondissement" et "quartier". Le nom de "quartier" vient du fait que, au Moyen-Age, la ville de Paris était divisée en quatre parties. Aujourd'hui chaque arrondissement comprend quatre quartiers dont les plus connus des touristes sont le Marais et le Quartier Latin. Un quartier est un espace dans lequel l'architecture, les magasins, etc. se ressemblent. C'est pourquoi aux Etats-Unis, le *French Quarter* de la Nouvelle-Orléans est si distinct du reste de la ville. A Paris, le quartier du Marais est un trésor historique. C'est là que se trouve le Musée Carnavalet qui fut, pendant un certain temps, la demeure de Madame de Sévigné et qui aujourd'hui abrite une collection d'oeuvres d'art ainsi que d'objets de l'époque révolutionnaire. Dans ce quartier se trouve aussi la maison de Victor Hugo. C'est dans le Quartier Latin, ainsi dénommé parce qu'on y a parlé latin jusqu'à la Révolution Française, que se trouve la célèbre université connue dans le monde entier: La Sorbonne.

VOCABULAIRE

arrondissements	*the different subdivisions of Paris*
à cette époque	*at that time*
élargit	*expanded*
faubourgs	*suburbs*
le sens	*the direction*
les aiguilles d'une montre	*the hands of a watch*
confondre	*confuse*
quartier	*quarter*
la demeure	*the house*
abrite	*houses*
Madame de Sévigné	*noblewoman of the XVIIth century*
	mostly known for the letters she wrote to her
	daughter and friends depicting life at that time.

6

The Pluperfect

Que savez-vous déjà?
What Do You Know Already?

Circle the correct answer in the pluperfect.

1. Simone (voir) le professeur avant la classe.
   (a) avait vu   (b) a vu

2. Nous (aller) chez Colette.
   (a) sommes allés   (b) étions allés

3. Je (dire) rien.
   (a) Je n'avais rien dit   (b) Je n'ai rien dit

4. Quand je suis arrivé, ils (finir) le dîner.
   (a) finissaient   (b) avaient fini

5. Elle a dit qu'elle (lire) ce livre.
   (a) avait lu   (b) a lu

6. Il (ne pas comprendre) le premier exercice.
   (a) n'a pas compris   (b) n'avait pas compris

7. Est-ce que tu (voyager) seul?
   (a) voyageais   (b) avais voyagé

8. La voiture qu'il (acheter) était immense.
   (a) avait achetée   (b) a achetée

The **plus-que-parfait** corresponds to the pluperfect in English. It describes a past action or event that occurred before another past action or event.

In the name of the verb itself, **plus-que-parfait**, you have the word **parfait**, which refers to the **imparfait**.

69

Why? Because, in order to form the **plus-que-parfait**, as in the **passé composé**, the auxiliary verbs **avoir** and **être** are used. However, unlike the **passé composé** where these verbs are conjugated in the present tense, in the **plus-que-parfait** they are conjugated in the imperfect tense before being followed by the past participle of the principal verb.

Compare

Passé composé:	*Hier,* ***j'ai étudié*** *jusqu'à minuit.*
Plus-que-parfait:	*Hier,* ***j'avais fini*** *mes devoirs quand mes parents sont arrivés.*

Subject → imperfect of avoir or être → past participle

Nous	avions	fini
Elles	avaient	parlé
Tu	étais	parti
Elle	était	allée
Je	m'étais	promené
Ils	s'étaient	amusés

When using the verb **être** the rules of agreement of the past participle that are used in the **passé composé** apply.

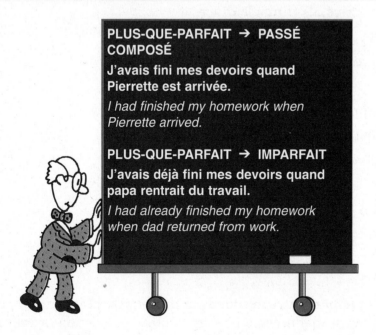

PLUS-QUE-PARFAIT → PASSÉ COMPOSÉ

J'avais fini mes devoirs quand Pierrette est arrivée.

I had finished my homework when Pierrette arrived.

PLUS-QUE-PARFAIT → IMPARFAIT

J'avais déjà fini mes devoirs quand papa rentrait du travail.

I had already finished my homework when dad returned from work.

Juxtaposed Sentences
Phrases juxtaposées

Antoine était fatigué: il avait travaillé jusqu'à minuit.
Antoine was tired: he had worked until midnight.

- **Après un pronom relatif**
  (See the chapter on relative pronouns.)

  Elle m'a parlé du film qu'elle avait vu.
  She spoke to me about the movie that she had seen.

  J'ai vu le film dont elle avait parlé.
  I saw the movie of which she had spoken.

- **Après parce que**

  Ils étaient fatigués parce qu'ils avaient couru.
  They were tired because they had been running.

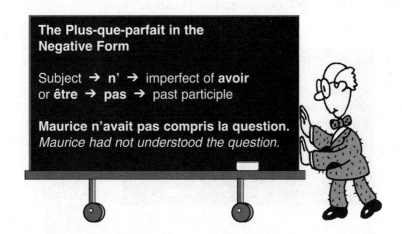

The Plus-que-parfait in the Negative Form

Subject → n' → imperfect of **avoir** or **être** → **pas** → past participle

Maurice n'avait pas compris la question.
Maurice had not understood the question.

QUICK PRACTICE

I. **Les mésaventures de Maurice. Monsieur Desjardins raconte ce qui était arrivé à son fils Maurice un jour pendant les vacances (au plus-que-parfait).**

1. Il (pleuvoir) _____ ce jour-là.

2. Maurice (avoir) _____ un accident de bicyclette.

3. Il (ne pas être) _____ sérieusement blessé.

4. La bicyclette (se casser) _____ .

5. Nous lui (dire) _____ de ne pas sortir sous cette pluie, mais il (ne pas vouloir) _____ nous écouter!

II. Laissez libre cours à votre imagination *(let your imagination run freely)*, **et complétez les phrases suivantes en vous servant du plus-que-parfait.**

1. Michel n'a pas fait ses devoirs hier parce qu'il _____ .

2. Ils sont arrivés à neuf heures, ils _____ .

3. Martine _____ parce qu'elle était paresseuse.

4. J'ai acheté la voiture dont _____ .

5. Ils m'ont dit que l'accident _____ .

The **Plus-que-parfait** and **Conjunctions of Time**
Le plus-que-parfait et les conjonctions de temps

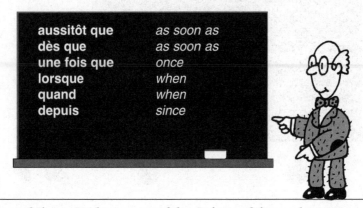

aussitôt que	*as soon as*
dès que	*as soon as*
une fois que	*once*
lorsque	*when*
quand	*when*
depuis	*since*

Conjunction of time → plus-que-parfait → imparfait or plus-que-parfait

Aussitôt qu'il avait fini ses devoirs, mon frère allait au stade.
As soon as he had finished his homework, my brother went to the stadium.

Quand ils étaient venus nous voir, ils n'avaient pas encore annoncé leurs fiançailles.
When they had come to see us, they hadn't yet announced their engagement.

Words and Expressions Often Used with the Plus-que-parfait

la semaine précédente	*the previous week*
le mois précédent	*the previous month*
la veille	*the previous night, the eve*
le jour d'avant	*the previous day*
le jour précédent	*the previous day*
il y avait (+ period of time + que)	*period of time + ago*
	pluperfect + for + period of time

Ils avaient fait leurs valises la veille de leur voyage.
They had packed their suitcases on the eve of their trip.

La semaine précédente ils avaient acheté leurs billets d'avion.
The previous week, they had bought their airplane tickets.

Il y avait trois ans qu'ils n'avaient pas fait de ski.
They had not skied for three years.

Passé composé, Imparfait, and Plus-que-parfait: Order
Le passé composé, l'imparfait, et le plus-que-parfait: Ordre

> plus-que parfait / passé composé → présent
> . . . imparfait . . .

Elle avait fini ses devoirs quand nous sommes arrivés.
She had finished her homework when we arrived.
(One action was completed before the other one occurred.)

Le film avait déjà commencé quand elle a trouvé sa place.
The movie had already begun when she found her seat.
(One action had already begun when the other one occurred.)

**Natalie racontait l'histoire à Thierry parce qu'il n'avait pas
lu le livre.**
Natalie was telling Thierry the story because he had not read the book.
(One action happened as a result of a previous past action.)

III. Complétez les mots suivants pour former des phrases. Servez-vous des temps du passé.

Modèle: Quand je/finir/le dîner/je/faire toujours/la vaisselle.
Quand j'avais fini le dîner, je faisais toujours la vaisselle.

1. le repas/toujours/préparer/papa.

2. Je/ne pas reconnaître/Marie/quand/je/la voir/au congrès.*(conference)*

3. Les Lemaître/déjà/rentrer/de voyage/ quand/je/les voir.

4. Je/voir/Carole/le jour de Noél/ La veille/elle/se fiancer.

5. Une fois que/Alain/finir/ses devoirs/ il/ sortir/toujours/avec ses amis.

6. Il /vouloir/aller au restaurant/parce que/ il/ne pas encore manger.

7. Il y avait/une semaine/qu'elle/être/malade.

IV. Mettez les verbes entre parenthèses aux temps du passé qui conviennent.

FAIT-DIVERS
News Item

Un accident *(avoir lieu)* la semaine dernière devant les Galeries Lafayette. Une jeune femme qui *(faire)* beaucoup d'emplettes *(tomber)* avec tous ses paquets près de la porte. Comme elle *(ne pas pouvoir)* se relever, on *(devoir)* appeler une ambulance qui *(la transporter)* à l'hôpital … avec tous ses paquets! Elle *(tenir)* beaucoup à ce qu'elle *(acheter)*… mais *(ne pas se rendre compte)* que son sac a main *(rester)* sur le trottoir. Folle d'inquiétude et oubliant la douleur que sa cheville lui *(causer)*, elle *(téléphoner)* aux Galeries pour voir si quelqu'un *(le trouver)*. A sa grande surprise, un passant obligeant venait de remettre le sac aux objets trouvés! A ce moment, le médecin *(arriver)* et *(lui dire)* qu'elle *(n'avoir)* qu'une entorse *(sprain)* au pied. Encore une histoire qui finit bien!

V. En vous servant de l'exemple ci-dessus, racontez l'histoire d'un accident. Employez le passé composé, l'imparfait et le plus-que-parfait.

MOTS CROISÉS
Le plus-que-parfait

Across

3. Nous _____ (avoir—2 words)

5. Tu _____ (lire—2 words)

7. Nous _____ (parler—2 words)

9. Il _____ (vivre—2 words)

10. Vous _____ (finir—2 words)

11. J' _____ (faire—2 words)

12. Elle _____ (venir—2 words)

13. Elle _____ (arriver—2 words)

Down

1. Il _____ (pleuvoir)

2. Elle _____ (courir—2 words)

4. Elle _____ (aller—2 words)

6. Il _____ (attendre—2 words)

8. Tu _____ (être—2 words)

10. Nous _____ (prendre—2 words)

Culture Capsule 5

Louis XIV avait résumé en quelques mots la loi de son règne: *"C'est la loi parce que je le veux!"*. Plus tard, avant la Révolution, Voltaire avait remarqué que les villages en France n'étaient pas tous soumis aux mêmes lois.

Promulgué le 21 mars 1804 (30 ventôse de l'an XII), le Code Napoléon réglemente la vie civile de tous les Français. Il existe toujours en France, plus de 200 ans après sa création par l'empereur Napoléon Premier, alors qu'il n'était que Premier Consul. Appelé simplement Bonaparte, celui-ci nomme d'abord une commission de rédacteurs pour rédiger le "Code Civil des Français". Après avoir été examiné par le Conseil d'Etat, le texte est ensuite promulgué comme loi. Il est aujourd'hui à la base du droit moderne. En le créant, Napoléon s'était appuyé sur la loi des Romains (Code de Justinien). Ce projet qui avait été envisagé au début de la révolution onze ans plus tôt unifie les pratiques de l'Ancien Régime et les principes républicains de liberté, égalité, fraternité.

Un objectif de ce nouveau code était de créer un guide que tout citoyen puisse comprendre et ainsi connaitre ses droits. Un deuxième objectif était d'échapper à la tutelle de l'Eglise en déclarant que le mariage relevait de la loi civile et que le divorce était legal. Un troisième objectif visait à ce que la propriété immobilière ne soit plus soumise aux droits féodaux: *"La propriété est le droit de jouir et de disposer des choses de la manière la plus absolue, pourvu qu'on n'en fasse pas un usage prohibé par les lois ou par les règlements"*.

Au cours des ans, le Code Napoléon a subi certaines modifications. Ainsi, la "puissance paternelle" est devenue "la puissance parentale" et la femme, qui, à son mariage, avait les droits d'un enfant mineur, aujourd'hui jouit des mêmes droits que son époux. Le Code Napoléon a inspiré plusieurs autres pays. N'oublions pas qu'aux Etats-Unis, la Louisiane a un système légal réglementé par le Code Napoléon.

Citons enfin cette phrase célèbre du petit empereur: *"Ma vraie gloire n'est pas d'avoir gagné quarante batailles; Waterloo effacera le souvenir de tant de victoires; ce que rien n'effacera, ce qui vivra éternellement, c'est mon Code Civil"*.

VOCABULAIRE

avait résumé	*had summarized*
la loi	*the law*
soumis	*subject (to the same law)*
rédacteurs	*writers (in this context)*
rédiger	*write/draft*
s'était appuyé	*had relied*
envisagé	*contemplated*
échapper à la tutelle	*get away from under the thumb*
les droits	*the rights*

7

Pronominal Verbs

Que savez-vous déjà?
What Do You Know Already?

(?)

Match the items of the two columns.

1. Pierre _____ toujours à minuit.   a. me brosse

2. Nous _____ pendant les vacances.   b. s'aiment

3. Je _____ les dents.   c. s'est habillée

4. Il _____ chaque matin à 6 heures.   d. nous sommes promenés

5. Ils _____ depuis toujours.   e. se couche

6. Elle _____ pour aller au bal.   f. s'appelle

7. Nous _____ dans le parc.   g. me demande

8. Il _____ Nicolas.   h. nous sommes amusés

9. Elle _____ les mains.   i. se réveille

10. Je _____ si c'est une bonne idée.   j. s'est lavé

As their name indicates, pronominal verbs are always accompanied by a pronoun. There are three categories of pronominal verbs:

- **Reflexive verbs**
- **Reciprocal verbs**
- **Pronominal verbs that are neither reflexive nor reciprocal**

WHAT IS A REFLEXIVE VERB?

A reflexive verb is a verb where an action is done by one person on himself or herself, as in *I dress myself*. When used without the pronoun, the action is on someone else. Whether with or without the pronoun, the verb keeps the same meaning.

Je m'habille.—J'habille ma petite fille.

A reflexive verb is often used to express an emotion: *to worry* = **s'inquiéter.**

WHAT IS A RECIPROCAL VERB?

A reciprocal verb requires two or more people. They reciprocate the action, as in *We look at each other*. When used without a pronoun, the action is performed without reciprocity, but retains the same meaning whether it is reciprocal or not.

Nous nous regardons.—Nous regardons le train qui passe.
We look at each other.—We look at the passing train.

WHAT IS A PRONOMINAL VERB THAT IS NEITHER REFLEXIVE NOR RECIPROCAL?

- **Verbs that can only be used pronominally**

    S'empresser = *to hurry to accomplish something or to please someone, usually zealously*

    Il s'empresse auprès de cette jeune fille.
    He is eager to please this young woman.

- **Verbs that have a passive meaning**

    S'employer = *to be used*

    Ce mot ne s'emploie plus aujourd'hui.
    This word is no longer used nowadays.

- **Verbs that have a different meaning when used pronominally**

    Se passer = *to happen* ➔ **passer** = *to pass, go by, to spend time*

    Qu'est-ce qui se passe?
    What's happening?

The Reflexive or Reciprocal Pronouns
Les pronoms réfléchis et réciproques

SUBJECT PRONOUNS	REFLEXIVE/RECIPROCAL PRONOUNS	
je	me	*myself*
tu	te	*yourself*
il	se	*himself*
elle	se	*herself*
on	se	*oneself*
nous	nous	*ourselves/each other*
vous	vous	*yourselves/each other*
ils	se	*themselves/each other/one another*
elles	se	*themselves/each other/one another*

For the infinitive, the pronoun **se** is always used: **se laver, se coucher**

For the imperative, there are three forms only: **toi, nous,** and **vous**

SOME COMMON REFLEXIVE VERBS

s'amuser	*to have fun*	**amuser**	*to entertain*
se cacher	*to hide oneself*	**cacher**	*to hide something*
se laver	*to wash oneself*	**laver**	*to wash + direct object*
se lever	*to get up*	**lever**	*to raise (physically)*
s'habiller	*to get dressed*	**habiller**	*to dress + direct object*
se déshabiller	*to get undressed*	**déshabiller**	*to undress + direct object*
se brosser les dents	*to brush one's teeth*	**brosser**	*to brush + direct object*
se raser	*to shave*	**raser**	*to shave + direct object*
se coucher	*to go to bed*	**coucher**	*to put to bed*
se réveiller	*to wake up*	**réveiller**	*to wake up someone*
se promener	*to take a walk*	**promener**	*to take someone for a walk*

Stéphanie s'habille toujours après le petit-déjeuner.
Stephanie always gets dressed after breakfast.

Stéphanie habille sa fille.
Stephanie dresses her daughter.

COMMON RECIPROCAL VERBS

Remember: They can only be conjugated in the plural form!

s'embrasser	*to kiss one another or each other*
se regarder*	*to look at one another or each other*
se parler*	*to speak (talk) to one another or each other*
s'aimer	*to love one another or each other*
s'écrire	*to write one another or each other*
se rencontrer	*to meet*
se téléphoner	*to call (telephone) one another or each other*

*Can be used in the singular form as in "I look at myself" or "I speak to myself."

When not used pronominally, these verbs retain the same meaning but must be followed by a direct or indirect object.

embrasser	*to kiss*
regarder	*to look*
parler (à/de)	*to speak (talk) to/about*
aimer	*to love*
écrire	*to write*
rencontrer	*to meet*
téléphoner (à)	*to telephone*

PRONOMINAL VERBS THAT ARE NEITHER REFLEXIVE NOR RECIPROCAL

s'évanouir	*to faint*		
se moquer (de)	*to make fun of*	*Used only*	
se souvenir (de)	*to remember*	*pronominally!!!*	
se taire	*to keep quiet, silent*		
s'appeler	*to be called (named)*	appeler	*to call*
se dire	*to tell (say to) oneself*	dire	*to tell (say)*
se passer	*to happen*	passer	*to pass, go by, spend time*
se trouver	*to be placed (located)*	trouver	*to find*
s'entendre	*to get along with*	entendre	*to hear*
se demander	*to wonder*	demander	*to ask*
se tromper	*to be mistaken*	tromper	*to fool, deceive/to be unfaithful*

Placement of Pronouns
La place des pronoms

PRESENT TENSE AND SIMPLE TENSES	
Subject → pronoun → verb	
Je me couche	Nous nous couchons
Tu te couches	Vous vous couchez
Il/elle/on se couche	Ils/elles se couchent

THE IMPERATIVE		
Verb in the imperative → pronoun		
Couche-toi	Couchons-nous	Couchez-vous

PASSÉ COMPOSÉ AND COMPOUND TENSES	
Subject → pronoun → auxiliary verb → past participle	
→ All pronominal verebs use être as an auxiliary verb ←	
Je me suis couché(e)	Nous nous sommes couché(e)s
Tu t'es couché(e)	Vous vous êtes couché(e)(s)
Il /elle/on s'est couché(e)	Ils/elles se sont couché(e)s

Agreement of the Past Participle
L'accord du participe passé

All pronominal verbs take the auxiliary verb **être**. However, the rules of agreement are different from other verbs taking **être** in compound tenses. Before deciding if there is an agreement, we need to know if the pronominal verb, when used in the nonpronominal form, is followed or not by the preposition **à**.

Regarder is not followed by **à**: **Je regarde la télévision.** (*direct*)
Some other verbs: **voir, aimer, détester, rencontrer.**

Téléphoner is followed by **à**: Je téléphone **à** mes amis. (*indirect*)
Some other verbs: **écrire, dire, parler, donner.**

- **When me, te, se, nous, vous is a *direct* object, there will be agreement with the subject**

    Nous nous sommes regard**és**.
    We looked at each other.   (*regarder*)

- **When me, te, se, nous, vous is an *indirect object*, there is no agreement with the subject**

    Nous nous sommes téléphon**é**.
    We telephoned each other.   (*téléphoner à*)

- **When me, te, se, nous, vous is a direct object but is followed by another direct object, there is no agreement**

    Compare: Elle s'est lav**ée**.   *She washed.*
                Elle s'est lav**é les mains**.   *She washed her hands.*

- **When the direct object precedes the verb, even if the reflexive/ reciprocal pronoun is indirect, there will be agreement with the subject**

    Compare: Carole s'est offert **une robe** de couturier.
                Carole offered herself a designer dress.   (*offrir à*)

    La robe que Carole s'est offert**e** est très chère.
    The dress that Carole offered herself is very expensive.

Note: You will notice that these are the same rules that are used with verbs using the auxiliary verb **avoir** in compound tenses.

*Q*UICK *P*RACTICE

I. Complétez les phrases suivantes au présent avec un des verbes ci-dessous, soit le verbe simple, soit le verbe pronominal.

Modèle: passer/se passer
         Elle _____ chaque jour devant le parc. Qu'est-ce qui _____ ?
         Elle passe chaque jour devant le parc. Qu'est-ce qui se passe?

1. trouver/se trouver

   Ma cousine _____ en Algérie. Elle _____ ce pays magnifique.

2. entendre/s'entendre

Nous _____ toujours nos voisins crier. Je ne pense pas qu'ils _____ .

3. laver/se laver

Nous _____ les mains avant de diner, mais nous ne _____ pas la vaisselle après!

4. tromper/se tromper

Josette _____ toujours de rue quand elle vient me voir.

5. acheter/s'acheter

Louis _____ une bague de fiançailles à Dorothée.

II. **Faites des phrases complètes en mettant le premier verbe à la forme correcte du passé composé et le deuxième verbe, s'il y en a un, à l'imparfait ou au présent, selon le cas.**

Modèle: la voiture / que Michèle /s'acheter / être / belle.
La voiture que Michèle s'est achetée est belle.
Le musée / que je / visiter / être / magnifique.
Le musée que j'ai visité était magnifique.

1. Hier / Suzanne / se promener / dans le village.

2. Les élèves / que je / voir/ venir de France.

3. Ils / se regarder.

4. Elle / se trouver / dans une rue / qu'elle / ne pas connaître.

5. Nous / se tromper / d'adresse / hier.

6. L'actrice / s'évanouir / à la fin de la pièce.

7. Nous / s'amuser / à la fête.

8. Elle / se brosser / les cheveux / avant de sortir.

9. Vous /se rencontrer / quand / vous / être / à l'université.

10. Elle / se réveiller /de très bonne heure (*very early*).

III. **Monsieur Rodin donne des ordres d'abord à sa fille, Colette, et puis à ses deux fils, Louis et Paul. Mettez les verbes suivants à la forme correcte de l'impératif.**

Modèle: Se coucher—Couche-toi/couchez-vous.

1. Se réveiller

2. Se laver

3. S'habiller

4. Se dépêcher

5. Se souvenir d'appeler grand-mère

Pronominal Verbs After Aller/Vouloir/Pouvoir
Les verbes pronominaux après "avoir/vouloir/pouvoir"

When a pronominal verb is used in conjunction with verbs such as **aller**, **vouloir**, or **pouvoir**, the reflexive pronoun is used before the pronominal verb.

Subject →	aller/vouloir/pouvoir →	reflexive pronoun →	infinitive of pron. verb
↓	↓	↓	↓
Nous	allons	**nous**	amuser
Il	veut	**se**	coucher

QUICK PRACTICE

IV. **Monsieur Charpentier essaie de convaincre ses enfants d'aller à la campagne cet été. Refaites les phrases suivantes en mettant les verbes entre parentheses à la forme correcte.**

1. Nous (aller—s'amuser).

2. Maman (aller—se reposer)

3. Vous (pouvoir—se baigner) tous les jours.

4. Vous (aller—se coucher) tard.

5. Vous (pouvoir—se réveiller) quand vous voulez

The Negative Form
La forme négative

PRESENT/SIMPLE TENSES (such as the imperfect)

Subject →	ne →	reflexive pronoun →	verb →	negative expression →	rest of the sentence
↓	↓	↓	↓	↓	↓
Tu	**ne**	**te**	réveilles	**pas**	avant midi
Nous	**ne**	**nous**	rencontrons	**jamais**	avant midi

PASSÉ COMPOSÉ/COMPOUND TENSES

Subject →	ne →	reflexive pronoun →	auxiliary →	negative expression →	main verb
↓	↓	↓	↓	↓	↓
Vous	**ne**	**vous**	êtes	**pas**	dépêchés
Elle	**ne**	**s'**	est	**jamais**	trompée

IMPERATIVE

Ne →	reflexive pronoun →	verb →	negative expression
↓	↓	↓	↓
Ne	te	dépêche	**pas**
Ne	vous	trompez	**plus**

WITH ALLER/VOULOIR/POUVOIR/DEVOIR

Subject →	ne →	aller/vouloir/pouvoir →	negative expression →	reflexive →	verb pronoun
↓	↓	↓	↓	↓	↓
Vous	**ne**	voulez	**pas**	**vous**	taire

QUICK PRACTICE

V. Thierry ne veut pas obéir à sa mère. Il répond négativement à ce qu'elle lui dit en se servant de "pas" ou "jamais".

1. Thierry, lave-toi les mains avant le diner.

   Non, _____

2. Brosse-toi les dents!

   Non, _____

3. Tu vas te coucher à dix heures ce soir.

Non, _____

4. Tu dois te réveiller à six heures demain matin.

Non, _____

5. Tu vas t'acheter un nouveau livre d'anglais.

Non, _____

VI. Mettez les phrases suivantes à la forme négative.

1. Jean et Kevin, cachez-vous tout le temps!

2. Albert, achète-toi un anorak très cher!

3. Maman, téléphonons-nous tous les jours!

4. Chéri, embrassons-nous devant tout le monde!

5. Vanessa, moque-toi de mes amis!

The Interrogative Form
La forme interrogative

SIMPLE TENSES				
THE INTERROGATIVE WITH EST-CE QUE				
Est-ce que → subject → reflexive pronoun → verb → rest of the sentence				
Est-ce que → tu → te → lèves → à sept heures?				
THE INTERROGATIVE USING THE INVERSION				
Reflexive pronoun → inversion verb/subject → rest of the sentence				
Vous → entendez-vous → avec Pierre?				
COMPOUND TENSES				
THE INTERROGATIVE WITH EST-CE QUE				
Est-ce que → subject → reflexive pronoun → auxiliary verb → past participle				
Est-ce que → vous → vous → êtes → amusés				
THE INTERROGATIVE USING THE INVERSION				
Reflexive pronoun → inversion auxiliary verb/subject → past participle				
Vous → êtes-vous → amusés				

Reminder: In an inversion, when a verb ends with a vowel and is followed by the pronoun **il** or **elle**, a **t** must be used between the verb and the pronoun.

TIP

When there is a noun, such as the name of a person, in the interrogative sentence, that name or noun is usually included. It is placed AFTER Est-ce que in the long form of the interrogative or BEFORE the inversion in the short form of the interrogative.

Name or noun → inverted sentence → rest of the sentence

Caroline → se réveille-t-elle → tous les jours à la même heure?
La petite fille → s'est-elle amusée → dans le parc?

QUICK PRACTICE

VII. **Michèle raconte à sa copine Delphine un film d'amour qu'elle a vu la veille** *(the evening before)*, **Delphine lui pose des questions (inversion) et Michèle lui répond. Les verbes sont au passé composé sauf** *(unless)* **si un autre temps est indiqué après le verbe.**

Michèle   Tu sais Delphine, j'ai vu un film superbe hier soir: Un amour d'été.

Delphine   Je n'ai pas le temps d'aller le voir, de quoi est-ce qu'il (s'agir—present) _____ ?

Michèle   Eh bien, un jeune médecin, Hervé, et une jeune actrice, Aline, (se rencontrer) _____ dans une gare. Ils (se regarder) _____ mais ils (ne pas se parler) _____ .

Delphine   Comment (se voir) _____ d'abord?

Michèle   Les deux avaient les mêmes valises, et Aline (se tromper) _____ et a pris la valise d'Hervé.

Delphine   Oh, je vois ce qui (se passer) _____ . Mais alors, quand (s'apercevoir) _____ de leur erreur et quand (se parler) _____ ?

Michèle   Eh bien, une fois dans le train, ils (se rendre compte) _____ de ce qui était arrivé.

Delphine   (s'aimer) _____ tout de suite?

Michèle   Non, ils (ne pas s'aimer) _____ immédiatement. Après avoir échangé les valises, ils . . .

Delphine   Ne dis plus rien! Maintenant j'ai envie d'aller le voir . . . même si je n'ai pas le temps!

VIII. A vous de parler! Avec un(e) camarade, discutez de vos dernières vacances en vous servant de verbes pronominaux. Les réponses peuvent être négatives ou affirmatives.

Modèle: Est-ce que tu t'es souvent promenée avec des copains?
Non, je ne me suis pas promenée avec des copains, mais tous les matins je me promenais seule à la plage.

(Exemples de verbes: s'amuser, se promener, se coucher, se réveiller, se baigner, se trouver, se demander, s'entendre)

IX. Mettez le verbe qui convient au passé composé dans les phrases suivantes, sauf si autrement (otherwise) **indiqué.**

Se salir to get dirty	**Se cacher** to hide
Se mettre à* to begin to do something	**Se disputer** to argue
S' amuser to have fun	**Se détendre** to relax
Se trouver to be located at	**Se reposer** to rest
Se maquiller to put makeup on	**S'embrasser** to kiss

1. Ce matin, quand Nicole _____ , elle a oublié de mettre son rouge à lèvres.

2. Maman _____ hier après-midi parce qu'elle était trop fatiguée.

3. En voyant le clown, Paul _____ rire.

4. Sa villa _____ au bord de la mer. (imparfait)

5. Le petit garçon _____ derrière un arbre et son père ne pouvait pas le trouver.

6. Nous _____ toujours quand nous allons au cirque (circus). (présent)

7. Marie-Ange _____ en jouant dans le jardin et maintenant, elle doit prendre un bain.

8. Je _____ avec mon frère parce qu'il a égratigné (scratched) ma voiture quand il l'a empruntée (borrowed it).

9. Nous _____ lorsque nous faisons du yoga. (présent)

10. Les français _____ toujours sur les deux joues (cheeks). (présent)

***Se mettre à** + infinitive = to begin doing something. The expression **se mettre à table** means to sit down to eat.

X. Mettez les verbes entre parenthèses soit au passé composé soit à l'imparfait:

FAIT-DIVERS
News Item

Nice, le 10 juin

Hier soir, vers 19h30, en sortant du café "Chez Edouard" un homme (*trébucher*) sur un caillou, (*tomber*) et (*se tordre*) la cheville. Un agent de police qui (*se trouver*) là (*se précipiter*) pour l'aider. L'homme (*le remercier*) et (*se lever*) sans trop de douleur. Il (*se diriger*) ensuite rapidement vers sa voiture. Peu après, l'agent (*remarquer*) sur le trottoir un portefeuille qui avait dû tomber de la poche de l'inconnu. Il (*essayer*) de le rattraper mais sans succès. L'homme (*être*) déjà hors de vue. En examinant le portefeuille, l'agent (*pouvoir*) identifier la victime de l'incident. Quelle n'(*être*) sa surprise de découvrir que ce dernier n'(*être*) autre que Marius Couturier, recherché depuis plusieurs mois pour vol à main armée! Quelques heures plus tard, le malfaiteur (*être*) arrêté.

LES VERBES PRONOMINAUX

```
H  S  F  L  B  I  M  V  L  R  S  C  J  Y  S
M  A  E  I  D  R  L  R  H  V  E  J  I  G  E
Y  Y  B  M  R  N  L  Z  F  E  T  E  W  U  T
E  F  Y  I  B  J  K  S  E  N  R  M  L  J  A
W  S  S  X  L  R  P  V  T  X  O  E  P  D  I
G  X  M  M  B  L  A  K  K  O  M  L  H  P  R
V  P  V  R  X  O  E  S  P  M  P  A  I  E  E
E  N  W  B  T  E  S  T  S  S  E  V  G  M  F
C  O  O  E  Y  V  O  M  O  E  R  E  P  G  N
S  H  A  B  I  L  L  E  R  I  R  F  W  H  B
M  X  S  D  R  E  Y  Z  X  I  G  X  W  R  T
Y  H  V  D  G  X  L  B  J  G  T  L  U  T  G
E  V  E  L  E  S  L  I  E  Z  A  W  F  O  O
E  E  V  E  L  T  S  E  S  E  L  L  E  B  R
L  K  K  H  T  H  L  D  O  C  O  C  E  L  D
```

ELLE S'EST LEVEE	JE ME LAVE	SE TROMPER
HABILLE-TOI	S'EMBRASSER	S'HABILLER
IL SE LEVE	SE TAIRE	

Culture Capsule 6

Le baccalauréat (appelé plus familièrement bac) est une institution qui date du début du dix-neuvième siècle. Quoiqu'on en retrouve des traces au Moyen-Age, ce n'est que sous Napoléon 1er, en 1808, que ce diplôme couronne la fin des études secondaires. A l'époque, les candidats devaient être âgés de seize ans ou plus et cet examen ne comportait que des épreuves orales. En 1830, la première épreuve écrite est introduite: le candidat peut choisir entre la composition française ou la traduction d'une oeuvre classique. En d'autres termes, seules les études humanistes font partie de l'épreuve. En 1821, les sciences sont ajoutées. Plus tard, en 1874, le baccalauréat série Lettres va se diviser en deux parties séparées par une année d'intervalle. Au vingtième siècle, la série moderne et la série technique sont offertes. Le baccalauréat technologique est créé en 1985 pour répondre aux exigences de la vie moderne. Il réunit une formation générale et une formation technologique.

Après avoir subi une série de transformations, la double finalité du baccalauréat se traduit aujourd'hui dans la poursuite d'études supérieures aussi bien que dans celle de débouchés professionnels immédiats. Les épreuves sont en effet d'une part générales et d'autre part professionnelles.

A noter: Les bacheliers étaient tous du sexe masculin jusqu'en 1861, date à laquelle la première femme, Julie Daubié, s'est présentée à l'examen.

VOCABULAIRE

couronne	*crowns*
débouchés professionnels	*career opportunities*
épreuves	*exams*
uniquement	*only*
ajoutées	*added*
bachelier, bachelière	*person who has a baccalauréat*

8

The Infinitive

Choose the correct answer.

1. _____ les devoirs avant de se coucher; c'est important.

   (a) finir   (b) finissant

2. Je vais _____ demain matin.

   (a) pars   (b) partir

3. Elle regarde les enfants _____ .

   (a) jouant   (b) jouer

4. Je ne peux pas _____ ce chapitre.

   (a) comprendre   (b) comprends

5. Elle _____ à Juliette.

   (a) téléphone   (b) téléphoner

6. Nous _____ avant 7 heures.

   (a) ne pouvons sortir pas   (b) ne pouvons pas sortir

7. Je te dis de _____ la fenêtre.

   (a) ne pas ouvrir   (b) n'ouvrir pas

8. J'étudie beaucoup afin de _____ .

   (a) réussis   (b) réussir

The Present Infinitive
L'infinitif présent

In French, the infinitive or the name of the verb falls into several categories, based on its ending:

Regular verbs	-er	parler *to speak*	*(verbes du 1er groupe)*
	-ir	finir *to finish*	*(verbes du 2ème groupe)*
	-re	attendre *to wait for*	*(verbes du 3ème groupe)*
Irregular verbs	-er	aller *to go*	
	-ir	ouvrir *to open*	
	-re	boire *to drink*	
	-oir	vouloir *to want*	

Different uses of the infinitive:

- **The infinitive as a noun corresponds to the English *-ing* form used as a noun**

  Traveling is a luxury. → **Voyager** est un luxe.

- **To replace the imperative in recipes**

  Add two eggs. → **Ajouter** deux oeufs.

- **After some prepositions such as** avant de, afin de, pour, sans

before leaving	→	**avant de partir**
in order to study	→	**afin d'étudier**
(in order) to succeed	→	**pour réussir**
without waiting	→	**sans attendre**

- **After some verbs that express wishes, perception, will, opinion, and motion**

aller *to go*	**espérer** *to hope*	**regarder*** *to watch*
aimer *to like*	**faillir** *to have a near*	**savoir** *to know how*
courir *to run*	miss	**souhaiter** *to wish*
croire *to believe*	**il faut** *it is necessary*	**sentir*** *to feel*
descendre *to go*	**laisser*** *to let, allow*	*(abstract meaning*
down	**monter** *to go up*	*only)*
désirer *to wish*	**oser** *to dare*	**venir** *to come*
devoir *to have to*	**penser** *to think*	**voir*** *to see*
détester *to detest*	**pouvoir** *to be able*	**vouloir** *to want*
entendre* *to hear*	**préférer** *to prefer*	

The verbs *entendre, laisser, regarder, sentir, voir* **can be used before the infinitive and the noun or before the noun and the infinitive.**

Je <u>laisse jouer</u> les enfants.　　**or**　Je <u>laisse</u> les enfants <u>jouer</u>.
I let the children play.

J'<u>entends sonner</u> la cloche.　　**or**　J'<u>entends</u> la cloche <u>sonner</u>.
I hear the bell ring.

Il <u>regarde courir</u> les élèves.　　**or**　Il <u>regarde</u> les élèves <u>courir</u>.
He watches the students running.

Elle <u>sent venir</u> l'orage.　　**or**　Elle <u>sent</u> l'orage <u>venir</u>.
She feels the storm coming.

Nous <u>voyons arriver</u> les copains.　**or**　Nous <u>voyons</u> les copains <u>arriver</u>.
We see the friends arrive.

<u>Laisse parler</u> la petite fille.　　**or**　<u>Laisse</u> la petite fille <u>parler</u>.
Let the little girl speak.

In the negative form, the two parts of the negative surround the conjugated verb:

Elle <u>ne</u> sent <u>pas</u> venir l'orage.　**or**　Elle <u>ne</u> sent <u>pas</u> l'orage venir.

<u>Ne</u> laisse <u>pas</u> parler la petite fille.　**or**　<u>Ne</u> laisse <u>pas</u> la petite fille parler.

In the passé composé, the above verbs do not agree with the direct object pronoun when followed by an infinitive:

Compare

J'ai <u>laissé les enfants</u> avec Corinne.　➔　Je <u>les</u> ai <u>laissés</u> avec Corinne.
I left the children with Corinne.　　*I left them with Corinne.*

J'ai <u>laissé jouer les enfants</u>.　　➔　Je <u>les</u> ai <u>laissé jouer</u>.
I let the children play.　　　*I let them play.*

Il court annoncer la nouvelle.	*He runs to announce the news.*
Nous désirons voir ce film.	*We wish to see this movie.*
Je vais aller au cinéma.	*I am going to go to the movies.*
Nous devons arriver avant 8h.	*We must arrive before 8 o'clock.*
Elle aime danser.	*She likes to dance.*
Je ne sais pas parler allemand.	*I don't know how to speak German.*
Elle est montée chercher le dictionnaire.	*She went up to get the dictionary.*
Ils sont venus voir maman.	*They came to see mom.*
Nous avons pu répondre aux questions.	*We were able to answer the questions.*
Je préfère sortir avec eux.	*I prefer going out with them.*
Il voulait acheter une voiture.	*He wanted to buy a car.*
Ils ont failli avoir un accident.	*They almost had an accident.*
Je pense faire un voyage en été.	*I think I will take a trip in the summer.*
Elle est partie faire des courses.	*She left to go shopping.*
Tu as osé conduire pendant l'orage.	*You dared to drive during the storm.*
Il faut étudier pour l'examen.	*It is necessary to study for the exam.*

- When using a direct or an indirect object pronoun, or both, they go between the two verbs.

Je préfère écrire la rédaction.	→	Je préfère l'écrire.
Il voulait conduire la voiture.	→	Il voulait la conduire.
Il faut parler au professeur.	→	Il faut lui parler.
Il va annoncer la nouvelle au directeur.	→	Il va la lui annoncer.
Va annoncer la nouvelle au directeur.	→	Va la lui annoncer.
Ne va pas voir le film.	→	Ne va pas le voir.

- What about the negative form?

In the infinitive the two parts of the negative (ne...pas, ne...jamais, ne...rien, ne...plus, ne...pas encore) precede the verb when the negation pertains to the verb in the infinitive.

Elle est sûre de ne pas se tromper.	→	She is sure that she is not mistaken.
J'ai peur de ne jamais comprendre.	→	I am afraid I will never understand.
Je préfère ne pas écrire la rédaction.	→	I prefer not to write the composition.
Il me conseille de ne plus insister.	→	He advises me not to insist anymore.
Il vaut mieux ne rien lui dire.	→	It is better not to tell him anything.

In some instances the negation surrounds the verb that precedes the infinitive because the negation pertains to the first verb.

Il ne voulait pas conduire la voiture.	→	He did not want to drive the car.
Il ne va pas chanter.	→	He is not going to sing.
Je ne pense pas visiter le musée.	→	I don't think I will visit the museum.

When using ne...personne and ne...aucun, the two parts of the negative surround the infinitive.

Elle est triste de ne voir aucun de ses amis à la soirée.
She is sad that she doesn't see any of her friends at the party.

J'ai peur de ne rencontrer personne pendant la croisière.
I am afraid I will meet no one during the cruise.

In the negative imperative form, the two parts of the negative precede the infinitive.

Ne pas ouvrir la porte!	➔	*Don't open the door!*
Ne pas traverser!	➔	*Don't cross!*

- **What about pronominal or reflexive verbs?**

The reflexive pronoun comes between the conjugated verb and the infinitive.

Je vais **m'**habiller.	➔	*I am going to get dressed.*
Je **ne** vais **pas m'**habiller.	➔	*I am not going to get dressed.*

QUICK PRACTICE

I. Dans les phrases suivantes remplacez le verbe conjugué par l'infinitif:

Modèle: Nous allons à la plage/ça fait du bien.
         Aller à la plage, ça fait du bien.

1. Vous nagez beaucoup/c'est bon pour la forme.

2. Elles voyagent souvent/ça forme la jeunesse.

3. Nous réfléchissons avant de parler/c'est sage.

4. Je sais quand il faut répondre/c'est une bonne idée.

5. Ils cherchent la bonne réponse/ce n'est pas facile.

II. Ajoutez "avant de, afin de, pour ou sans" dans les phrases suivantes:

1. Il n'aime pas sortir _____ mettre le chapeau.

2. Elle est allée au cinéma _____ faire ses devoirs.

3. J'ai promis d'étudier _____ pouvoir sortir ce soir.

4. J'ai pris le petit-déjeuner _____ aller à l'école.

5. Il faut bien écouter le professeur _____ comprendre la leçon.

III. Traduisez les mots entre parenthèses:

1. (Listening) _____ , c'est un art.

2. (Reading) _____ le journal tous les jours, c'est important pour moi.

3. Elle est sortie sans (closing) _____ la porte.

4. Je préfère (not to go out) _____ sans les copains.

5. J'aime (watching) _____ la télévision.

IV. Refaites les phrases en suivant l'exemple:

Modèle: Je laisse/le crayon tombe.
Je laisse tomber le crayon.
Je laisse le crayon tomber.

1. J'entends/les enfants jouent dans le jardin.

2. Ils voient/le train arrive.

3. Nous regardons/les chevaux courent.

4. Je sens/un mal de tête venir.

5. Elle laisse/les enfants dorment.

Causative Construction of Faire
La construction causative de "faire"

The **causative construction** means that the subject has (causes) someone else (to) do the action. When followed by a noun, this noun is a direct object. When followed by two nouns, one is a direct object and the other is an indirect object.

- **One noun**

Le professeur fait écrire **les élèves**. →	*The teacher has (makes) the students write.*
J'ai fait réciter **le poème**. →	*I had the poem recited (by someone).*

- **Two nouns**

The indirect object can be introduced by a form of **à** or by **par**. When using **à**, **au**, **à la**, **aux**, the person who is the subject of the sentence gives the order. When **par** is used, the person who is the subject has someone else do the work in his or her place.

> Le professeur fait écrire **la rédaction** *(dir. obj.)* aux **élèves** *(ind. obj.)*.
> *The teacher has the students write the composition.*

> J'ai fait réciter **le poème** *(dir. obj.)* aux **enfants** *(ind. obj.)*.
> *I had the children recite the poem.*

> J'ai fait réparer **la voiture** par **un mécanicien**.
> *I had the car repaired by a mechanic.*

- **When using a direct or an indirect object pronoun, or both, where do they go?**

Both the direct and indirect object pronouns precede the verb **faire**, except in the imperative affirmative.

> Tu fais réciter le poème aux enfants.
> Tu **le leur** fais réciter.   ➔ Fais-le-leur réciter!
> Tu fais réparer la voiture par le mécanicien.
> Tu **la lui** fais réparer   ➔ Fais-la-lui réparer!

- **What does faire faire mean?**

➔ **faire faire** = *to have someone do (or make) something.*

> **Je fais faire les devoirs aux enfants.**
> *I have the children do the homework.*

- **What about se faire faire?**

➔ **se faire faire** = *to have something done for you.*

> **Elle s'est fait faire une robe par une excellente couturière.**
> *She had a dress made for her by an excellent dressmaker.*

TIP
Note that when using se faire faire in a compound tense such as the passé composé, the past participle <u>never</u> agrees with the subject.

V. Refaites les phrases suivantes en ajoutant le verbe "faire" ou "se faire" au passé composé.

Modèle: Maman/couper les cheveux.
Maman s'est fait couper les cheveux.
Papa/sortir le chien.
Papa a fait sortir le chien.

1. L'actrice/faire un costume original.

2. Le film/rire les enfants.

3. Les gâteaux/grossir la jeune fille.

4. Je/faire une autre clé pour le bureau.

5. Elle/ne pas manger la purée au bébé.

VI. Remplacez les noms par des pronoms objets.

Modèle: Je pense vendre la voiture.—Je pense la vendre.

1. Nous espérons voir le film demain.

2. Elle a fait chanter les élèves.

3. Elle a fait chanter la chanson aux élèves.

4. Ne faites pas sortir les valises.

5. J'ai laissé tomber mes livres.

The Past Infinitive
L'infinitif passé

The past infinitive has a compound form. Just like any compound tense, there is an auxiliary verb that precedes the conjugated verb. In the **passé composé** the auxiliary verb is in the present (**je suis allé, j'ai fini**), in the past infinitive the auxiliary verbs **avoir** and **être** are in the **infinitive**.

Elle est heureuse d'**avoir fini** l'examen.
She is happy to have finished the exam.

Ils sont désolés d'**être arrivés** en retard.
They are sorry that they arrived late.

The past infinitive follows the same rules of agreement as the compound tenses.

- **The past infinitive is always used after** *après*

> **Après avoir lu** le livre, je l'ai prêté à Paul.
> *After having read the book, I lent it to Paul.*

> **Après être sortie** de la maison, elle a vu qu'il pleuvait.
> *After having left the house, she saw that it was raining.*

AVANT DE	+	PRESENT INFINITIVE
APRÈS	+	PAST INFINITIVE

- **The past infinitive of a pronominal or reflexive verb is used with the reflexive pronoun**

> **Après s'être habillée,** elle a pris le petit-déjeuner.
> *After getting dressed, she had breakfast.*

> **Après nous être couchés,** nous avons entendu un bruit dans la cuisine.
> *After having gone to bed, we heard a noise in the kitchen.*

> **Après m'être dépêché,** je me suis rendu compte que j'étais en avance.
> *After having hurried, I realized that I was early.*

QUICK PRACTICE

VII. Transformez les phrases suivantes en ajoutant "avant de" ou "après" avant le verbe.

Modèle: Il range ses affaires/il sort avec Natalie. (après)
Après avoir rangé ses affaires, il est sorti avec Natalie.

1. Elle ouvre la fenêtre/elle allume la radio. (après)

2. Ils se dépêchent/ils ont quand même râté le metro. (après)

3. Elle achète une bicyclette/elle empruntait celle de la voisine. (avant)

4. Je sors/j'ai mis mon manteau. (avant)

5. Ils ont fini l'examen/ils sont allés au cinéma. (après)

The Infinitive Preceded by the Prepositions A and De
L'infinitif precédé de "à" et "de"

- **Some expressions require de before an infinitive**

  Il est difficile de → Il est difficile de répondre à la question.
  It is difficult to answer the question.

  Il est important de → Il est important d'acheter les billets.
  It is important to buy the tickets.

  Il est nécessaire de → Il est nécessaire d'avoir un parapluie.
  It is necessary to have an umbrella.

- **Whenever you use *of* + *...ing* in English, in French you use de + the infinitive**

  The idea of traveling. → L'idée **de voyager**.
  The importance of reading. → L'importance **de lire**.

- **Whenever you use *to* + *infinitive* in English, meaning something that must be done to something, in French you use à + the infinitive**

  I have many books to buy. → J'ai plusieurs livres **à acheter**.

- **Some verbs are followed by the prepositions à and de before the infinitive (see the chapter on Prepositions)**

  J'ai appris **à** conduire à l'âge de 16 ans.   *I learned to drive when I was 16.*
  Il a refusé **de** sortir avec nous.   *He refused to go out with us.*

QUICK PRACTICE
VIII. Traduisez les phrases suivantes.

1. It is important to listen to them.

2. She has a job to do.

3. The thought (*la pensée*) of losing is terrible.

4. I have three books to read this semester.

5. It is easy to talk with her.

L'infinitif

Across

6. I must read (3 words)

8. Without speaking

9. To have someone study (2 words)

10. You hope to see (3 words)

Down

1. Nothing (2 words)

2. After having finished (3 words)

3. To let play (2 words)

4. Add some milk (recipe—3 words)

5. In order to (2 words)

7. Never

Culture Capsule 7

Le Verlan ou langue à l'envers est un langage faussement attribué aux jeunes banlieusards des années 70. Quoique ces derniers l'aient adopté pour éviter le contrôle social, ce procédé d'inversion date de beaucoup plus longtemps. Ainsi, Béroul (1190) dans son "Roman de Tristan" transforme le prénom de son héros en Tantris. Ce qui est sûr, c'est que les jongleries verbales, en tout cas, sont et ont toujours été très populaires en France. Le Dictionnaire Universel de Furetière, en 1690, explique ainsi une locution: "On dit, c'est verjus ou jus vert pour dire: c'est la même chose". Au XVIème siècle la famille royale des Bourbon devient "*les Bonbour*" et les "*sans-souci*" (en réalité les "sans six-sous") étaient des gens très pauvres, des sans-le-sou. Plus tard, on appelle le roi Louis Quinze, "*Séquinzouille*"… une sorte de verlan pas trop respectueux, il faut l'admettre! Au XIXème siècle, Toulon se transforme en "*Lontou*". Les exemples sont très nombreux.

Aujourd'hui, le verlan connait beaucoup de succès auprès des jeunes et son emploi dans les films et les chansons l'ont fait entrer dans le langage familier. Dans les années 90, on a pu voir aux Etats-Unis un film français qui avait pour titre "Les ripoux" (les pourris = the rotten ones).

Exemples de verlan:

tromé	= métro
laisse béton	= laisse tomber *(drop it)*
meuf	= femme
keuf	= flic *(cop)*
je tréren	= je rentre
soirce	= ce soir
un skeud	= un disque
un Séfran	= un Français
chanmé	= méchant *(mean)*
tigen	= gentil
méfu	= fumer
zyva	= vas-y *(go ahead)*

VOCABULAIRE

à l'envers	*in reverse*
faussement	*falsely*
banlieusards	*people who live in the suburbs*
jongleries verbales	*verbal juggling*
fait les délices	*delighted*
respectueux	*respectful*
admettre	*admit*

9

The Passé Simple and the Passive Voice

Que savez-vous déjà?
What Do You Know Already?

Can you fill in the blanks with the correct form of the **passé simple** *of the verb indicated in parentheses?*

1. Nous (parler) _____ de nos vacances.

2. Il (naître) _____ en 1802.

3. Ils (ouvrir) _____ la fenêtre.

4. Vous (aller) _____ au cinéma.

5. Elle (finir) _____ ses devoirs.

6. J'(oublier) _____ mon parapluie.

7. Tu (attendre) _____ le train.

8. Je (dire) _____ la vérité.

The Passé Simple (The Simple Past)
Le passé simple

The **passé simple** or simple past is a literary tense that replaces the **passé composé** in most novels and classical plays. Although mainly used in its written form, it can still be found today in some official speeches. While many students are intimidated by it, the **passé simple** is, like its name indicates, quite *simple*.

For regular verbs, the **passé simple** of **-er**, **-ir**, and **-re** endings of the infinitive are dropped and are replaced by the **passé simple** endings as follows:

	-ER verbs	-IR verbs	-RE verbs
Je	— ai	— is	— is
Tu	— as	— is	— is
Il/elle/on	— a	— it	— it
Nous	— âmes	— îmes	— îmes
Vous	— âtes	— îtes	— îtes
Ils/elles	— èrent	— irent	— irent

NOTE: Only the **nous** and **vous** forms require a circumflex accent (**accent circonflexe**) on the vowels preceding **mes** or **tes** endings.

The following three regular verbs show standard **passé simple** conjugations.

PAR**LER**	**FINIR**	ATTEND**RE**
Je parl**ai**	Je fin**is**	J'attend**is**
Tu parl**as**	Tu fin**is**	Tu attend**is**
Il parl**a**	Il fin**it**	Il attend**it**
Elle parl**a**	Elle fin**it**	Elle attend**it**
On parl**a**	On fin**it**	On attend**it**
Nous parl**âmes**	Nous fin**îmes**	Nous attend**îmes**
Vous parl**âtes**	Vous fin**îtes**	Vous attend**îtes**
Ils parl**èrent**	Ils fin**irent**	Ils attend**irent**
Elles parl**èrent**	Elles fin**irent**	Elles attend**irent**

Verbs ending in **-cer** or **-ger** such as **commencer** and **manger** have a slightly different ending:

COMMENCER	**MANGER**
Je commen**çai**	Je mang**eai**
Tu commen**ças**	Tu mang**eas**
Il commen**ça**	Il mang**ea**
Elle commen**ça**	Elle mang**ea**
On commen**ça**	On mang**ea**
Nous commen**çâmes**	Nous mang**eâmes**
Ils commen**cèrent**	Ils mang**èrent**
Elles commen**cèrent**	Elles mang**èrent**

NOTE: The **ils** and **elles** forms do not change.

IMPARFAIT AND PASSÉ SIMPLE

The rules that apply to the use of the **passé composé** and the **imparfait** together apply also when the **passé simple** is used instead of the **passé composé**.

Elle faisait ses devoirs lorsque ses parents arrivèrent.
She was doing her homework when her parents arrived.

PASSÉ SIMPLE OF IRREGULAR VERBS

There are two easy ways to conjugate irregular verbs in the passé simple. The first one is to memorize the first person singular of the verb in the passé simple and continue with the following endings:

Je	→	—s
Tu	→	—s
Il/elle/on	→	—t
Nous	→	—^mes
Vous	→	—^tes
Ils/elles	→	—rent

There are two sets of endings in the **passé simple** of irregular verbs. All irregular verbs end in the first person singular either in **-us** or in **-is**.

LIRE	ÉCRIRE
Je **lus**	j'**écrivis**
Tu lu**s**	tu écrivi**s**
Il/elle/on lu**t**	il/elle on écrivi**t**
Nous l**ûmes**	nous écriv**îmes**
Vous l**ûtes**	vous écriv**îtes**
Ils/elles lu**rent**	Il/elles écrivi**rent**

Another way of conjugating an irregular verb in the **passé simple** is to use the past participle of the verb and replace the last letter by the endings of the **passé simple**.

Infinitif	Participe Passé	Passé Simple
Avoir	eu	j'eus, tu eus, il eut
Boire	bu	je bus, tu bus, elle but
Connaître	connu	je connus, tu connus, elle connut
Courir	couru	je courus, tu courus, elle courut
Croire	cru	je crus, tu crus, elle crut
Devoir	dû	je dus, tu dus, elle dut
Dire	dit	je dis, tu dis, elle dit
Falloir	fallu	il fallut
Lire	lu	je lus, tu lus, elle lut
Mettre	mis	je mis, tu mis, elle mit
Partir	parti	je partis, tu partis, elle partit

Infinitif	Participe Passé	Passé Simple
Prendre	pris	je pris, tu pris, elle prit
Plaire	plu	il plut
Pouvoir	pu	je pus, tu pus, elle put
Recevoir	reçu	je reçus, tu reçus, elle reçut
rire	ri	je ris, tu ris, elle rit
Savoir	su	je sus, tu sus, elle sut
Sentir	senti	je sentis, tu sentis, elle sentit
Sortir	sorti	je sortis, tu sortis, elle sortit
Valoir	valu	il valut
Vivre	vécu	je vécus, tu vécus, elle vécut
Vouloir	voulu	je voulus, tu voulus, elle voulut

There are also some irregular verbs that differ from the past participle. You must therefore study the first or third person singular of the verb in the **passé simple**; the other persons follow suit (**s, s, t, ^mes, ^tes, rent**).

Conduire	je conduisis, tu conduisis, elle conduisit
Couvrir	je couvris, tu couvris, elle couvrit
Écrire	j'écrivis, tu écrivis, elle écrivit
Étre	je fus, tu fus, il fut
Faire	je fis, tu fis, elle fit
Offrir	j'offris, tu offris, elle offrit
Mourir	je mourus, tu mourus, elle mourut
Naître	je naquis, tu naquis, il naquit
Souffrir	je souffris, tu souffris, elle souffrit
Voir	je vis, tu vis, il vit

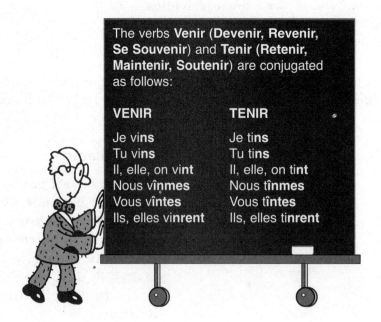

The verbs **Venir (Devenir, Revenir, Se Souvenir)** and **Tenir (Retenir, Maintenir, Soutenir)** are conjugated as follows:

VENIR	**TENIR**
Je vins	Je tins
Tu vins	Tu tins
Il, elle, on vint	Il, elle, on tint
Nous vînmes	Nous tînmes
Vous vîntes	Vous tîntes
Ils, elles vinrent	Ils, elles tinrent

QUICK PRACTICE

I. Un conte de fées (*a fairy tale*)**: Racontez le conte de fées en mettant les verbes entre parenthèses aux formes correctes du passé simple et de l'imparfait:**

Il (être) _____ une fois une jeune princesse qui (être) _____ très malade. Tous les médecins ne (savoir) _____ pas quoi faire. Alors, son père le roi, fou d'inquiétude, (annoncer) _____ à tout le royaume *(kingdom)*, que celui qui (aller) _____ trouver un remède pour guérir *(cure)* la belle princesse l'épouserait. Plusieurs jeunes gens (essayer) _____ de chercher le médicament magique, mais sans aucun succès. Or, dans la forêt, il y (avoir) _____ un jeune bûcheron *(woodcutter)* qui (vivre) _____ avec sa vieille grand'mère. Celle-ci (connaître) _____ toutes les plantes de la forêt. Quand elle (apprendre) _____ que la jeune princesse (être) _____ si malade, elle (appeler) _____ son petit-fils et lui (dire) _____ : "Va dans la forêt, derrière le grand sapin *(pine tree)* à gauche de la petite clairière *(clearing)*. Il y a une plante jaune et verte, avec des petites fleurs roses. Apporte-moi trois plantes".

Le jeune bûcheron (faire) _____ immédiatement ce que sa grand'mère (vouloir) _____ . Elle (prendre) _____ les plantes et (commencer) _____ à les faire cuire dans un chaudron *(cauldron)* énorme. Elle les (faire) _____ cuire pendant deux jours. Au bout *(at the end)* de deux jours, elle (prendre) _____ cette soupe, (la mettre) _____ dans un récipient de verre, et (dire) _____ à son petit-fils: "Va au palais du roi et demande au roi de donner ce bouillon à la princesse".

Le jeune homme (aller) _____ voir le roi et lui (donner) _____ le bouillon de sa grand'mère. Le roi (se rendre) _____ dans la chambre où sa fille (dormir) _____ . Il la (réveiller) _____ et lui (donner) _____ une tasse de bouillon. Dix minutes plus tard, la jeune princesse (se lever)_____ et (demander) _____ une autre tasse. Après la deuxième tasse, elle (vouloir) _____ boire une troisième, et une quatrième. Après avoir fini tout le bouillon, elle (dormir) _____ pendant dix heures. Quand elle (se réveiller) _____ , elle (vouloir) _____ manger car elle (avoir) _____ très faim. Le roi (faire) _____ venir le médecin et celui-ci (être) _____ très surpris. La princesse (être) _____ en parfaite santé.

Quelques jours plus tard, on (célébrer) _____ le mariage de la princesse et du bûcheron.

The Passive Voice
La voix passive

The passive voice in French, just as in English, requires the use of the verb to be followed by the past participle.

My brother **repairs** the car. → The car **is** repaired by my brother.

In the active voice, the verb *to repair* is conjugated in the present tense. In the passive voice, the verb *to be* is conjugated in the present tense and is followed by the past participle. It is exactly the same in French.

Mon frère **répare** la voiture. → La voiture **est** réparée par mon frère.

In the active voice, the verb **réparer** is conjugated in the present tense. In the passive voice, the verb **être** is conjugated in the present tense and is followed by the past participle.

THE PASSIVE VOICE AND THE OTHER TENSES

Just as in English, the other tenses follow the same rule. If the verb conjugated in the active voice is in the **passé composé**, then, in the passive voice, the verb **être** is in the **passé composé**.

LA VOIX PASSIVE AU PASSÉ

The tense of the verb in the active voice becomes the tense of the auxiliary verb être in the passive voice.

VOIX ACTIVE	VOIX PASSIVE
Passé Composé	
Pierre **a expliqué** la leçon.	La leçon **a été** expliquée par Pierre.
Pierre explained the lesson.	*The lesson was explained by Pierre.*
Imparfait	
Pierre **expliquait** la leçon.	La leçon **était** expliquée par Pierre.
Pierre was explaining the lesson.	*The lesson was being explained by Pierre.*
Plus-que-parfait	
Pierre **avait expliqué** la leçon.	La leçon **avait été** expliquée par Pierre.
Pierre had explained the lesson.	*The lesson had been explained by Pierre.*

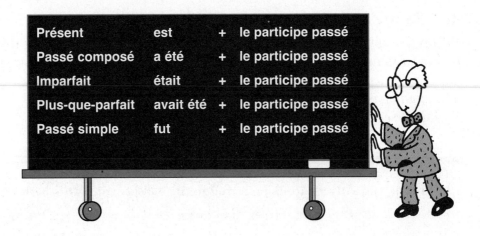

Présent	est	+	le participe passé
Passé composé	a été	+	le participe passé
Imparfait	était	+	le participe passé
Plus-que-parfait	avait été	+	le participe passé
Passé simple	fut	+	le participe passé

LE PASSIF AVEC "PAR" ET "DE"

- **Par**

  In general, **par** is used when there is a physical action or whenever there is a concrete action.

  > **Le livre a été écrit par mon professeur.**
  > *The book was written by my teacher.*

  > **Le chateau de sable a été détruit par les vagues.**
  > *The sand castle was destroyed by the waves.*

- **De**

  Some expressions are always followed by **de**:

  > **être entouré de** (*to be surrounded by*)
  > **être rempli de** (*to be full of, to be filled with*)
  > **être couvert de** (*to be covered by/with*)
  > **être orné de** (*to be decorated with*)

  De is also used before a noun without an article:

  Compare: **La glace est dévorée par le petit garcon.**
  The ice cream is devoured by the little boy.

  > **Elle est dévorée de chagrin.**
  > *She is devoured by her sorrow. (She is full of sorrow.)*

  NOTE: The verb **aimer** can be used with either **par** or **de**.

  Elle est aimée **de** tout le monde.   *She is loved by everybody.*
  Elle est aimée **par** tout le monde.   *She is loved by everybody.*

LE FAUX PASSIF

When the verb indicates an action that is being accomplished, or the result of an action, it is neither followed by **par** or by **de**. It is the same in English.

The window is closed.	→	**La fenêtre est fermée.**
Dinner is served.	→	**Le diner est servi.**

> **TIP**
> In French, the active voice is preferred to the passive voice. It is better to say
> **Pierre a ouvert la porte rather than** La porte a été ouverte par Pierre.

LE PRONOM PERSONNEL "ON"

The indefinite pronoun **on** is often used with an active verb instead of using the passive voice.

French is spoken here.	→	**Ici on parle français.**

INTRANSITIVE VERBS

Intransitive verbs are verbs that are never followed by a direct object. They are followed by the preposition à. For example, **parler à, répondre à, demander à, obéir à**.

The student was spoken to.	→	**On a parlé à l'élève.**
The letter was answered.	→	**On a répondu à la lettre.**
Aimée was asked to sing.	→	**On a demandé à Aimée de chanter.**

QUICK PRACTICE

II. Le professeur raconte aux élèves un évènement important de l'Histoire de France. Mettez ce qu'il dit à la voix passive:

1. Le peuple de Paris a attaqué la Bastille le 14 juillet 1789.

2. Le gouverneur de la Bastille a donné l'ordre de tirer sur la foule (*the crowd*).

3. On a baissé le pont-levis (*the drawbridge*) de la forteresse.

4. La foule a exécuté le gouverneur.

5. La France a choisi le 14 juillet comme fête nationale en 1880.

III. Traduisez les phrases suivantes:

1. Christophe was always surrounded by friends.

2. Colette had been asked to drive to school.

3. The house was destroyed by the tornado (*la tornade*).

4. The answer to this problem has not been found.

5. The castle was built in 1600.

IV. Travail oral à deux. Donnez une phrase à la voix passive et votre partenaire vous la redonne à la voix active:

1. La porte a été fermée par les étudiants.

2. Le tableau a été peint en 1850.

3. Le problème est résolu par le professeur.

4. La tour fut construite par plusieurs hommes.

5. Le professeur est aimé de ses élèves.

LE PASSÉ SIMPLE

```
J  K  Y  M  O  G  A  S  D  T  N  Z  G  T  T
R  G  O  A  U  Y  S  R  E  D  F  E  P  N  T
M  L  F  N  T  D  B  U  T  M  V  H  S  E  V
E  E  I  G  E  N  M  N  F  G  I  L  S  R  Z
V  Q  D  E  V  J  E  A  F  Z  P  D  U  E  J
M  L  S  A  N  R  L  R  S  D  V  A  R  S  W
S  C  L  S  I  L  A  I  I  T  F  T  C  N  T
O  M  B  U  U  Q  M  T  F  V  N  O  H  A  L
E  A  Q  T  X  R  L  P  T  J  I  D  R  D  Z
I  A  L  L  A  Z  E  A  R  E  W  R  W  K  S
N  O  U  V  R  I  R  E  N  T  N  O  C  U  X
O  A  J  J  Q  W  F  E  M  R  Q  D  J  E  Z
R  X  P  W  C  K  U  L  B  U  N  F  I  J  J
K  S  R  K  U  N  M  I  Y  M  Q  X  M  S  F
T  D  I  O  J  N  N  V  Y  W  S  X  E  X  K
```

ALLAI	DIMES	MANGEAS
ATTENDIS	ECRIVIRENT	NAQUIRENT
CRUS	FALLUT	OUVRIRENT
DANSERENT	FUS	

10

The Future and the Conditional

What Do You Know Already?

*Can you fill in the blanks with the correct form of the future tense
of the verb indicated in parentheses?*

1. Nous (aller) _____ en France la semaine prochaine.

2. Est-ce que tu (finir) _____ tes devoirs avant le dîner?

3. Le directeur (commencer) _____ son discours à huit heures.

4. Il (venir) _____ nous voir très bientôt.

5. Si j'ai le temps, je (prendre) _____ une semaine de vacances.

*Can you fill in the blanks with the correct form of the present conditional
tense of the verb indicated in parentheses?*

6. Elle croyait que nous (être) _____ en retard.

7. Nous (pouvoir) _____ venir mardi.

8. Si j'étais riche je (donner) _____ beaucoup d'argent aux pauvres.

9. Il (manger) _____ toute la salade s'il avait faim.

10. (aimer) _____ -tu voir ce film avec moi?

The Simple Future
Le futur simple

SIMPLE FUTURE OF REGULAR VERBS			
-er verbs	➔ Subject	+ infinitive of verb (**parler**)	+ future endings
-ir verbs	➔ Subject	+ infinitive of verb (**finir**)	+ future endings
-re verbs	➔ Subject	+ infinitive minus e (**attendr**)	+ future endings

The future endings are the endings of the verb **avoir** in the present tense: **ai, as, a, ons, ez, ont.**

The following three regular verbs show the identical endings of the future tense.

PARLER	FINIR	ATTENDRE
Je parler**ai**	Je finir**ai**	J'attendr**ai**
Tu parler**as**	Tu finir**as**	Tu attendr**as**
Il/elle parler**a**	Il/elle finir**a**	Il/elle attendr**a**
Nous parler**ons**	Nous finir**ons**	Nous attendr**ons**
Vous parler**ez**	Vous finir**ez**	Vous attendr**ez**
Ils/elles parler**ont**	Ils/elles finir**ont**	Ils/elles attendr**ont**

SPELLING CHANGES IN THE FUTURE TENSE

- Verbs that end in **yer** in the infinitve, such as **essayer**. The **yer** becomes **ier** before adding the future ending.*

  essayer *to try*

J'essaierai	Nous essaierons
Tu essaieras	Vous essaierez
Elle/il essaiera	Elles/ils essaieront

- In the future, the verbs **jeter** and **appeler** double the consonant that precedes the ending and the verb **acheter** has an *accent grave* on the first *e*.

jeter *to throw*	**appeler** *to call*	**acheter** *to buy*
Je jetterai	J'appellerai	J'achèterai
Tu jetteras	Tu appelleras	Tu achèteras
Il/elle jettera	Il/elle appellera	Il/elle achètera
Nous jetterons	Nous appellerons	Nous achèterons
Vous jetterez	Vous appellerez	Vous achèterez
Ils/elles jetteront	Ils/elles appelleront	Ils/elles achèteront

*The verb **payer** can be conjugated with **y** (**je payerai**) or with **i** (**je paierai**).

Although the following verbs have irregular stems, the endings are still **ai, as, a, ons, ez, ont**.

Infinitive	Future Stem
aller	**ir** (to go)
apercevoir	**apercevr** (to see or perceive)
avoir	**aur** (to have)
courir	**courr** (to run)
devoir	**devr** (to have to, to owe)
envoyer	**enverr** (to send)
être	**ser** (to be)
faire	**fer** (to make, to do)
pouvoir	**pourr** (to be able to, can)
savoir	**saur** (to know)
s'asseoir	**assier** or **assoir** (to sit)
venir	**viendr** (to come)
voir	**verr** (to see)
vouloir	**voudr** (to want)

IMPERSONAL VERBS

| Il faut. | **Il faudra.** | *It will be necessary.* |
| Il pleut. | **Il pleuvra.** | *It will rain.* |

> **TIP**
> The pronunciation of some -er ending verbs can vary in the future. If two different consonants precede the -er ending in the infinitive, such as in parler, the e is pronounced: je par/le/rai. However, if only one consonant precedes the -er ending, the e is not pronounced: je jette/rai.

QUICK PRACTICE

I. Nicolas et Serge parde de leurs projets pour l'été. Mettez tous les verbes en caractères gras (*bold letters*) au futur simple.

1. Je **vais** en Italie. Et toi?

2. Eh bien, moi, je **rends** visite à une amie qui vit à Nice.

3. Moi, je **visite** beaucoup de musées. Et toi, que **fais**-tu?

4. Je sais qu'elle **veut** aller à la plage tous les jours.

5. J'espère pour toi qu'il ne **pleut** pas!

6. Tu sais, s'il pleut, nous **allons** au cinéma!

7. Moi, je **vais** à Rome où je **vois** un tas de monuments.

8. **Vas**-tu seulement à Rome?

9. Non, je **passe** une semaine à Venise.

10. Ah, j'y suis allé l'année dernière; tu **aimes** beaucoup cette ville.

When, As soon as, Once
Quand, Lorsque, Dès que, Aussitôt que, Une fois que

Quand, lorsque, dès que, aussitôt que, and **une fois que** are always followed by the same tense as the verb in the other part of the sentence.

Elle **est** heureuse quand elle **sort** avec ses amis. → present/present
She is happy when she goes out with her friends. present/present

Elle **était** heureuse quand elle **sortait** avec ses amis. → imperfect/imperfect
She was happy when she was going out with her friends. imperfect/imperfect

Elle **sera** heureuse quand elle **sortira** avec ses amis. → future/future
She will be happy when she goes out with her friends. → future/present

ENGLISH	FRENCH
When is followed by the **present**.	**Quand/lorsque** are followed by the **future.**
When I see Louis, I will talk to him.	**Quand je verrai** Louis, je lui parlerai. **Lorsque je verrai** Louis, je lui parlerai.
This applies also to **as soon as** (**dès que – aussitôt que**) and **once** (**une fois que**).	
As soon as I see Louis, I will talk to him.	**Dès que je verrai** Louis, je lui parlerai. **Aussitôt que je verrai** Louis, je lui parlerai.
Once I see Louis, I will talk to him.	**Une fois que je verrai** Louis, je lui parlerai.

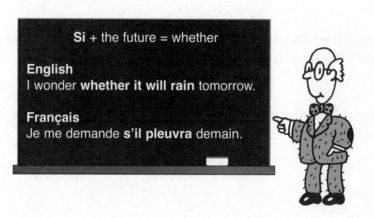

Si + the future = whether

English
I wonder **whether it will rain** tomorrow.

Français
Je me demande **s'il pleuvra** demain.

QUICK PRACTICE

II. Traduisez les phrases suivantes.

1. When they want to go to the restaurant, they will telephone me.

2. As soon as they arrive, I will give them the present (*le cadeau*).

3. I wonder whether Jeanne will come on Sunday.

4. I am not sure whether they will go to New York.

5. He will go to school when the bus arrives.

III. Mettez le verbe à la forme qui convient:

Modèle: Quand elle (avoir) _____ une voiture, elle sera plus libre.
Quand elle aura une voiture, elle sera plus libre.

1. Aussitôt qu'ils (arriver) _____ nous pourrons dîner.

2. Dès qu'il (faire beau) _____ j'irai à la plage.

3. Quand il (pleuvoir) _____ ma grand-mère ne sort pas.

4. Il jouait toujours au football quand il (être) _____ jeune.

5. Lorsque j'(avoir faim) _____ je mange!

IV. Conversation: Discutez de vos projets pour le week-end prochain avec un ami. *(j'irai, je ferai, je verrai, etc.)*

V. Rédaction: Imaginez votre ville dans cent ans. Qu'est-ce qui sera différent?

The Future Perfect
Le futur antérieur

The **futur antérieur** describes something that happens in the future before another future event.

I will have had dinner before seven o'clock.

The future perfect is a compound tense. Like all compound tenses, it is formed by an auxiliary verb and the past participle of the verb. The auxiliary verb is in the future.

SUBJECT	AUXILIARY VERB	PAST PARTICIPLE
Nous *We*	aurons *will have*	fini *finished*
Nous *We*	serons *will have*	partis* *left*

*When the verb être is used as an auxiliary verb, the past participle agrees in gender and number with the subject.

Does the rule about **quand, lorsque, dès que, aussitôt que, une fois que** apply in the future perfect? Yes. If the action occurred before another future action, then the first event will be in the future perfect, or **futur antérieur**, and the second event will be in the **futur simple**.

When you have studied the poem, you will recite it (*you must have studied it before you can recite it*).
Une fois que tu auras étudié le poème, tu le réciteras.
or
Tu réciteras le poème une fois que tu l'auras étudié.

Pendant que (*while, during*) and **tandis que** (*whereas*) are used with the future.

J'irai en France tandis qu'il ira en Chine.
I will go to France whereas he will go to China.

Après que (*after*) is used with the future perfect.

Je te téléphonerai après que mes amis seront partis.
I will call you after my friends have left.

Quick Practice

VI. Mettez les verbes entre parenthèses soit au futur simple, soit au futur antérieur.

1. Lorsque Frédéric (comprendre) _____ l'explication, il (pouvoir) _____ faire ses devoirs.

2. Avant de revenir aux Etats-Unis, Françoise (traverser) _____ plusieurs pays.

3. Dès que je (voir) _____ le professeur, je lui (donner) _____ ma rédaction.

4. Je/j'(économiser) _____ assez d'argent avant la fin de l'été.

5. Une fois que tu (recevoir) _____ la lettre de Corinne, tu (pouvoir) _____ y répondre.

The Present Conditional
Le conditionnel présent

Verbs in the **conditionnel présent** and verbs in the **futur simple** share the same stems. However, in the **conditionnel présent** the endings are those of the **imparfait**.

FUTURE ENDINGS			PRESENT CONDITIONAL ENDINGS		
Je	infinitive +	ai	Je	infinitive +	ais
Tu		as	Tu		ais
Elle/il		a	Elle/il		ait
Nous		ons	Nous		ions
Vous		ez	Vous		iez
Elles/ils		ont	Elles/ils		aient

NOTE: Verbs with irregular stems in the future have these same stems in the present conditional:

Futur Simple		Conditionnel Présent	
J'irai à l'école.	*I will go to school.*	J'irais à l'école.	*I would go to school.*
Tu verras un film.	*You will see a movie.*	Tu verrais un film.	*You would see a movie.*
Il sera là.	*He will be there.*	Il serait là.	*He would be there.*
Elle fera une robe.	*She will make a dress.*	Elle ferait une robe.	*She would make a dress.*
Nous irons le voir.	*We will go see him.*	Nous irions le voir.	*We would go see him.*
Vous devrez venir.	*You will have to come.*	Vous devriez venir.	*You would have to come.*
Ils/Elles courront.	*They will run.*	Ils/Elles courraient.	*They would run.*

- The conditional is used as a form of politeness.

  Je voudrais un café, s'il vous plait.
  I would like a coffee, please.

  Pourriez-vous ouvrir la porte?
  Could you open the door?

- In the indirect discourse, the conditional is used in the second part when the principal verb is in the past tense.

  Elle a annoncé qu'elle partirait bientôt.
  She announced that she would leave soon.

  Nous pensions qu'ils viendraient avec nous.
  We thought that they would come with us.

VII. La petite Vanessa adore rêver à son avenir. Elle en parle à sa grand-mère. Mettez les verbes entre parenthèses au conditionnel présent:

1. J'(aimer) _____ être une belle princesse.

2. J'(épouser) _____ le prince charmant.

3. Je (vivre)_____ dans un merveilleux palais.

4. J'(avoir)_____ beaucoup de serviteurs.

5. J'(acheter)_____ des robes magnifiques.

6. Je (voir)_____ tous les pays du monde.

7. Je (porter) _____ des bijoux très chers.

8. Je (pouvoir) _____ acheter des cadeaux superbes à mes amis.

9. Je (dormir) _____ dans un lit à baldaquin (*canopy bed*).

10. Je (recevoir)_____ mes amis dans un salon élégant.

The Past Conditional
Le conditionnel passé

The past conditional is a compound tense; it is conjugated with the auxiliary verb **avoir** or **être** in the **present conditional** and followed by the past participle of the principal verb.

SUBJECT	AUXILIARY VERB	PAST PARTICIPLE
Nous *We*	aurions *would have*	fini. *finished.*
Nous *We*	serions *would have*	partis.* *left.*

*When the verb **être** is used as an auxiliary verb, the past participle agrees in gender and number with the subject.

LES PHRASES CONDITIONNELLES		
SI + PRÉSENT	→	PRÉSENT/FUTUR/IMPÉRATIF
Si tu as le temps	→	tu peux aller au cinéma.
		tu pourras aller au cinéma.
		Va au cinéma!
If you have the time		*you can go to the movies.*
		you will be able to go to the movies.
		Go to the movies!
SI + IMPARFAIT	→	CONDITIONNEL PRÉSENT
Si tu avais le temps	→	tu irais au cinéma.
If you had the time		*you would go to the movies.*
SI + PLUS-QUE-PARFAIT	→	CONDITIONNEL PASSÉ
Si tu avais eu le temps	→	tu serais allé au cinema.
If you had had the time		*you would have gone to the movies.*

- Like the present conditional, the past conditional is used after the conjunction **que** when the principal verb is in the past.

    Je pensais que tu aurais aimé ce film.
    I thought that you would have liked this movie.

- The present and past conditional are used to report a rumor, a fact that has yet to be confirmed.

    Madame Chevalier est en retard; elle aurait des problèmes avec sa voiture.
    Mrs. Chevalier is late; she could have car problems.

    Un tremblement de terre aurait détruit tout un village au Japon.
    An earthquake may have destroyed an entire village in Japan.

- The past conditional is used when a wish did not come true.

    Elle aurait voulu nous accompagner, mais son mari était malade.
    She would have liked to accompany us, but her husband was ill.

    J'aurais aimé les inviter, mais ils étaient en Afrique.
    I would have liked to invite them, but they were in Africa.

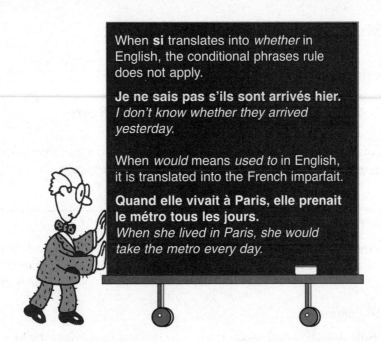

When **si** translates into *whether* in English, the conditional phrases rule does not apply.

Je ne sais pas s'ils sont arrivés hier.
I don't know whether they arrived yesterday.

When *would* means *used to* in English, it is translated into the French imparfait.

Quand elle vivait à Paris, elle prenait le métro tous les jours.
When she lived in Paris, she would take the metro every day.

QUICK PRACTICE

VIII. Complétez les phrases suivantes au temps qui convient:

1. S'il pleut, les enfants (ne pas sortir).

2. La leçon (être) difficile, si le professeur ne l'avait pas expliquée.

3. Si vous (être) en retard, dépêchez-vous!

4. Je me demande si elle (finir) ses devoirs ce matin.

5. Si tu avais le temps, tu (pouvoir) faire une promenade.

6. Si vous aviez écouté les informations, vous (savoir) qu'on annonçait un orage.

7. Sais-tu si elle (venir) demain?

8. Selon le journal, une tornade (dévaster) la ville.

9. Je viendrai te voir si je (quitter) le travail avant sept heures.

10. (pouvoir) vous fermer la fenêtre s'il vous plaît?

IX. Rédaction: Si vous gagniez à la loterie, que feriez-vous pour réaliser vos rêves?

To Have to, Must, Owe
Devoir

The verb **devoir** may mean **to owe**.

Je dois 10 euros à Jacques.   *I owe Jacques 10 euros.*

As an auxiliary verb, **devoir** has different meanings depending on the tense in which it is used.

PRÉSENT = Obligation, probability, *or* intention

Je dois acheter un dictionnaire.	*I have to (must) buy a dictionary.*
Il n'est pas à l'école; il doit être malade.	*He isn't at school; he must be sick.*
Je dois finir avant midi.	*I must (intend to) finish before noon.*

FUTUR = Obligation

Nous devrons quitter avant midi.	*We will have to leave before noon.*

IMPARFAIT = Intention, obligation, *or* probability in the past

Nous devions aller à la montagne mais nous n'avons pas pu.
We intended to go to the mountain, but we couldn't.

Nous devions toujours faire nos devoirs avant le diner.
We always had to do our homework before dinner.

Elle n'était pas en classe ce jour-là; elle devait être malade.
She wasn't in class on that day; she must have been sick.

PASSÉ COMPOSÉ = Obligation *or* probability

Ils ont dû quitter avant midi.	*They had to leave before noon.*
Ils ne sont pas ici; ils ont dû partir tôt.	*They are not here; they must have left early.*

CONDITIONNEL PRÉSENT = Advice *or* suggestion

Tu devrais prendre un parapluie; on dit qu'il va pleuvoir.
You should take an umbrella; they said it was going to rain.

CONDITIONNEL PASSÉ = Reproach *or* regret

Tu aurais dû prendre un parapluie.	*You should have taken an umbrella.*
J'aurais dû étudier avant l'examen.	*I should have studied before the exam.*

X. Transformez les phrases suivantes en vous servant du verbe "devoir" au temps qui convient.

Modèle: Je suis obligé d'ouvrir la fenêtre—Je dois ouvrir la fenêtre.

1. Elle *was obliged* annuler son voyage.

2. Quand j'avais douze ans, *I had to* lire une histoire à ma petite soeur chaque soir.

3. Si tu veux réussir à l'examen demain, tu *should* étudier sérieusement ce soir.

4. J'ai eu une mauvaise note à l'examen, *I should have* étudier hier soir.

5. Patrick n'est pas venu à la fête; il *must have* oublier!

Le futur et le conditionnel

Across

2. Je (will pay)

4. You should (2 words—fam.)

6. Ils (will go)

8. Elles (will send)

9. Vous (would want)

11. Nous (will have arrived)

12. Je (would speak)

Down

1. Il (would be necessary)

3. Tu (will have finished)

5. Tu (would know)—savoir

7. Whereas (2 words)

10. Nous (would finish)

Culture Capsule 8

Les Antilles françaises comptent aujourd'hui la Guadeloupe, Basse-Terre, la Martinique, la Désirade, Grande-Terre, Marie-Galante, les îles de la Petite Terre et des Saintes, Saint-Barthélémy et une partie de l'île de Saint-Martin (partagée avec les Antilles néerlandaises).

Il ne faut pas oublier que c'est Christophe Colomb qui, le premier, découvrit les Antilles. Ce n'est qu'au début du 17ème siècle que les Français envoyèrent des expéditions vers le Nouveau Monde. En 1635, les Français arrivent en Martinique, puis en Guadeloupe où, au milieu du 17ème siècle se développe l'industrie sucrière. Cela entraîne l'importation d'esclaves africains et, avec eux, de leur culture et leur musique.

Grâce à la musique les esclaves peuvent communiquer entre eux. C'est de là que nous vient le **Zouk**, musique qui devient de plus en plus populaire dans le monde entier. A l'origine, surtout à la **Martinique**, le zouk était une fête où l'on dansait. Cependant, vers la fin des années 70, les artistes africains, descendants des anciens esclaves, ont créé avec des artistes français le genre musical que nous connaissons aujourd'hui et qui est la musique antillaise par définition. À la **Guadeloupe**, la musique traditionnelle est le **Gwo-ka** qui doit son nom au mot africain pour "tambour" ou "n'goka". Il s'agit d'une musique à forme répétitive, avec de l'improvisation et des échanges entre le soliste et les autres membres de l'assistance. Plusieurs rythmes font partie du *Gwo-ka* dont un rythme guerrier ou Lewoz, une danse pour célébrer la récolte de la canne à sucre ou Kagenbel sans oublier le Roulé qui se moque du maître blanc.

VOCABULAIRE

partagée	*shared*
néerlandaises	*dutch*
l'industrie sucrière	*the sugar industry*
les esclaves	*the slaves*
de plus en plus	*more and more*
les années 70	*the seventies*
tambour	*drum*

11

The Subjunctive

Que savez-vous déjà?
What Do You Know Already?

?

What is the present subjunctive of the following verbs?

1. tu (être) _____

2. nous (manger) _____

3. elle (faire) _____

4. je (sentir) _____

5. vous (finir) _____

6. ils (lire) _____

7. tu (avoir) _____

8. il (entendre) _____

9. elles (parler) _____

10. nous (nager) _____

Both indicative and subjunctive are moods. While the indicative (present, future, past tenses, etc.) designates a conjugated verb that reflects an objective fact, the subjunctive designates a conjugated verb that reflects obligation, necessity, wish, doubt, emotion, uncertainty, or prohibition.

The Present Subjunctive
Le subjonctif présent

The present subjunctive of a verb can be obtained by taking the third person plural of the present indicative of regular verbs, dropping the **ent** ending and replacing it by the subjunctive endings **e, es, e, ions, iez, ent**.

REGULAR VERBS such as **aimer** *(to love/like)* **finir** *(to finish)* **attendre** *(to wait for)*

-er verbs → Ils aim**ent** → aim →

que j'aime	que nous aim**ions**
que tu aim**es**	que vous aim**iez**
qu'il/qu'elle aime	qu'ils/qu'elles aim**ent**

-ir verbs → Ils finiss**ent** → finiss →

que je finisse	que nous finiss**ions**
que tu finiss**es**	que vous finiss**iez**
qu'il/qu'elle finisse	qu'ils/qu'elles finiss**ent**

-re verbs → Ils attend**ent** → attend →

que j'attende	que nous attend**ions**
que tu attend**es**	que vous attend**iez**
qu'il/qu'elle attende	qu'ils/qu'elles attend**ent**

For verbs ending in ier such as étudier, the i preceding the ending is doubled for the 1st and 2nd persons plural: Il faut que nous étudiions.

NOTE: For the verbs of the first group (**-er**), the 1st, 2nd, and 3rd persons singular and the 3rd person plural are the same as in the present indicative. For the verbs of the second (**-ir**) and third (**-re**) groups, the 3rd person plural is the same as in the present indicative.

For all three groups, the **nous** and **vous** forms have the endings of the **imparfait**.

Il faut que Renée finisse ses devoirs.
It is necessary that Renée finish her homework.

Il faut que nous regardions cette emission.
It is necessary that we watch this program.

Il faut que je réponde à cette lettre.
It is necessary that I answer this letter.

Il faut que Michel vende sa voiture.
It is necessary that Michel sell his car.

Il faut que vous appeliez votre grand-mère.
It is necessary that you call your grandmother.

QUICK PRACTICE

I. Le père de Julien et Vanessa est furieux parce que ses enfants sont paresseux. Il leur dit ce qu'il faut faire:

1. Vanessa, il faut que tu (nettoyer) ta chambre!

2. Julien et Vanessa, il faut que vous (ranger) vos affaires!

3. Julien, il faut que tu (écouter) quand je te dis de faire quelque chose!

4. Julien et Vanessa, il faut que vous (jeter) ces papiers à la poubelle!*

5. Julien et Vanessa, il faut que vous (téléphoner) à vos grands-parents!

IRREGULAR VERBS WITH A REGULAR SUBJUNCTIVE					
Most irregular verbs have a regular subjunctive.					
dire *to say or tell*	→ ils dis**ent**	→ dis	→	que je dise que tu dis**es** qu'/elle/il dise	que nous dis**ions** que vous dis**iez** qu'elles/ils dis**ent**
ouvrir *to open*	→ ils ouvr**ent**	→ ouvr	→	que j'ouvre que tu ouvr**es** qu'elle/il ouvre	que nous ouvr**ions** que vous ouvr**iez** qu'elles/ils ouvr**ent**
courir *to run*	→ ils cour**ent**	→ cour	→	que je coure que tu cour**es** qu'elle/il coure	que nous cour**ions** que vous cour**iez** qu'elle/ils cour**ent**

*poubelle: *garbage can.*

130 Complete French Grammar Review

IRREGULAR VERBS WITH AN IRREGULAR SUBJUNCTIVE

- For some irregular verbs, the subjunctive is irregular because the root of the verb changes for **je, tu, il, elle, on, ils, elles**, and the imperfect indicative is used for the **nous** and **vous** forms.

Infinitive	Irregular Root	Subjunctive	
aller	aill	que j'aille	que nous **allions**
to go		que tu ailles	que vous **alliez**
		qu'il/elle aille	qu'ils/elles aillent
vouloir	veuill	que je veuille	que nous **voulions**
to want		que tu veuilles	que vous **vouliez**
		qu'il/elle veuille	qu'ils/elles veuillent

- For some irregular verbs such as **faire**, **pouvoir**, and **savoir**, the irregular root is **the same** for all persons, but the subjunctive endings still apply.

faire	fass	que je fasse	que nous fassions
to do, make		que tu fasses	que vous fassiez
		qu'il/elle fasse	qu'ils/elles fassent
pouvoir	puiss	que je puisse	que nous puissions
can, be able		que tu puisses	que vous puissiez
		qu'il/elle puisse	qu'ils/elles puissent
savoir	sach	que je sache	que nous sachions
to know		que tu saches	que vous sachiez
		qu'il/elle sache	qu'ils/elles sachent

- The verbs **avoir** and **être** are completely irregular.

avoir		**être**	
to have		*to be*	
que j'aie	que nous ayons	que je sois	que nous soyons
que tu aies	que vous ayez	que tu sois	que vous soyez
qu'il/elle ait	qu'ils/elles aient	qu'il/elle soit	qu'ils/elles soient

- Note the impersonal verbs **pleuvoir**, **neiger**, and **falloir** *(to rain, to snow, to be necessary)*

qu'il pleuve	qu'il neige	qu'il faille

Il faut que j'aille chez le médecin.	*It is necessary that I go to the doctor's.*
Il faut que tu saches ce poème.	*It is necessary that you know this poem.*
Il faut qu'il veuille étudier.	*It is necessary that he want to study.*
Il faut que nous puissions sortir.	*It is necessary that we be able to go out.*
Il faut que vous fassiez attention.	*It is necessary that you pay attention.*
Il faut que vous ayez de la monnaie.	*It is necessary that you have change.*
Il faut que je sois en bonne santé.	*It is necessary that I be in good health.*

Is the subjunctive always used with **il faut que**? No. Here are some other impersonal expressions that express *necessity, obligation, possibility, impossibility, doubt, regret,* and *emotion,* and therefore require the subjunctive:

il est important que	*it is important that*
il est nécessaire que	*it is necessary that*
il est bon que	*it is good that*
il est douteux que	*it is doubtful that*
il est utile que	*it is useful that*
il est inutile que	*it is useless that*
il est indispensable que	*it is indispensable that*
il est possible que	*it is possible that*
il est impossible que	*it is impossible that*
il est normal que	*it is normal that*
il est peu probable que*	*it is not likely that*
il n'est pas probable que	*it is not likely that*
il est regrettable que	*it is regrettable that*
il est préférable que	*it is preferable that*
il est dommage que	*it is a pity that*
il est étonnant que	*it is surprising that*
il est triste que	*it is sad that*
il semble que*	*it seems that*
il vaut mieux que	*it is better that*
il est temps que	*it is time that*

Il est important que vous soyez à l'heure pour votre rendez-vous.
It is important that you be on time for your appointment (date).

Il est possible qu'ils veuillent venir à cette soirée.
It is possible that they'll want to come to this party.

Il est dommage qu'elle ne puisse pas assister à ce spectacle.
It is a pity she will not be able to attend this show.

Il vaut mieux que tu prennes ton imper parce qu'il va pleuvoir.
It is better that you take your raincoat because it is going to rain.

Are all impersonal expressions followed by the sujunctive? No. When an impersonal expression reflects certainty or a polite way of expressing certainty, the indicative is used, exept when the exressions are negative or interrogative.

il est vrai que	*it is true that*
il est certain que	*it is certain that*
il est probable que	*it is probable that*
il est évident que	*it is evident that*
il est clair que	*it is clear that*
il paraît que	*it appears that*
il me semble que	*it seems to me that*

*Note that the affimative form of this expression **il est probable que** requires the indicative, **not** the subjunctive.
**When using il me semble que (*it seems to me that*), the indicative is used.

QUICK PRACTICE

II. Refaites les phrases suivantes en ajoutant l'expression entre parenthèses et en faisant les changements nécessaires:

1. (il est important)   tu viens avant neuf heures.

2. (il est possible)   elle est malade.

3. (il est inutile)   vous prenez le métro.

4. (il est clair)   il ne comprend pas.

5. (il est temps)   je fais mes devoirs.

6. (il est préférable)   vous ouvrez la fenêtre.

7. (il est probable)   ils savent la vérité.

8. (il est dommage)   elle ne peut pas partir en vacances.

9. (il vaut mieux)   il ne pleut pas.

10. (il paraît)   ils sont en Afrique actuellement.

III. Complétez les phrases suivantes avec la forme des verbes entre parenthèses:

1. il est indispensable que Patrick ...
   (faire attention, finir le chapitre, répondre aux questions)

2. il peu probable qu'ils ...
   (avoir le temps, pouvoir arriver avant midi, dormir jusqu'à 9 heures)

IV. Refaites les phrases suivantes avec "il faut + l'infinitif". Employez un pronom objet tel que "me, te, etc.":

Modèle: *Il est nécessaire qu'elle ait* une voiture.—Il lui faut une voiture.

1. *Il faut que nous achetions* une autre voiture.

2. *Il faut qu'elle parte* à six heures.

3. *Il faut que tu dises* la vérité à ton père.

4. *Vous avez besoin d'*un parapluie.

5. *J'ai besoin de* deux pommes pour cette recette.

VERBS THAT ARE FOLLOWED BY THE SUBJUNCTIVE

Verbs that express emotion, desire, wish, obligation, prohibition, doubt, requirement, permission, regret, and are followed by **que** require the subjunctive, such as:

aimer *to love, like*	**douter** *to doubt*	**refuser** *to refuse*
attendre *to wait for*	**s'étonner** *to be surprised*	**regretter** *to regret*
s'attendre à *to expect*	**exiger** *to require*	**souhaiter** *to wish*
craindre *to fear*	**interdire** *to forbid*	**tenir à** *to insist*
défendre *to forbid*	**permettre** *to allow*	**vouloir** *to want*
demander *to ask*	**préférer** *to prefer*	

Verbs such as **s'attendre à** and **tenir à** are followed by **ce que** after the preposition **à**.

Je m'attends à ce qu'ils fassent leurs devoirs.
I expect them to do their homework.

Je tiens à ce que vous veniez avec nous.
I insist that you come with us.

Il demande que nous répondions à la question.
He asks that we answer the question.

J'aimerais que vous veniez nous voir.
I would like for you* to come see us.

Ils veulent que nous sortions avec eux.
They want us* to go out with them.

Je doute qu'elle reçoive cette lettre aujourd'hui.
I doubt that she will receive this letter today.

*Some verbs that require the subjunctive, such as *to want* (**vouloir**) are not followed by *that* in English.

I want **you** to read this book.   ➔ Je veux **que tu** lises ce livre.

NOT   ~~Je te veux lire ce livre.~~

She would like **for us** to go see her on Saturday.
➔ Elle aimerait **que nous** allions la voir samedi.

NOT   ~~Elle aimerait pour nous d'aller la voir samedi.~~

What happens when the subject of the verb and the object are one and the same? It is just like in English. The infinitive is used.

I would like to go to the beach   ➔ **J'aimerais aller à la plage.**
I refuse to go to the beach.   ➔ **Je refuse d'aller à la plage.****

VERBAL EXPRESSIONS THAT ARE FOLLOWED BY THE SUBJUNCTIVE

être content	*to be happy*	être triste	*to be sad*
être heureux	*to be happy*	être malheureux	*to be unhappy*
être fâché	*to be angry*	être furieux	*to be furious*
être désolé	*to be sorry*	être surpris	*to be surprised*
avoir peur	*to be afraid*	avoir envie	*to wish for*
avoir honte	*to be ashamed*	c'est dommage	*it's too bad*

Je suis surpris qu'il soit absent.   *I am surprised that he is absent.*
Elle est heureuse que tu viennes. *She is happy that you are coming.*

Mais ➔ **Elle est heureuse de venir.** *She is happy to come.*

When a verb is normally followed by a preposition before an infinitive, such as **refuser de, that preposition must be included.

PENSER, CROIRE, ESPÉRER, IL EST CERTAIN, IL EST SÛR, IL EST ÉVIDENT, ETC.

In the affirmative form → Indicative
In the interrogative and negative forms → Subjunctive*

Je pense qu'il est malade.	*I think that he is ill.*
~~**Penses-tu qu'il soit malade?**~~	*Do you think that he is ill?*
Je ne pense pas qu'il soit malade.	*I don't believe that he is ill.*

The same rule applies to expressions such as **il est certain, il est clair, il est évident**, etc. which, when used affirmatively, require the indicative, but when used in the negative and interrogtive forms require the subjunctive.

Il est certain qu'elle est heureuse.	*It is certain that she is happy.*
Est-il certain qu'elle soit heureuse?	*Is it certain that she is happy?*
Il n'est pas certain qu'elle soit heureuse.	*It is not certain that she is happy.*

QUICK PRACTICE

V. Monsieur Hubert pose des questions à Madame Hubert au sujet de leurs enfants Philippe et Louisette. Elle répond soit négativement, soit positivement.

Modèle: – Philippe veut aller à la plage sans nous.
– Ah, non, je ne veux pas qu'il aille à la plage sans nous. *ou*
– Oui, je veux bien qu'il aille à la plage sans nous.

1. Les enfants ont envie d'aller voir cette pièce musicale.

   Je veux bien qu'ils _____

2. Louisette voudrait boire un citron pressé.

   Ah, non, c'est le troisième, je ne veux pas qu'elle _____

3. Philippe ne sait pas sa leçon de chimie.

   Eh bien, j'exige qu'il _____

4. Philippe et Louisette font leurs devoirs.

   Je suis heureuse qu'ils _____

5. Louisette veut voir cette emission à la télé.

   Ah, non, je ne veux pas qu'elle _____.

*When speaking, the indicative is often used instead of the subjunctive in the interrogative and negative forms: **Penses-tu qu'il est malade? Je ne pense pas qu'il est malade.**

VI. Refaites les phrases suivantes en vous servant du subjonctif ou de l'indicatif:

1. Ma soeur/espérer/nous/aller/jouer au tennis.

2. Monique/s'étonner/ils/être en retard.

3. Papa/exiger/nous/faire nos devoirs.

4. Maman/vouloir/je/prendre/mon imper.

5. Marie-Christine/être triste/nous/ne pas pouvoir/aller voir cette pièce.

6. Je/souhaiter/elle/faire attention.

7. Nous/penser/elle/être chez elle.

8. Pierre/ne pas croire/Suzanne/être fâchée.

9. Je/insister/il/venir à l'heure en classe.

10. Elle/s'étonner/je/ne pas comprendre.

VII. Conversation: Avec un ami ou une amie, discutez de tout ce que vous devez faire à la maison en utilisant "Il faut que" and "il ne faut pas que". (*faire la vaisselle, sortir la poubelle, ranger mes affaires, etc.*)

CONJUNCTIONS THAT REQUIRE THE SUBJUNCTIVE

à condition que	*provided that*	en attendant que	*until*
à moins que*	*unless*	jusqu'à ce que	*until*
afin que	*in order that*	malgré que	*although*
avant que*	*before*	pour que	*so that*
bien que	*although*	pourvu que**	*provided that*
de crainte que*	*for fear that*	quoique	*although*
de peur que*	*for fear that*	sans que	*without*

Je vais mettre la table maintenant afin que tout soit prêt à leur arrivée.
I will set the table now in order that everything will be ready when they arrive.

J'étudierai jusqu'à ce que je comprenne ce chapitre.
I will study until I understand this chapter.

Nous irons à la plage demain à condition qu'il fasse beau.
We will go to the beach tomorrow provided the weather is nice.

Bien qu'il pleuve, nous allons faire un pique-nique.
Although it is raining, we will have a picnic.

*à moins que, avant que, de crainte que** and **de peur que** are usually followed by **ne** (*le ne pléonastique*), but this is not compulsory. It does not reflect a negative and there is no **pas** after the verb.

Je ne veux pas sortir de crainte qu'il **ne** pleuve *ou* de crainte qu'il pleuve.
I don't want to go out for fear that it might rain.

pourvu que at the beginning of a sentence means *Let's hope that*. However, in a subordinate clause, it means *provided that*.

Pourvu qu'il ne pleuve pas demain!
Let's hope it will not rain tomorrow!

Nous irons à la plage demain pourvu qu'il ne pleuve pas.
We will go to the beach tomorrow provided it doesn't rain.

Do all conjunctions followed by **que** require the subjunctive? No. After the following conjunctions, the indicative is used: **après que, aussitôt que, dès que, pendant que, tandis que, parce que, puisque.**

THE SUBJUNCTIVE IN A PRINCIPAL CLAUSE

It corresponds to *may* in English.

Qu'ils viennent à l'heure!	*May they come on time!*
Qu'ils cessent de faire du bruit!	*May they stop making noise!*

THE SUBJUNCTIVE IN SENTENCES THAT EXPRESS UNCERTAINTY OR DOUBT

Je cherche quelqu'un qui puisse réparer ce meuble ancien.
I am looking for someone who can repair this antique piece of furniture.

Connais-tu quelqu'un qui sache réparer ce meuble ancien?
Do you know someone who can repair this antique piece of furniture?

Je n'ai pas encore trouvé quelqu'un qui sache réparer ce meuble ancien.
I haven't yet found someone who can repair this antique piece of furniture.

QUICK PRACTICE

VIII. Refaites les phrases suivantes:

Modèle: Il fera /ses devoirs/avant que/son père/vient
Il fera ses devoirs avant que son père (ne) vienne.

1. Bien que/elle/être malade/elle/faire/ses devoirs.

2. Je/expliquer/encore une fois/pour que/vous/comprendre.

3. Ils/aller à la plage/à condition que/faire beau.

4. Connaître/vous/ quelqu'un qui/savoir/le chinois?

5. Elle/s'occuper de/le chien des voisins/jusqu'à ce que/ils/revenir.

6. Je répondrai à ses lettres/pourvu que/il/m'écrire.

7. Michel range ses affaires/de peur que/sa mère/être furieuse.

8. J'ai lu le livre/en attendant que/le film/sorte.

The Past Subjunctive
Le subjonctif passé

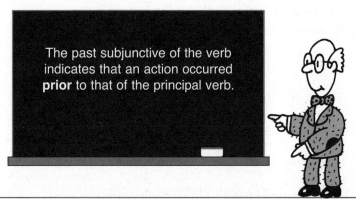

The past subjunctive of the verb indicates that an action occurred **prior** to that of the principal verb.

SUBJECT		SUBJUNCTIVE OF AVOIR OR ÊTRE	PAST PARTICIPLE
Que	nous	ayons	voyagé
Qu'	elle	soit	allée

Il veut que nous ayons fini avant midi.
He wants us to be finished before noon.

C'est dommage que tu n'aies pas vu Pierrette hier.
It is too bad that you did not see Pierrette yesterday.

Je doute qu'ils se soient réveillés à six heures.
I doubt that they woke up at six o'clock.

Il est possible qu'elle soit allée chez Jean-Claude.
It is possible that she went to Jean-Claude's house.

Il ne croit pas qu'ils se soient dépêchés.
He doesn't believe that they hurried.

Nous regrettons que tu sois parti avant le diner.
We regret that you left before dinner.

QUICK PRACTICE

IX. Refaites les phrases suivantes au subjonctif présent ou au subjonctif passé:

Modèle: Nous sommes désolés/vous êtes malade.
Nous sommes désolés que vous soyez malade.

Je suis surprise/vous avez perdu son adresse.
Je suis surprise que vous ayez perdu son adresse.

1. C'est dommage/vous n'êtes pas allé les voir.

2. J'ai peur/il a oublié le rendez-vous.

3. Je suis heureuse/ils sont ici.

4. Mon professeur veut/nous sommes toujours à l'heure.

5. Il est possible/Patrick/a déjà visité ce musée.

6. Elle est contente/nous sommes allés la voir.

7. Je suis désolé/vous n'avez pas pu rester plus longtemps.

8. Fabienne est heureuse/sa fille a eu une bonne note.

9. Il faut /il fait attention.

10. Elle doute/Pierre est en Europe.

Le subjonctif

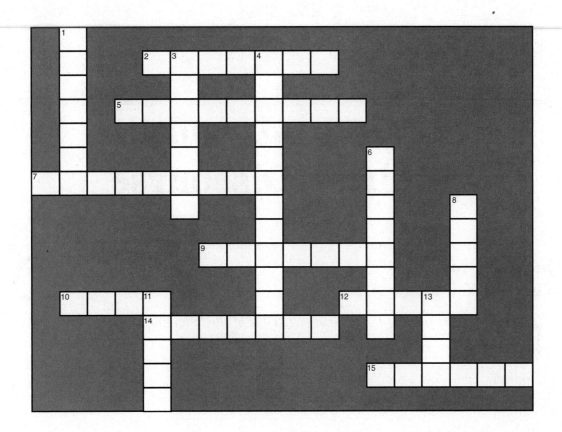

Across

2. Qu'elle _____ (finir)

5. Que nous _____ (etudier)

7. Qu'ils _____ (vouloir)

9. Que nous _____ (aller)

10. Que tu _____ (être)

12. Qu'il _____ (vendre)

14. Que nous _____
(voir—subj. passé)

15. Que tu _____
(pouvoir—subj. passé)

Down

1. Il est _____ (pity)

3. Il es _____ (useless)

4. Qu'elle _____ (aller—subj. passé)

6. Que vous _____ (pouvoir)

8. Que je vous _____ (parler)

11. Qu'elle _____ (savoir)

13. Que je _____ (dire)

12

The Present Participle, the Gerund, and the Indirect Discourse

---

Que savez-vous déjà?
What Do You Know Already? (?)

What is the correct form of the present participle of the following verbs?

1. connaître _____

2. parler _____

3. dire _____

4. avoir _____

5. finir _____

6. aller _____

7. attendre _____

8. écrire _____

9. venir _____

10. partir _____

The Present Participle
Le participe présent

     The present participle of a verb is formed by taking the **nous** form of the verb in the present tense, dropping the **ons** ending and replacing it by **ant**. The **ant** ending corresponds to the *ing* ending in English.

INFINITIVE	PRESENT	PRESENT PARTICIPLE
aimer	aim**ons**	aim**ant**
finir	finiss**ons**	finiss**ant**
attendre	attend**ons**	attend**ant**
dire	dis**ons**	dis**ant**
voir	voy**ons**	voy**ant**
apprendre	appren**ons**	appren**ant**
boire	buv**ons**	buv**ant**
manger	mange**ons**	mange**ant**
commencer	commenç**ons**	commenç**ant**

Do all present participles follow this rule? Yes, except for three irregular present participles:

avoir	**avons**	**ayant**
être	**sommes**	**étant**
savoir	**savons**	**sachant**

Voulant partir en Italie, elle regardait un tas de brochures de voyage.
Wanting to go to Italy, she was looking at a lot of travel brochures.

Étant malade, je n'ai pas pu sortir avec mes copains.
Being ill, I was not able to go out with my friends.

Sachant qu'il était déjà vingt-deux heures, je n'ai pas voulu leur téléphoner.
Knowing that it was already 10 P.M. I didn't want to call them.

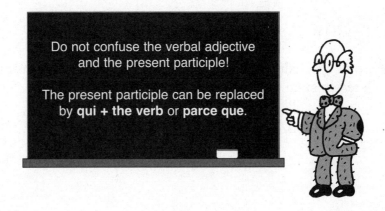

Do not confuse the verbal adjective and the present participle!

The present participle can be replaced by **qui + the verb** or **parce que**.

Stéphanie, **suivant** les conseils de son médecin, a pris une semaine de congé.
Stephanie, following her doctor's advice, took a week off.

ou **Stéphanie qui suit les conseils de son médecin, a pris une semaine de congé.**
Stephanie, who follows her doctor's advice, took a week off.

Etant fatiguée, Stéphanie est allée voir son médecin.
Being tired, Stephanie went to see her doctor.

ou **Parce qu'elle était fatiguée, Stéphanie est allée voir son médecin.**
Since (because) she was tired, Stephanie went to see her doctor.

The verbal adjective agrees in gender and number with the noun it modifies.

La semaine **suivante**, Stéphanie est retournée au travail.
The following week, Stephanie returned to work.

And in the negative form **NE + PARTICIPE PRÉSENT + PAS** is the rule. So all English verbs ending in *ing* translate into the French present participle? Not exactly.

- When two verbs follow each other in English and the second one ends in *ing*, it is translated by the French infinitive:

     We like dancing. → **Nous aimons danser.**

   And NEVER use the French present participle when translating an action in progress.

     I am dancing. → **Je danse.**

     NOT   ~~Je suis dansant.~~

- Some English words ending in *ing* are used as nouns and should be translated as such.

     Dancing is always in fashion. → **La danse** est toujours à la mode.

I. Refaites les phrases suivantes en employant le participe présent:

1. J'ai vu Dominique *qui courait* dans la rue.

2. Vincent, *qui aimait* le tennis, voulait devenir joueur professionnel.

3. J'ai rencontré mon professeur *qui sortait* de la boulangerie.

4. Ma cousine, *qui ne sait pas* parler anglais, va suivre un cours d'été.

5. Les étudiants, *qui sortaient* de l'université, ont vu l'accident.

II. Traduisez:

1. This story is interesting.

2. Running is an excellent sport.

3. My brother likes reading.

4. The children are playing.

5. Knowing it was raining, she took her umbrella.

The Past Form of the Present Participle
Le participe parfait

Present Participle of Avoir **or** Étre **+ Past Participle**

As for all compound tenses, when using the verb **être**, the past participle agrees in gender and number with the subject. In the negative form, the two parts of the negative surround the present participle and precede the past participle.

N' **+ Present Participle of** Avoir **or** Étre **+** Pas **+ Past Participle**

Ayant décidé d'aller à la soirée, Françoise voulait acheter une nouvelle robe.
Having decided to go to the party, Françoise wanted to buy a new dress.

Line, **étant sortie** avec ses copains, n'avait pas envie de rentrer de bonne heure.
Line, having gone out with her friends, didn't feel like going home early.

N'ayant **pas** encore vu ce film, je veux absolument le voir ce week-end.
Not having seen this movie yet, I absolutely want to see it this week-end.

Emma, **n'**étant **pas** arrivée à l'heure, avait manqué son train.
Emma, not having arrived on time, had missed her train.

The Gerund
Le gérondif

En + Present Participle

The gerund often answers the question *how*. In English, **en** + present participle is translated by *by, while, upon* + present participle.

She reads while listening to music.   ➔ **Elle lit en écoutant la musique.**
How does she read? She reads while listening to music.

One learns by listening.   ➔ **On apprend en écoutant.**
How does one learn? One learns by listening.

She fell upon arriving.   ➔ **Elle est tombée en arrivant.**
When did she fall? She fell upon arriving.

• The gerund describes two actions that take place simultaneously.

   Il chante en conduisant.   *He sings while driving.*

• The gerund describes the way something is done or the result of something.

   On apprend en étudiant.   *One learns by studying.*

• The gerund describes a condition necessary for something to occur.

   En pratiquant, on finit par exceller.
   By practicing, one ends up excelling.

• **Tout en** + present participle is used to reinforce an idea in relation to another idea.

   Elle faisait ses devoirs tout en mangeant.
   She was doing her homework (and all the) while she was eating.

   Il s'habillait tout en parlant au téléphone.
   He was getting dressed (and all the) while he was talking on the telephone.

What is the difference between these two sentences?

J'ai rencontré Paul en sortant du cinéma.

and **J'ai rencontré Paul sortant du cinéma.**

In the first example, I met Paul as **I** was leaving the movie theater. In the second example, I met Paul as **he** was leaving the theater.

QUICK PRACTICE

III. Mettez le verbe entre parenthèses à l'une des formes suivantes: le participe présent, le gérondif ou l'adjectif verbal:

1. J'ai pleuré d'émotion (apprendre) que j'avais réussi.

2. Il n'a pas beaucoup gagné (vendre) sa voiture.

3. Les élèves (courir) devant l'école s'amusaient beaucoup.

4. Nicole est une jeune fille (sourire).

5. Il est devenu plus sage (grandir).

6. Paulette, (penser) qu'il allait pleuvoir, a pris son parapluie.

7. Il ne faut pas parler (manger).

8. La petite fille (réciter) le poème, s'appelle Micheline.

9. Corinne agaçait le professeur (bavarder) constamment.

10. Mes parents, (être) fatigués, ont décidé de rentrer à la maison.

IV. Traduisez:

1. Having studied until midnight

2. Having arrived early

3. Having left at noon

4. Having been ill

5. Having opened the window

The Indirect Discourse
Le discours indirect

In the direct discourse someone makes a statement or asks a question (*she says: " "*). It is reported verbatim, as a quotation. In the indirect discourse, it is the person reporting who is speaking (*she says that . . .*).

Direct	→	Il dit: "Sara est absente aujourd'hui".	*(quote)*
		He says: "Sara is absent today."	
Indirect	→	Il dit **que** Sara est absente aujourd'hui.	*(relative pronoun)*
		He says that Sara is absent today.	
Direct	→	Je me demande: "Sara est-elle malade?"	*(quote)*
		I wonder: "Is Sara ill?"	
Indirect	→	Je me demande **si** Sara est malade.	*(si)*
		I wonder if (whether) Sara is ill.	
Direct	→	Je me demande: "**Avec qui ont-ils voyagé**?"	*(inversion)*
		I wonder: "With whom did they travel?"	
Indirect	→	Je me demande **avec qu'ils ont voyagé**.	*(no inversion)*
		I wonder with whom they traveled.	
Direct	→	Il demande: "**Avec quoi vas-tu écrire**?"	*(inversion)*
		He asks: "With what are you going to write?"	
Indirect	→	Il demande **avec quoi je vais écrire**.	*(no inversion)*
		He asks with what I am going to write.	
Direct	→	Je demande: "**Quelle heure est-il**?"	*(inversion)*
		I ask: "What time is it?"	
Indirect	→	Je demande **quelle heure il est**.	*(no inversion)*
		I ask what time it is.	
Direct	→	Elle suggère: "Allons au cinéma".	*(quote)*
		She suggests: "Let's go to the movies."	
Indirect	→	Elle suggère **d'**aller au cinéma.	*(de)*
		She suggests going to the movies.	
Direct	→	Elle exige: "Faites attention!"	*(imperative)*
		She says: "Pay attention!"	
Indirect	→	Elle exige **que nous fassions** attention.	*(subjunctive)*
		She requires that we pay attention.	
Direct	→	Je demande: "**Qu'est-ce qui** se passe?"	*(quote)*
		I ask: "What is happening?"	
Indirect	→	Je demande **ce qui** se passe.	*(pronoun)*
		I ask what is happening.	

There is no change in the sentence when using the interrogative pronoun **qui**.

Direct → **Je demande: "Qui est venu?"**
I ask: "Who came?"

Indirect → **Je demande qui est venu.**
I ask who came.

QUICK PRACTICE

V. Mettez les phrases suivantes à la forme indirecte:

Modèle: Elle dit: Tu es à l'heure.—Elle dit que je suis à l'heure.

1. Il demande: "Avec qui sortez-vous?"

2. Elle dit: "Je suis fatiguée".

3. Nous demandons: "Sont-ils occupés?"

4. Elle nous dit: "Allez au parc!"

5. Je me demande: "Vont-ils à la plage?"

6. Elle demande: "Qui vient avec nous?"

7. Son père ordonne: "Tais-toi".

8. Il me conseille: "Lis ce livre".

9. Elle me demande: "Quel film veux-tu voir?"

10. Il me dit: "N'oublie pas ton sac".

The Indirect Discourse and Other Tenses
Le discours indirect et autres temps

DISCOURS DIRECT	DISCOURS INDIRECT
passé composé Il a dit: "J'ai mangé une pomme". *He said: "I ate an apple."*	*plus-que-parfait* Il a dit qu'il avait mangé une pomme. *He said that he had eaten an apple.*
imparfait Elle a dit: "J'étais furieuse". *She said: "I was furious."*	*imparfait* Elle a dit qu'elle était furieuse. *She said that she was furious.*
plus-que-parfait Elle a demandé : "Avais-tu oublié?" *She asked: "Had you forgotten?"*	*plus-que-parfait* Elle a demandé si j'avais oublié. *She asked if I had forgotten.*
futur Il a déclaré: "Je n'irai pas au club". *He declared: "I will not go to the club."*	*conditionnel présent* Il a déclaré qu'il n'irait pas au club. *He declared that he would not go to the club.*

futur anterieur
Elle a dit: "Je n'aurai pas fini à 3h".
*She said: "I will not have finished at
   3 o'clock."*
	conditionnel passé
	Elle a dit qu'elle n'aurait pas fini à 3 h.
	*She said that she would not have finished at
	   3 o'clock.*

conditionnel présent Il a dit: "Je n'aimerais pas être en retard". *He said: "I would not like to be late."*	*conditionnel présent* Il a dit qu'il n'aimerait pas être en retard. *He said he would not like to be late.*
conditionnel passé Elle a dit: "J'aurais voulu les voir". *She said: "I would have liked to see them."*	*conditionnel passé* Elle a dit qu'elle aurait voulu les voir. *She said that she would have liked to see them.*

> **TIP**
> **Adverbs of time often need to change in the indirect discourse.**
>
> | | | | | |
> |---|---|---|---|---|
> | demain | → le lendemain | après-demain | → | le surlendemain |
> | aujourd'hui | → ce jour-là | hier | → | la veille |
> | avant-hier | → l'avant-veille | ce matin | → | ce matin-là |
> | cette semaine | → cette semaine-là | ce soir | → | ce soir-là |

VI. Transformez les phrases en discours indirect:

Modèle: Il m'a demandé: "As-tu compris?"—Il m'a demandé si j'avais compris.

1. Le professeur a dit: "J'expliquerai ce problème".

2. Elle m'a demandé: "Avec qui viendras-tu?"

3. Il a écrit: "J'aimerais vous inviter".

4. Je me demande: "Avec quoi vont-ils écrire?"

5. Elle m'a expliqué: "Je n'ai pas compris".

6. Il suggère: "Finis avant le dîner".

7. Elle a demandé: "Avez-vous oublié la réponse?"

8. Elle m'a dit: "J'ai vu Pierre hier".

9. Mon père exige: "Fais tes devoirs!"

10. Maman a dit: "La lettre est arrivée ce matin".

Le participe présent

```
V  T  M  L  D  W  F  V  G  X  F  O  H  T  Q
X  I  N  U  W  X  J  Z  V  C  Y  T  Z  N  E
F  O  V  A  E  W  S  A  L  B  A  X  T  A  D
H  X  J  D  V  O  L  T  F  E  W  G  F  Y  O
Q  H  H  B  G  U  N  J  I  J  B  V  H  O  X
U  W  N  H  P  A  B  T  N  A  L  I  I  V  J
N  Z  U  Z  E  A  U  V  I  V  X  H  C  C  G
W  R  M  G  Y  M  D  J  S  R  N  Q  J  H  A
H  H  N  G  F  T  C  K  S  C  F  J  T  Y  P
M  A  T  N  A  S  I  D  A  W  M  N  J  R  E
M  A  K  W  Z  Q  P  G  N  H  A  X  S  P  I
P  N  P  B  I  Q  R  B  T  Y  D  E  K  H  N
A  C  P  O  G  R  D  J  A  T  R  C  X  Z  O
V  V  I  L  X  T  E  T  A  N  T  H  R  X  P
H  F  E  N  S  A  C  H  A  N  T  X  O  T  D
```

AYANT	EN SACHANT	MANGEANT
BUVANT	ETANT	VOYANT
DISANT	FINISSANT	

Culture Capsule 9

apoléon Premier voulait faire de Paris la capitale de l'Europe, projet qui n'a jamais été réalisé. Malgré la construction des ponts d'Iena et d'Austerlitz, ainsi que de celles de la rue de Rivoli et de la colonne Vendôme, c'est à Napoléon III que l'on doit la vraie urbanisation de la ville. Jusqu'alors Paris, avec ses rues étroites, insalubres, et mal famées, est une ville du Moyen-Age. Vers 1200 Philippe Auguste avait fait paver les rues de Paris avec, au milieu, une rigole d'évacuation. Le premier égout souterrain situé rue Montmartrene ne fut construit qu'en 1370.

A part les quelques renovations entamées sous le règne de Napoléon Premier, il est impossible d'y circuler facilement, surtout avec une population croissante. Napoléon III fait alors appel au préfet de la Seine, le Baron George Eugene Haussmann, pour diriger les travaux de rénovation. Celui-ci démolit et rebâtit sans compter, faisant tout ce qui était nécesaire à l'embellissement de la ville. Il fait élargir les rues, percer des avenues et créer des parcs et jardins magnifiques. C'est de cette époque que datent les boulevards ainsi que les avenues et les vastes places qui font la gloire de Paris tels que les Champs Elysées et la place de l'Étoile. Par souci d'hygiène aussi, Haussmann confie à l'ingénieur Belgrand la construction d'un aqueduc qui fait venir l'eau potable provenant de sources d'eau fraîche. En outre, en 1850 le baron Haussmann fait construire près de 600 kms d'égouts.

Il faut cependant reconnaître que les raisons qui ont poussé Napoléon III à entamer ces rénovations ne portaient pas uniquement sur l'embellissement de la capitale. Les grandes rues et avenues ne pouvaient pas se couvrir facilement de barricades et permettaient aux troupes armées d'arriver sans obstacles. Il n'avait pas oublié les révolutions parisiennes!

VOCABULAIRE

jusqu'alors	*until then*
étroites	*narrow*
entamées	*started*
croissante	*increasing*
fait alors appel	*calls then*
embellissement	*embellishment*
élargir	*widen*
par souci	*worrying about*
confie	*entrusts*
eau potable	*drinkable water*
égouts	*sewers*

PART III:
Reviewing and Practicing the Other Parts of Speech

13

Articles

Que savez-vous déjà?
What Do You Know Already?

Can you fill in the blanks with the correct form of the indicated article?

Definite		*Indefinite*	
1. _____ amis		6. _____ maison	
2. _____ élève		7. _____ portes	
3. _____ réponse		8. _____ professeur	
4. _____ livre		9. _____ restaurants	
5. _____ fenêtres		10. _____ femme	

Definite and Indefinite Articles
Les articles définis et indéfinis

In French, nouns are either masculine or feminine. Unlike English there is no neuter gender (*it*).

• **The definite article**
In English, the definite article *the* applies to masculine, feminine, and plural nouns. In French, there is a different article for each; in the plural, feminine and masculine words take the same article.

NOTE: When a noun begins with a vowel or a mute **h** (**h** that is not pronounced, such as "**homme**"), the definite articles **le** and **la** change to **l'**.

MASCULINE	FEMININE	PLURAL
le garçon	la table	les garcons, les tables
l'ami	l'amie	les amis, les amies

- **The indefinite article**

In English, the indefinite article *a* applies to masculine and feminine, nouns (a man, a woman). In the plural, there is no indefinite article. In French, there is a different indefinite article for masculine, feminine, and plural, with no change for words beginning with a vowel or a mute **h**. The indefinite article **des** can sometimes be translated into *some*.

MASCULINE	FEMININE	PLURAL
un garçon	une table	des garcons, des tables
a boy	*a table*	*boys, tables*

General Uses of the Articles
Quand utiliser un article

CONTRACTIONS OF THE DEFINITE ARTICLE WITH THE PREPOSITIONS À AND DE		
Masculine	Feminine	Plural
à + le → au (à l')	à + la → à la (à l')	à + les → aux
de + le → du (de l')	de + la → de la (de l')	de + les → des

Je vais à la plage.   Je viens de la plage.
Je vais au cinéma.   Je viens du cinéma.
Je parle à la dame.   Je parle de la dame.
Je parle au professeur.   Je parle du professeur.
Je parle aux élèves.   Je parle des élèves.
Je parle à l'élève.   Je parle de l'élève.

THE DEFINITE ARTICLE EXPRESSES

- **The possessive:** with the preposition de

    La robe **de la** jeune fille est bleue.
    The dress of the young woman is blue.

- **Names of peoples or animals when expressing a generality**

    Les américains aiment voyager.   *Americans like to travel.*
    Les lions sont féroces.   *Lions are ferocious.*

- **Abstract nouns**

    La gentillesse de cette femme est exemplaire.
    The kindness of this woman is exemplary.

The Partitive Article
Le partitif

The partitive article is used before a noun to express a quantity that cannot be measured. In English, it is translated as *some* or *any*, or omitted altogether.

I bought some milk.	→ J'ai acheté **du** lait.
Would you like some apple pie?	→ Voulez-vous **de la** tarte aux pommes?
I bought some apples.	→ J'ai acheté **des** pommes.
I bought apples.	→ J'ai acheté des pommes.
Do you have any apples?	→ Avez-vous **des** pommes?
Do you have apples?	→ Avez vous des pommes?

After the verbs **aimer, détester, préférer, adorer,** the definite article must be used instead of the partitive.

Compare:
J'achète du lait. *I buy (some) milk.*
J'aime le lait. *I like milk.*

WHEN DO UN, UNE, DES, DU, DE L', AND DE LA BECOME DE?

• In the negative form

As-tu **un** cahier de vocabulaire? Non, je **n'**ai **pas de** cahier de vocabulaire.
Veut-elle toujours **des** bonbons? Non, elle **ne** veut **jamais de** bonbons.
A-t-il **de l'**argent? Non, il **n'**a **pas d'**argent.

With the verb **être** there is no change in the negative form:

C'est un film policier.	→ Ce **n'est pas un** film policier.
Ce sont des roses.	→ Ce **ne sont pas des** roses.

NOTE: **ne...que** is not a negative. It means *only*.

Il **n'**a **que des** problèmes. *He has only problems.*

- **With expressions of quantity, weights, and measures**

beaucoup de	*a lot of, many, much*
assez de	*enough*
autant de	*as much, as many*
moins de	*less*
plus de	*more*
trop de	*too much*
une bouteille de	*a bottle of*
un kilo de	*a kilo of*
une livre de	*a pound of*
un verre de	*a glass of*
une tasse de	*a cup of*
une douzaine de	*a dozen of*
une boite de	*a box of*
un litre de	*a liter of*
un mètre de	*a meter of*

J'ai **trop de** devoirs aujourd'hui!
I have too much homework today!

Il a acheté **une bouteille de** vin.
He bought a bottle of wine.

Donnez-moi **une tasse de** café.
Give me a cup of coffee.

Elle voudrait **une douzaine de** roses.
She would like a dozen roses.

Compare: a cup of coffee → une tasse **de** café
a coffee cup → une tasse **à** café

TIP
La plupart (*most of*) is used with des although it is a quantity!
Bien de (*a lot of*) is used with the article although it is a quantity!

La plupart des jeunes aiment ce chanteur.
Most young people like this singer.

Tu as **bien de la** chance d'aller à ce concert.
You have a lot of luck (much luck) to be going to this concert.

Ils ont **bien des** problèmes avec leurs enfants.
They have a lot of problems with their children.

- **When something is made <u>of</u> or <u>for</u> something**

un livre de géologie	*a geology book*
une robe de soie (or **en soie**)	*a silk dress*

- **When a plural adjective <u>precedes</u> the noun**

  de belles pommes   mais   **des** pommes **pourries**
  beautiful apples   *rotten apples*

TIP

Do not confuse the indefinite article des with the contraction of de + les!

Compare

Elle a des lunettes de soleil.	Elle n'a pas de lunettes de soleil.
She has sunglasses.	*She doesn't have sunglasses.*
Il parle des films français.	Il ne parle pas des films français.
He speaks about the French movies.	*He doesn't speak about **the** French movies.*

Special Uses of the Definite Article
Utilisation de l'article défini

- **The definite article is used before a day of the week to imply repetition**

  Le lundi je vais à l'université à 9 heures.
  On Mondays I go to the university at 9 o'clock.

  NOTE: For a specific day of the week, nothing comes before the name of the day: *On Monday* → **Lundi**.

- **To express measures of weight or speed**

  Ces pommes coûtent 1 euro **le** kilo.
  *These apples cost 1 euro **per** kilo.*

  Il a roulé à 70 kilomètres à **l'**heure.
  *He drove at 70 kilometers **per** hour.*

- **With parts of the body instead of a possessive adjective**

  Elle a **les** cheveux blonds et **les** yeux verts.
  She has blond hair and green eyes.

- **With the names of languages**

  J'ai étudié **le** chinois quand j'étais en Chine.
  I studied Chinese when I was in China.

- **With names of academic subjects**

  Cette année, j'apprends **la** chimie.
  This year, I am learning chemistry.

- **Before the name of a person's profession followed by his/her name**

  Le docteur Dubois est allé à l'hôpital.
  Dr. Dubois went to the hospital.

  → However, when addressing that person, there is no article:
  Bonjour Dr. Dubois. *Good morning, Dr. Dubois.*

- **Before a family name**

  Les Dupont, les Lemaire *(there is no s at the end of the name).*

OMISSION OF THE ARTICLE

- **When the verb parler is used with the name of a language**

  Il parle français. *He speaks French.*

  Compare with: **Il étudie le français.** *He studies French.*

- **Before a specific day of the week**

  Lundi, je vais voir ma tante. *On Monday, I will see my aunt.*

- **In an address**

  10, avenue Colbert

- **In a heading**

  Acte I, scène 1—Chapitre trois
  Act 1, Scene 1—Chapter Three

- **After sans**

  Il est sorti sans parapluie.
  He went out without an umbrella.

- **After avec for abstract things**

    Il attend toujours avec patience.
    He always waits patiently (with patience).

    BUT: **Il prend son café avec du sucre.** *He takes his coffee with sugar.*

- **After en and a geographical name**

    En Australie, on parle anglais.
    In Australia, they speak English.

- **In some proverbs**

    Oeil pour oeil, dent pour dent.
    An eye for an eye, a tooth for a tooth.

- **Before the name of a profession, religion or nationality, after the verb être**

    Il est professeur.   Elle est catholique.
    He is a teacher.   *She is a catholic.*

    SPECIAL EXPRESSION: *One and the other* = **l'un et l'autre**

QUICK PRACTICE

I. Dans ce fait-divers (*news item*), le journaliste, qui était en retard, a oublié tous les articles! Mettez-les pour lui s'il le faut.

Hier, pendant _____ discours du Premier Ministre, _____ jeune femme s'est levée et a crié: "Vous nous avez menti!" _____ homme qui était assis à côté d'elle et qui était probablement son mari, a essayé de la calmer, mais elle a levé _____ bras en criant: "Vous nous racontez _____ histoires qui ne sont pas vraies!" _____ Premier Ministre a répondu: "De quoi parlez-vous, Madame?" Elle a dit "Vous avez dit _____ peuple que _____ argent destiné _____ arts n'allait pas être touché!"

   Le Premier Ministre a répondu en riant: "Mais bien sûr, madame, c'est _____ vérité. Pour moi, _____ théâtre, _____ cinéma, _____ musique sont très importants. D'ailleurs, ma femme est _____ pianiste. Je vous promets que nous ne touchons pas à _____ budget destiné aux arts!"

II. Mettez l'article défini, indéfini ou partitif, s'il y a lieu.

1. _____ patience est une vertu.

2. J'ai acheté _____ fleurs pour ma mère.

3. Elle aime _____ films étrangers.

4. La plupart _____ élèves sont dans la classe de gym.

5. Je n'ai pas _____ timbres.

6. Il y a _____ belles oranges au supermarché.

7. Elle aime son café sans _____ sucre.

8. Il a étudié _____ géologie à _____ université.

9. J'accepte votre invitation avec _____ plaisir.

10. Donnez-moi _____ boite _____ chocolats s'il vous plait.

III. Conversation
Pierre est allé au marché pour sa mère. Il rentre à la maison et sa mère lui demande ce qu'il a acheté. Traduisez ce que les deux ont dit:

"Pierre, where are the apples?"

"There were no apples; I bought oranges."

"Did you buy milk?"

"Yes, I bought two bottles of milk."

"Did you find the green beans (*les haricots verts*)?"

"Yes, but I don't like green beans."

"I know, but did you buy the green beans?"

"Yes, I bought the green beans and also the potatoes."

"And the cheeses?"

"Yes, here are (*voici*) the cheeses."

"But you bought only two cheeses!"

"I didn't have enough money."

THE ARTICLE BEFORE GEOGRAPHICAL NAMES

The names of continents, countries, states, provinces, as well as mountains and rivers, etc. are preceded by an article.

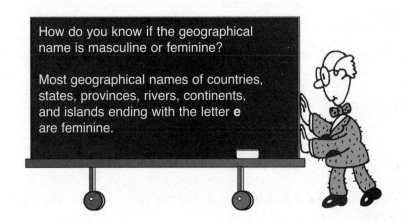

How do you know if the geographical name is masculine or feminine?

Most geographical names of countries, states, provinces, rivers, continents, and islands ending with the letter **e** are feminine.

NOTE: **In + feminine country, state**, etc. is translated by **En + feminine country.**

In + masculine country, state, etc. is translated by **Au + masculine country.**

Exception: **masculine countries, states**, etc. **beginning with a vowel (en Iran, en Alabama).**

Examples of Countries

La France, La Belgique, La Chine, La Norvège, La Suède

but

Le Canada, Le Japon, Le Maroc, Le Sénégal, Le Chili, Les Etats-Unis
Exception: **Le Mexique, Le Cambodge**

Rivers

La Seine, La Loire, La Tamise
Exception: **Le Danube, Le Rhône**

but

Le Saint-Laurent, Le Mississippi, Le Nil, Le Rhin

Provinces

La Bretagne, La Normandie

but

Le Berry

States

La Californie, la Floride, la Louisiane
Exception: Le Delaware, Le Tennessee

but

Le Colorado, Le Michigan, Le Texas → au Colorado, au Michigan, au Texas

NOTE: for masculine states, **dans le** can also be used (dans le Colorado, dans le Connecticut).

Islands
Some islands do not take an article before their name and follow the rule that applies to cities:

Hawaï, Tahiti, Cuba → à Hawaï, à Tahiti, à Cuba

but

à la Martinique, à la Guadeloupe

Continents
All the names of continents begin with a vowel and, in French, end with the letter **e**. Although the word *continent* is a masculine word, the names themselves are considered feminine. Sometimes these continents are grouped together to form five continents:

L'Europe, l'Asie, l'Afrique, l'Amérique et l'Océanie

↓

En Europe, en Asie, en Afrique, en Amérique et en Océanie

Sometimes, they are divided into seven:

L'Amérique du Nord, l'Amérique du Sud, l'Antarctique (ou Antarctide), l'Europe, l'Asie, l'Afrique et l'Océanie

	CITIES	MASCULINE COUNTRIES	FEMININE COUNTRIES	PLURAL COUNTRIES
to	à Paris	**au** Sénégal	**en** Italie	**aux** Etats-Unis
	à Dakar	**au** Danemark	**en** France	**aux** Pays-Bas*
	au Caire**	**au** Chili	**en** Angleterre	
	à la Nouvelle-Orléans***	**au** Japon	**en** Thaïlande	
from	de Lyon	**du** Canada	**de** Chine	**des** Etats-Unis
	de Chicago	**du** Portugal	**de** Belgique	**des** Pays-Bas
	du Caire**	**du** Maroc	d'Algérie	

NOTE
*Les Pays-Bas	The Netherlands
**au Caire	the city's name is Le Caire (in Arabic: Al Kahira), therefore à + le → au and de + le → du
***La Nouvelle-Orléans	The adjective nouvelle being in the feminine, à la must be used for *to* and de la must be used for *from*.

QUICK PRACTICE

IV. Vos amis sont tous partis à l'étranger pendant les dernières vacances, voici où ils sont allés:

Modèle: Paul/France/Paris—Paul est allé en France, à Paris.

1. Angélique/Sénégal/Dakar.

2. Patrick/Canada/Montréal.

3. Geneviève/Norvège/Oslo.

4. Jean-Pierre et Paulette/Angleterre/Londres.

5. David/Egypte/Le Caire.

V. Elise et son mari Benoît ont une auberge de jeunesse (*a youth hostel*) où il y a plusieurs étudiants étrangers. Ils vous disent d'où ils viennent:

Modèle: Nancy/Dallas/Etats-Unis—Nancy vient de Dallas aux Etats-Unis.

1. Salwa/Beyrouth/Liban

2. Holger/Stockholm/Suède

3. Mona/Le Caire/Egypte

4. Anna/Milan/Italie

5. Hiroshi/Tokyo/Japon

VI. LECTURE (*"L'éducation sentimentale" de Flaubert*)

Traduisez le passage suivant

Ils descendirent au pas le quartier Bréda; les rues, à cause du dimanche, étaient désertes, et des figures de bourgeois apparaissaient derrière des fenêtres. La voiture prit un train plus rapide; le bruit des roues[1] faisait se retourner les passants, le cuir de la capote[2] rabattue brillait, le domestique se cambrait[3] la taille, et les deux havanais[4] l'un près de l'autre semblaient deux manchons d'hermine[5] posés sur les coussins.

VII. Quel pays? Quelle ville?

1. *Le Havre*   Je vais_____ Havre.

2. *Paris*   Nous vivons _____ Paris.

3. *La Floride* Elle vient _____ Floride.

4. *Sydney*   Nous allons _____ Sydney.

5. *Le Maroc*   Nous partons _____ Maroc.

VIII. Rédaction

Imaginez que vous allez faire un grand voyage autour du monde. Quels pays et quelles villes allez-vous visiter?

[1]**roues**—wheels
[2]**capote**—hood or top
[3]**se cambrait la taille**—braced his chest
[4]**havanais**—small dogs
[5]**manchons d'hermine**—ermine (fur) muffs

```
V  I  X  N  P  Y  Q  Y  P  F  G  A  W  A  A
N  L  O  B  M  L  G  B  P  B  T  U  A  F  H
H  F  U  J  T  I  A  L  E  D  S  N  I  O  M
U  N  E  T  A  S  S  E  A  T  H  E  B  F  E
N  O  C  R  A  G  N  U  Z  J  Q  C  Y  T  N
D  E  B  E  A  U  X  L  I  V  R  E  S  R  B
V  G  A  P  U  D  R  Y  C  N  U  W  Y  O  R
Q  X  P  M  U  S  O  P  D  B  S  U  W  P  E
O  P  A  C  E  P  B  E  Q  L  Y  K  M  D  T
J  Z  A  I  Q  N  D  G  E  R  T  G  N  E  A
Q  F  Z  N  G  C  I  X  E  G  L  D  Z  C  G
E  P  M  A  L  Y  I  C  D  L  E  J  C  A  N
R  H  Q  N  W  P  M  I  U  V  X  F  G  F  E
A  U  M  E  X  I  Q  U  E  A  Y  L  J  E  O
P  A  R  L  E  R  A  N  G  L  A  I  S  U  P
```

AU CINEMA   EN BRETAGNE   UNE TASSE A THE

AU MEXIQUE   MOINS DE LAIT   UN GARCON

DE BEAUX LIVRES   PARLER ANGLAIS

DU CAFE   TROP DE CAFE

Culture Capsule 10

C'est le 24 juillet 1534 que Jacques Cartier, au cours de son premier voyage au Canada, plante une croix à Gaspé. Par ce geste, il prend officiellement possession du territoire au nom du roi de France, François 1er. Cette croix porte le blason royal: trois fleurs de lys sur un fond bleu.

L'enracinement français du territoire est accompli par Samuel de Champlain au début du siècle suivant. Il fait venir des familles, des soldats et des artisans ainsi que des jésuites. La colonie est instaurée. Cependant, la plupart des colons sont des hommes et, en 1663, la Nouvelle-France (les possession françaises du Canada) compte peu de femmes. Afin de peupler le territoire, le roi de France Louis XIV décide de recruter des jeunes femmes qui acceptent d'émigrer. Celles-ci sont souvent des veuves ou des orphelines, sans dot, mais avec un solide enseignement religieux. Appelées "Filles du Roy" car tous les frais de voyage et d'établissement en Nouvelle-France sont payés par le roi, ces jeunes femmes quittent la France pour ne plus jamais y revenir. Elles ont en général entre vingt et vingt-cinq ans. Il semble que grâce à elles, une vingtaine d'années après leur arrivée, la population de la Nouvelle-France ait triplé.

Jusqu'en 1673, plus de huit cent "Filles du Roy" arrivent au Canada. Elles viennent de Paris, de Normandie, de Bretagne, du Poitou, etc. Le jour de leur mariage, une somme appelée "la dot du roy" (*the king's dowry*) leur est (mais pas toujours) remise pour les aider dans leur nouvelle vie. Ces femmes sont les ancêtres de la plupart des Québécois d'aujourd'hui.

VOCABULAIRE

blason	*coat of arms*
enracinement	*establishment/taking root*
afin de	*in order to*
peupler	*populate*
veuves	*widows*
orphelines	*orphans*
les frais	*the expenses*
grâce à	*thanks to*
dot	*dowry*
la plupart	*most*

14

Nouns

Que savez-vous déjà?
What Do You Know Already?

(?)

True or false?

1. _____ **Enfants** is the plural of **enfant**.

2. _____ **Amies** is the plural of **ami**.

3. _____ **Bijoux** (*jewels*) is the plural of **bijou**.

4. _____ **Oeil** (*eye*) is the singular of **yeux**.

5. _____ **Médecine** is the feminine of **médecin** (*doctor*).

6. _____ The names of languages are always masculine.

7. _____ **Nez** (*nose*) is spelled the same way in the singular and in the plural.

8. _____ **Foule** is the feminine of **fou** (*crazy*).

9. _____ **Journaux** is the plural of **journal**.

10. _____ **Vie** (*life*) is always in the feminine singular.

The Gender of Nouns
Le genre des noms

- **Nouns with masculine ending**
  The following endings (with some examples) indicate a masculine noun.

age	le courage (*courage*)—le village (*village*)
cle	le siècle (*century*)—le spectacle (*performance*)
ème	le poème (*poem*)—le problème (*problem*)
ège	le cortège (*procession*)
eau	le poteau (*the pole*)
cre	le sucre (*the sugar*)
ier	le papier (*the paper*)

| isme | le communisme (*communism*) |
| asme | le sarcasme (*sarcasm*) |

Exceptions: **une image** (*an image, a reflection*)
une débâcle (*a collapse, a debacle*)

- **Special masculine nouns**

Letters of the alphabet
Un a, un b, un c, un d, un e, etc. . . .

Days of the week, months, and seasons
Le lundi, le mardi, le mercredi, le jeudi, le vendredi, le samedi,
le dimanche
Janvier, février, mars (le mois de janvier, etc.)
Le printemps, l'été, l'automne, l'hiver

Colors
Le bleu, le blanc, le rouge, le vert, le rose, le jaune, le mauve,
le noir, le gris

Languages
Le français, l'anglais, l'italien, le japonais, le chinois,
l'allemand, le russe

Metric weights, measures, and cardinal points
Le kilogramme, le gramme, le mètre, le centimètre

Directions
le nord, le sud, l'est, l'ouest

Countries and states not ending in e
Le Brésil, le Japon, le Canada (exception: le Mexique, le
Cambodge)

Metals
L'or, le cuivre, l'argent, le fer

Trees
Le chêne, le palmier, le sapin, le pommier

Cardinal numbers
Le dix, le onze, le douze, le vingt, le cent

Compound nouns
Le porte-feuille, le coffre-fort, le pourboire, le parapluie

Nouns derived from English
Le tee-shirt, le weekend

- **Feminine nouns**

  Most feminine nouns end in **e**, and some are formed by just adding an **e** to the masculine (as in: **un ami, une amie—un employé, une employée—un patient, une patiente**). The following noun endings have a feminine that is irregular:

en—enne	parisien—parisienne	*(parisian)*
eur—euse	danseur—danseuse	*(dancer)*
eur—rice	directeur—directrice	*(director)*
an—anne	paysan—paysanne	*(peasant)*
ou—olle	fou—folle	*(madman, madwoman)*
er—ère	fermier—fermière	*(farmer)*
on—onne	lion—lionne	*(lion—lioness)*

- **Special feminine nouns**

  People and animals

un homme—une femme	*(a man, a woman)*
un oncle—une tante	*(an uncle, an aunt)*
un mouton—une brebis	*(a sheep, a ewe)*
un taureau—une vache	*(a bull, a cow)*
un coq—une poule	*(a rooster, a chicken)*
un cheval—une jument	*(a horse, a mare)*

  Virtues

La bonté—la charité	*(kindness—charity)*

  Exceptions: **le courage**

  Countries ending with a mute e

  La France, la Russie, la Belgique, la Suisse, l'Amérique

  Exceptions: **le Mexique, le Cambodge**

  Automobiles

  La Citroën, la Renault, la Toyota, la Ford, la Cadillac

  Rivers ending in e

  La Seine, la Loire

  Exceptions: **le Rhône, le Danube**

  Nouns ending in ée **and** é

  La dictée, la journée, la société *(dictation, day, society)*

  Exceptions: **le lycée, le musée, le trophée** *(high school, museum, society)*

  Nouns ending in ie

  La vie, la sortie

  Exceptions: **le génie, l'incendie** *(genius, building fire)*

Nouns ending in ion
La passion, la nation, la révolution

Exceptions: **un avion, un camion** (*airplane, truck*)

Nouns ending in ison
La maison, la prison (*house, prison*)

Nouns ending in eur
La couleur, la douleur (*color, sorrow or pain*)

Exceptions: **le bonheur, le malheur** (*happiness, misfortune*)

- **Some nouns have the same form in the masculine and the feminine**

Un élève	Une élève	*A pupil*
Un artiste	Une artiste	*An artist*
Un touriste	Une touriste	*A tourist*
Un secrétaire	Une secrétaire	*A secretary*
Un malade	Une malade	*A sick person*

- **Nouns that are always feminine (referring to both sexes)**

Une victime	*A victim*
Une personne	*A person*

- **Nouns that are always masculine (referring to both sexes)**

Un auteur*	*An author*
Un écrivain**	*A writer*
Un médecin	*A doctor (physician)*
Un peintre	*A painter*
Un témoin	*A witness*
Un professeur***	*A teacher*

- **Nouns that are both masculine and feminine: these nouns change meaning as they change gender**

le crêpe (*the fabric: crepe*)	la crêpe (*pancake*)
le critique (*the critic*)	la critique (*the critique*)
le livre (*the book*)	la livre (*the pound*)
le manche (*the handle*)	la manche (*the sleeve*)
	la Manche (*the English Channel*)
le page (*the page boy*)	la page (*the page*)
le poêle (*the heater*)	la poêle (*the frying pan*)
le physique (*the physique*)	la physique (*physics*)

*In Québec, a woman author is referred to as **une auteure**.
In Québec, a woman writer is also referred to as **une écrivaine.
***In familiar language, a female teacher is often referred to as **la prof**.

le poste *(the job)*	**la poste** *(the post office)*
le mort *(the dead man)*	**la mort** *(death)*
le somme *(the nap, sleep)*	**la somme** *(the sum)*
le tour *(the tour, the trick)*	**la tour** *(the tower)*
le voile *(the veil)*	**la voile** *(the sail)*

> Several nouns follow no gender rule
>
> **la mer** *(the sea)*
> **le beurre** *(butter)*
> **le sacrifice** *(sacrifice)*
> **le vocabulaire** *(vocabulary)*
>
> Because of this, and because of the many exceptions, the best way to learn a new noun is to study it with its article.

QUICK PRACTICE

I. Mettez l'article qui convient (le, la ou l'):

1. Jean-Pierre étudie _____ russe.

2. Passez-moi _____ sucre s'il vous plait.

3. _____ bonté de Claire est célèbre.

4. _____ problème, c'est qu'ils ont oublié leur passeport.

5. _____ nation est en danger.

6. J'aime beaucoup _____ musée du Louvre.

7. Est-il allé chez _____ dentiste?

8. Ma couleur préférée est _____ bleu.

9. _____ avion est en retard.

10. _____ amie de Pierre s'appelle Lucie.

II. Choisissez l'article correct:

1. Il adore _____ natation (le/la).

2. J'ai acheté _____ poêle à frire (un/une).

3. Est-ce que as lu _____ critique de cette pièce (le/la)?

4. La mariée portait _____ voile (un/une).

5. Nous avons besoin d' _____ kilogramme de pommes (un/une).

6. J'ai beaucoup aimé _____ poème de Baudelaire (le/la).

7. Il a fait preuve d' _____ courage exemplaire (un/une).

8. _____ spectacle était superbe (le/la).

9. As-tu reçu _____ message de Catherine (le/la)?

10. _____ victime s'appelait Jean Duclos (le/la).

The Plural of Nouns
Le pluriel des noms

In French, most nouns form their plural by adding an **s**.

une femme	→	des femmes
un livre	→	des livres
la porte	→	les portes
le crayon	→	les crayons
la maison	→	les maisons
l'avion	→	les avions

TIP
Family names
In English, when referring to a family, an s is added at the end of the last name:

The Smiths, the Carpenters

In French, since the article is in the plural, no s is added to the last name:

Les Dupont, **les** Charpentier

The following are always used in the singular:

La vie (*life*), la foi (*faith*), la paix (*peace*), la mort (*death*)

Numbers and letters:

There are three two's in her address. = Il y a trois deux dans son adresse.
There are two l's in his name. = Il y a deux l dans son nom.

SPECIAL CASES

- **Nouns ending in s, x, or z do not change in the plural**

le mois	→	les mois	*(month/months)*
le nez	→	les nez	*(nose/noses)*
la voix	→	les voix	*(voice/voices)*

- **Most nouns that end in al in the singular have a plural form of aux**

cheval	→	chevaux	*(horse/horses)*
journal	→	journaux	*(newspaper/newspapers)*

Exceptions: les carnavals, les festivals, les recitals, les bals

- **Most nouns that end in ail in the singular have a plural form of ails except for**

travail	→	travaux	*(work/works)*
corail	→	coraux	*(coral/corals)*

- **Most nouns that end in au, eau, and eu in the singular add an x to form the plural**

tuyau	→	tuyaux	*(pipe/pipes* as in metal pipes)
bureau	→	bureaux	*(desk or office/desks or offices)*
jeu	→	jeux	*(game/games)*

Exceptions: **le pneu → les pneus** *(tire/tires)*

NOTE: The word **cheveu** is used in the plural in French unless it refers to one hair only.

She has blond hair = Elle a **les cheveux** blonds.*

- **Most nouns ending in ou in the singular add an s to form the plural**

le clou	→	les clous	*(nail/nails* as in metal nails)

Exceptions:		
	bijoux	*(jewels)*
	cailloux	*(pebbles)*
	choux	*(cabbages)*
	genoux	*(knees)*
	hiboux	*(owls)*
	joujoux	*(toys)*
	poux	*(lice)*

****Cheveux** is used only for hair that is on the head. For bodily hair, the word is **poils**.

- **Some nouns have irregular plurals**

mademoiselle	→	mesdemoiselles
madame	→	mesdames
monsieur	→	messieurs
un jeune homme	→	des jeunes gens
le ciel	→	les cieux
l'oeil	→	les yeux

Mademoiselle comes from **"ma"** demoiselle, or "*my*" (single) *lady*; therefore the plural is **"mes"** demoiselles, or "*my*" *ladies*. It is the same for **Madame**, which comes from **"ma"** dame, or "*my*" *lady*. **Monsieur** comes from **"mon"** sieur, or *my sire* (*lord*). However the meanings have changed to: Miss, Mrs., and Mr.

- **Nouns that are always used in the plural**

les ciseaux	(*scissors*)	les maths	(*math*)
les frais	(*expenses*)	les vacances	(*vacation*)

- **Compound nouns differ**
Nouns that are formed by verbs and nouns do not add **s** to the plural.

    le lave-vaisselle   →   les lave-vaisselle (*dishwashers*)

Nouns that are formed by nouns and adjectives take an **s** after the noun and one after the adjective.

    le grand-père   →   les grands-pères (*grandfathers*)

Nouns that are formed by a preposition and a noun do not take an **s** in the plural.

    un après-midi   →   des après-midi   (*afternoons*)

QUICK PRACTICE

III. Conversation à deux: Christophe et Rémi sont deux amis. Christophe dit à Rémi ce qu'il fait, et Rémi a fait plus de choses que son copain.

Modèle: (acheter/stylo) hier.   Christophe: J'ai acheté un stylo hier.
                             Rémi: Et moi, j'ai acheté trois stylos hier.

1. (voir/cheval) derrière la maison.

2. (rencontrer/jeune homme) qui parlait russe.

3. (avoir/pneu crevé) hier.

4. (jeter/caillou) dans la mer.

5. (lire/journal) hier.

6. (aller/bal) la semaine dernière.

7. (voir/hibou) sur une branche.

8. (offrir/cadeau) à Josette pour son anniversaire.

9. (visiter/château) pendant les vacances.

10. (peindre/tableau) en une semaine.

It Is
C'est ou Il est

- **C'est** and its plural **Ce sont** answer the questions
  Qu'est-ce que c'est? (*What is it?*) and **Qui est-ce?** (*Who is it?*)

Qu'est-ce que c'est?	**C'est un pneu.**
Qu'est-ce que c'est?	**Ce sont des pneus.**
Qui est-ce?	**C'est mon oncle.**

  C'est is used with a modifier (**un, une, des, mon, ma, mes,** etc.).

- **Il est** and **Elle est** answer the questions
  Où est-il (elle)? *(Where is he [she]?)* and **Comment est-il (elle)?**
  (How is he [she]?)

Où est-elle?	**Elle est en Europe.**
Comment est-elle?	**Elle est petite et brune.**

  Il est and **Elle est** are used without a modifier.

  Compare: **Il est** boxeur—**C'est un** boxeur

- **C'est** is used in the middle of a sentence or in a new sentence, referring to what precedes it

  Elle n'aime pas voyager? **C'est** vrai.
  She doesn't like to travel? It's true.

  Il est is used at the beginning of a sentence and refers to what comes after

  Il est vrai qu'elle n'aime pas voyager.
  It is true that she doesn't like to travel.

- **C'est** is used after an infinitive

  Elle n'aime pas voyager, c'est évident.
  She doesn't like to travel, it is obvious.

- **C'est** is used before a stress pronoun

Qui est-ce?	**C'est moi.**
Who is it?	*It is I.*

With names of profession, nationality, or religion

Il est chanteur
C'est **un** chanteur
C'est **un** chanteur **célèbre**

Elle est sénégalaise
C'est **une** sénégalaise
C'est **une jolie** sénégalaise

Ils sont bouddhistes
Ce sont **des** bouddhistes
Ce sont **des** bouddhistes **fervents**

QUICK PRACTICE
IV. Choisissez entre "c'est" et "il est" ou "elle est":

1. Mon cousin Georges? _____ un pilote.

2. Tu as vu ce film? _____ trop violent pour moi!

3. Sa mère? _____ professeur.

4. Qui a écrit cet essai? _____ Montaigne.

5. Elle n'a pas aimé ce livre? _____ incroyable!

6. _____ important que tu révises ce chapitre avant l'examen.

7. _____ la fille de Monsieur Leduc.

8. _____ son fiancé qui est en France actuellement.

9. Marguerite? _____ belge.

10. Marie-Claude est paresseuse? _____ vrai!

MOTS CROISÉS
Les noms

Across

3. An image (2 words)

6. An author (2 words)

7. The courage (2 words)

9. A victim (2 words)

10. The communism (2 words)

Down

1. The crepe (pancake—2 words)

2. The dancer (2 words)

4. The tower (2 words)

5. The apple tree (2 words)

7. _____ weekend

8. A witness (2 words)

15

Adjectives and Adverbs

Que savez-vous déjà?
What Do You Know Already?

(?)

Match the items in the two columns.

1. Il y a deux _____ filles devant le cinéma.   a. gentil

2. Mon professeur est _____ .   b. nouvel

3. J'ai les cheveux _____ .   c. ancien

4. Ils ont un _____ appartement.   d. bien

5. Quelle histoire _____ !   e. vite

6. Son _____ professeur ne travaille plus depuis 5 ans. f. vieille

7. Il parle _____ Français.   g. belles

8. Je cours _____ pour arriver avant la classe.   h. longs

9. _____ les élèves sont ici aujourd'hui.   i. intéressante

10. Cette femme est _____ ; elle a 90 ans.   j. tous

The Gender of Adjectives
Le genre des adjectifs

In English, adjectives are invariable: they are the same for masculine, feminine, and plural. In French, the **adjectif qualificatif** changes to reflect the feminine and the plural in several ways.

- **When the masculine adjective ends with the letter e, there is no change in the feminine**

facile	→	facile (fem.)
jeune	→	jeune (fem.)

Le poème est facile.   *The poem is easy.*
La leçon est facile.   *The lesson is easy.*

- **When the masculine ends with another vowel, a mute e is added to reflect the feminine**

    poli   →   polie

    Le garcon est poli.   *The boy is polite.*
    La petite fille est polie. *The little girl is polite.*

- **When the masculine ends with l, n, s, or t, the last consonant is often doubled and is followed by a mute e to reflect the feminine**

    bas   →   basse
    gentil   →   gentille
    italien   →   italienne
    gros   →   grosse
    coquet   →   coquette

    Un prix assez bas = *A rather low price*
    Elle parle à voix basse. = *She speaks in a low voice.*
    Pierre est gentil. = *Pierre is nice (kind).*
    Florence est gentille. = *Florence is nice (kind).*
    Pietro est italien. = *Pietro is Italian.*
    Anna est italienne. = *Anna is Italian.*
    Il est gros. = *He is fat.*
    Elle est grosse. = *She is fat.*
    Un jardin coquet = *A trim garden*
    Une femme coquette = *A stylish woman—A coquettish woman*

    Exceptions: gris (gray) →   grise
                    secret →   secrète
                    complet →   complète
                    petit →   petite

- **When an adjective ends in er in the masculine, the feminine is formed by changing er to ère**

    fier *(proud)*   →   fière
    étranger *(foreign)* →   étrangère

    Le jeune homme est fier. = *The young man is proud.*
    La jeune fille est fière. = *The young woman is proud.*
    Un élève étranger = *A foreign (male) student*
    Une élève étrangère = *A foreign (female) student*

- **When an adjective ends in eur or teur in the masculine, the feminine is formed by changing to euse**

      menteur *(liar)*   ➔   menteuse

      Un homme menteur = *a lying man*
      Une femme menteuse = *a lying woman*

Exceptions: supérieur ➔ supérieure *(superior)*
                  meilleur   ➔ meilleure   *(better)*
                  destructeur ➔ destructrice *(destructive)*

Un officier supérieur	➔	*A superior officer*
La mère supérieure	➔	*The mother superior*
Le livre est meilleur	➔	*The book is better*
La soupe est meilleure	➔	*The soup is better*
Un ouragan destructeur	➔	*A destructive hurricane*
Une tornade destructrice	➔	*A destructive tornado*

- **When an adjective ends in f in the masculine, the feminine is formed by changing f to ve**

    neuf *(brand-new)* ➔ neuve
    naïf *(naïve)*   ➔ naïve

Un complet neuf	➔	*A brand-new suit*
Une voiture neuve	➔	*A brand-new car*
Un enfant naïf	➔	*A naïve child*
Une personne naïve	➔	*A naïve person*

- **When an adjective ends in x in the masculine, the feminine is formed by changing x to se**

    heureux *(happy)*   ➔ heureuse
    merveilleux *(wonderful)* ➔ merveilleuse

un enfant heureux	➔	*a happy child*
une famille heureuse	➔	*a happy family*
un livre merveilleux	➔	*a wonderful book*
une histoire merveilleuse	➔	*a wonderful story*

Adjectives that don't fall into any of the previous categories include the following

blanc—blanche *(white)*
châtain—châtain *(chestnut brown)*
faux—fausse *(false, wrong)*
favori—favorite *(favorite)*
frais—fraîche *(fresh)*
franc—franche *(frank)*
grec—grecque *(Greek)*
long—longue *(long)*
malin—maligne *(clever/shrewd)*
public—publique *(public)*
roux—rousse *(redhead)*
sec—sèche *(dry)*

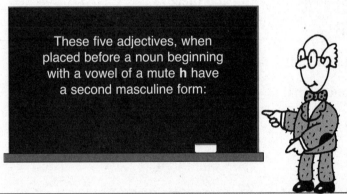

These five adjectives, when placed before a noun beginning with a vowel of a mute **h** have a second masculine form:

MASCULINE	MASCULINE *before a vowel or mute h*	FEMININE
beau *(handsome)*	bel	belle *(beautiful)*
fou *(crazy, mad)*	fol	folle
mou *(soft, weak, spineless)*	mol	molle
nouveau *(new)*	nouvel	nouvelle
vieux *(old)*	vieil	vieille

Son mari est beau. = C'est un bel homme.
Her husband is handsome. = He is a handsome man.

I. Mettez au féminin:

1. un téléphone public   /   une place _____ .

2. un film ennuyeux   /   une pièce _____ .

3. un homme méchant /   une femme _____ .

4. un enfant gentil   /   une petite fille _____ .

5. un livre cher   /   une maison _____ .

6. un film bête   /   une histoire _____ .

7. mon prof favori   /   ma pièce _____ .

8. il est doux   /   elle est _____ .

9. un chemisier noir   /   une jupe _____ .

10. mon examen final /   la décision _____ .

The Plural of Adjectives
Le pluriel des adjectifs

- **Most adjectives form the plural by adding an s to the masculine singular and the feminine singular**

MASCULINE SINGULAR	PLURAL	FEMININE SINGULAR	PLURAL
cruel	cruels	cruelle	cruelles
innocent	innocents	innocente	innocents
favori	favoris	favorite	favorites
long	longs	longue	longue

Un enfant innocent   →   Des enfants innocents
An innocent child   *Innocent children*

- **Masculine adjectives ending in x and s do not change in the plural**

Un homme heureux	→	Des hommes heureux
A happy man		*Happy men*

Un chapeau gris	→	Des chapeaux gris
A gray hat		*Gray hats*

- **Masculine adjectives ending in al and eau change into aux and eaux**

Un livre moral	→	Des livres moraux
A moral book		*Moral books*

Le nouveau chapitre	→	Les nouveaux chapitres
The new chapter		*New chapters*

Exceptions:	banal	→	banals
	fatal	→	fatals
	final	→	finals
	naval	→	navals

Placement of Adjectives in the Sentence
Où placer l'adjectif dans la phrase

Whereas in English adjectives precede the noun they modify, in French they usually follow the noun.

Un livre intéressant	Une amie loyale
An interesting book	*A loyal friend*

- **Some short adjectives usually precede the noun**

autre	*other*	beau	*beautiful, handsome*
bon	*good*	dernier	*last*
jeune	*young*	joli	*pretty*
large	*wide*	long	*long*
mauvais	*bad*	nouveau	*new*
petit	*small*	premier	*first*
vieux	*old*	vaste	*vast*

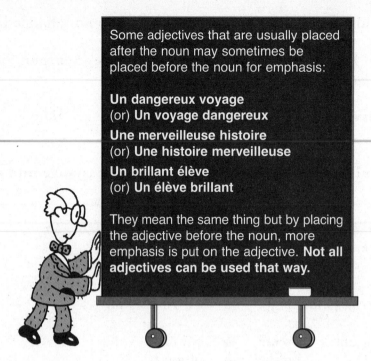

Some adjectives that are usually placed after the noun may sometimes be placed before the noun for emphasis:

Un dangereux voyage
(or) **Un voyage dangereux**

Une merveilleuse histoire
(or) **Une histoire merveilleuse**

Un brillant élève
(or) **Un élève brillant**

They mean the same thing but by placing the adjective before the noun, more emphasis is put on the adjective. **Not all adjectives can be used that way.**

- **Some adjectives can precede or follow the noun, but they change meaning when they change position**

Before	After
un ancien patron	un château ancien
a former boss	*an old castle*
une brave femme	une femme brave
a good woman	*a courageous woman*
un certain homme	un résultat certain
a certain man	*a sure result*
une chère amie	une robe chère
a dear friend	*an expensive dress*
un grand acteur	un homme grand
a great actor	*a tall man*
une grande fille	une fille grande
(un grand garçon)	(un garçon grand)
a big girl (a big boy) age-wise	*a tall girl, a tall boy*
une pauvre femme	une femme pauvre
a poor woman (to be pitied)	*a poor woman (who doesn't have money)*
un méchant garçon	un garçon méchant
a naughty boy	*a mean (naughty) boy*
le même jour	le jour même
the same day	*the very day*
une nouvelle voiture	une voiture nouvelle
a new car (new to you)	*a brand-new car*
le prochain voyage	le mois prochain
the next trip	*next month*

ma propre robe	**ma robe propre**
my own dress	*my clean dress*
le seul professeur	**un homme seul**
the only teacher	*a lonely man*
la semaine dernière	**la dernière semaine**
last week	*the last week (i.e., of the month, of the year)*

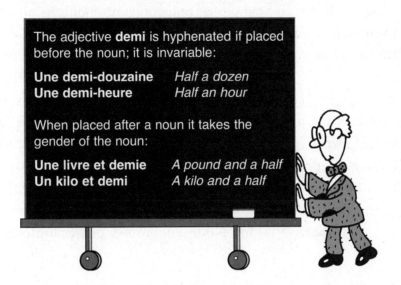

The adjective **demi** is hyphenated if placed before the noun; it is invariable:

Une demi-douzaine   *Half a dozen*
Une demi-heure   *Half an hour*

When placed after a noun it takes the gender of the noun:

Une livre et demie   *A pound and a half*
Un kilo et demi   *A kilo and a half*

QUELQU'UN, QUELQUE CHOSE, PERSONNE, RIEN

When followed by an adjective, **quelqu'un** (*someone*), **quelque chose** (*something*), **personne** (*nobody/ no one*), **rien** (*nothing*) require the preposition **de** before the adjective, which in this case is always masculine.

J'ai lu quelque chose de très étrange dans ce magazine hier.
I read something strange in this magazine yesterday.

Je n'ai rien d'important à faire ce week-end.
I have nothing important to do this weekend.

QUICK PRACTICE

II. Madame Juneau vient d'acheter une maison au bord de la mer. Elle la décrit à ses cousins. Changez les adjectifs masculins, s'il le faut:

Alors, voici comment ça s'est passé: nous nous promenions au bord de la mer.
Il faisait un temps (*magnifique*) _____ et nous n'avions aucune envie
de quitter ce (*beau*) _____ endroit pour retourner dans notre climat
(*pluvieux*) _____ . Soudain, Robert s'est écrié: "Regarde, Nadine, regarde
cette (*petit*) _____ maison en face de la plage, tu vois, elle est
à vendre!" Enfin, d'une chose à l'autre, nous sommes allés voir la propriétaire,
une femme (*gentil*) _____ avec qui nous avons tout de suite sympathisé
et quelques jours plus tard, la (*joli*) _____ maison nous appartenait.
Elle a le toit (*rouge*) _____ , des fenêtres assez (*grand*) _____
et, ce qui est (*merveilleux*) _____ , des palmiers (*adorable*)
_____ dans le jardin. Nous comptons y passer toutes nos vacances!

III. Placez correctement l'adjectif selon le contexte:

Modèle: *(ancien)* —**Le professeur** de Gilles a quitté le pays.
     L'ancien professeur de Gilles a quitté le pays.

1. (*même*)   —**Le jour** de son arrivée, il s'est mis à neiger.

2. (*propre*)   —Prends **ta voiture**, pas celle de ton père.

3. (*brave*)   —C'est **un soldat**, il n'a pas peur de se battre.

4. (*pauvre*)   —C'est **un garçon**, il ne peut pas s'acheter une voiture.

5. (*seule*)   —**La femme** que j'aime, c'est toi ma chérie.

IV. Traduisez cet exercice.

Adverbs
Les adverbes

Many adverbs in English are formed by adding *ly* to the adjective:

slow → slowly   complete → completely   attentive → attentively

Many adverbs in French are formed by adding **ment** to the feminine of an adjective that ends in a consonant. For a masculine adjective ending with **e**, the feminine is the same.

lent—lente	→	**lentement**
complet—complète	→	**complètement**
attentif—attentive	→	**attentivement**
honnête—honnête	→	**honnêtement**

While an adjective modifies a noun, an adverb modifies a verb, another adverb, or an adjective:

verb:	**Il conduit lentement.**	*He drives slowly.*
adverb:	**Il conduit très lentement.**	*He drives very slowly.*
adjective:	**Il est complètement fou.**	*He is completely crazy.*

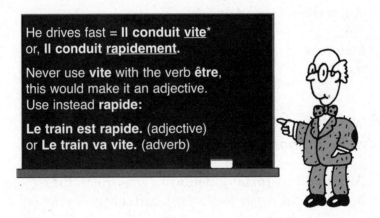

He drives fast = **Il conduit vite***
or, **Il conduit rapidement**.

Never use **vite** with the verb **être**, this would make it an adjective.
Use instead **rapide**:

Le train est rapide. (adjective)
or **Le train va vite.** (adverb)

SPECIAL CASES

- **For adjectives ending in ant or ent, the adverb endings are amment *and* emment**

const**ant**	→	const**amment**	*constantly*
évid**ent**	→	évid**emment**	*evidently*

> **TIP**
> Both **emment** and **amment** endings are pronounced **amment**.

*Although **vitement** was used in prior centuries, it is no longer accepted.

- For masculine adjectives ending in **i**, **é**, or **u**, the **ment** ending is added directly

Masculine	Adverb
vrai	vraiment
spontané	spontanément
absolu	absolument

- Some expressions use adjectives instead of adverbs

sentir bon	*to smell good*
coûter cher	*to cost a lot (to be expensive)*
parler haut	*to speak loudly*
voir clair	*to see clearly*

- Some adverbs have irregular endings

Masculine	Feminine	Adverb	
immense	immense	immensément	*immensely*
précis	précise	précisément	*precisely*

- Irregular adverbs

Adjective	Adverb	
bon	bien	*well*
mauvais	mal	*badly*
meilleur	mieux	*better*

OTHER ADVERBS

- *Adverbs of Time—*Adverbes de Temps

  Aujourd'hui (*today*), **demain** (*tomorrow*), **hier** (*yesterday*), **avant-hier** (*the day before yesterday*), **autrefois** (*in the past*), **maintenant** (*now*), **toujours** (*always*), **jamais** (*never*), **d'abord** (*first/at first*), **tard** (*late*), **tôt** (*early*), **désormais**, **dorénavant** (*from now on*), **souvent** (*often*), **bientôt** (*soon*), etc.

- *Adverbs of Place—*Adverbes de Lieu

  Ici (*here*), **là** (*there*), **dehors** (*outside*), **dedans** (*inside*), **près** (*near*), **loin** (*far*), **derrière** (*behind*), **partout** (*everywhere*), etc.

- *Adverbs of Quantity—*Adverbes de Quantité

  Assez (*enough*), **aussi** (*also*), **autant** (*as much*), **beaucoup** (*a lot, much*), **combien** (*how much*), **davantage** (*more*), **environ** (*approximately*), **moins** (*less*), **plus** (*more*), **presque** (*almost*), **tellement** (*so much*), **trop** (*too much*), etc.

- *Adverbs Used with Adjectives or Adverbs*

Très (*very*), fort (*very*), trop (*too*), bien (*well*), etc.

TIP
Adverbs of manner ending in ment can be replaced by avec plus the noun or d'une façon, d'un ton, d'un air plus the adjective:

Elle parle tristement. → Elle parle avec tristesse. → Elle parle d'un ton triste.
She speaks sadly. → She speaks with sadness. → She speaks with a sad tone of voice.

NOTE: This also applies when there is no adverb.

Elle parle d'un ton moqueur. → *She speaks with a mocking (sarcastic) tone of voice.*

Placement of Adverbs
Où placer l'adverbes

PRESENT TENSE

Adverbs that modify a verb are placed immediately after the verb in the present tense.

Je travaille constamment. *I work constantly.*

Adverbs that modify an adverb are placed immediately before the adverb they modify.

Tu travailles trop lentement. *You work too slowly.*

Adverbs that modify an adjective are placed immediately before the adjective they modify.

C'est un livre très amusant. *It's a very funny book.*

PASSÉ COMPOSÉ AND OTHER COMPOUND TENSES

Most adverbs are placed between the auxiliary verb (avoir or être) and the past participle.

Elle a déjà fini ses devoirs. *She already finished her homework.*
Nous avons beaucoup aimé ce film. *We liked this movie a lot.*

Most longer adverbs that end in ment follow the past participle.

Il a répondu intelligemment. *He answered intelligently.*

A few long adverbs can sometimes be placed before the past participle for emphasis.

Elle a gentiment accepté mon invitation. *She kindly accepted my invitation.*

In the near future, the adverb is usually placed before the infinitive.

Ils vont énormément apprécier cela. *They will appreciate this enormously.*

In a negative sentence, the adverb follows the negative.

Je n'ai pas bien compris.
Je ne cours pas vite.

QUICK PRACTICE

V. Répondez aux questions suivantes en utilisant un adverbe.

Modèle: Geneviève est-elle gentille quand elle parle avec Louis?
   —Oui, elle parle gentiment.

1. Est-ce que Bernard est méchant quand il parle?

2. Gabrielle a-t-elle répondu avec impatience?

3. Est-ce que le professeur est patient quand il explique la leçon?

4. Monsieur Dubois est-il nerveux quand il parle?

5. Cet homme était-il honnête quand il a répondu à la question?

VI. Refaites les phrases suivantes en plaçant correctement les mots ci-dessous.

sans succès	*profondément*	*prudemment*
mal	*davantage*	*absolument*
bien	*autrefois*	*d'un ton brusque*
constamment		

1. Je suis fatiguée parce que hier soir j'ai dormi.

2. Ils voyageaient beaucoup, mais plus maintenant.

3. Mes deux frères se disputent.

4. Ils s'aiment.

5. Il faut voir ce film; il est merveilleux.

6. Elle ne parle pas anglais.

7. Tu m'aimes? Et bien, moi je t'aime.

8. Elle conduit toujours.

9. Je ne sais pas pourquoi il parle toujours.

10. Il a essayé de comprendre.

Tout as Adjective, Adverb, or Pronoun
Tout: adjectif, adverbe ou pronom

Tout can be an adjective, an adverb, or a pronoun.

ADJECTIVE *(all, every, the whole)*

As an adjective, it varies in gender and number with the noun it modifies.

Masculine Singular	Masculine Plural	Feminine Singular	Feminine Plural
tout	tous	toute	toutes

Elle a mangé tout le bifteck.	*She ate the whole steak.*
Il a plu toute la semaine.	*It rained all week.*
Je travaille tous les jours.	*I work every day.*
Je les vois toutes les semaines.	*I see them every week.*
Ils sont restés toute la soirée.	*They stayed the whole evening.*

TIP
Tout *or* **Toute** **is often used before the noun in the singular without an article. It means** *any,* *all,* **or** *every.*

Tout élève doit être attentif.	*Every student must be attentive.*
Toute réponse est importante.	*Every answer is important.*

PRONOUN *(everything, all, all of them)*

Tous sont ici aujourd'hui.	*All of them are here today.*
Elles sont toutes en retard.	*They are all late.*

Expressions with **tout ce qui, tout ce que, tout ce dont:**

Tout ce qui est difficile	*Everything that is difficult*
Tout ce que j'aime	*Everything that I love (like)*
Tout ce dont elle a peur	*Everything that she fears*

ADVERB *(all, very)*

In the masculine, the adverb **tout** is invariable.

Il est tout content. Ils sont tout contents.

In the feminine, **tout** is invariable if the feminine adjective that follows begins with a vowel or a mute **h.**

Elle est tout heureuse.	*She is very happy.*
Elles sont tout heureuses.	*They are very happy.*

If the feminine adjective that follows begins with a consonant, then **tout** becomes **toute** or **toutes.**

Elle est toute belle.	*She is very pretty.*
Elles sont toutes belles.	*They are very pretty.*

Pronunciation of Tous

Pronunciation of **tous** varies according to the meaning.

Ils ont tous les problèmes que leurs parents avaient.
↓
Do not *pronounce the* **s**.

Translation: *They **have all the problems** that their parents had.*

Ils ont tous les problèmes que leurs parents avaient.
↓
Pronounce *the* **s**.

Translation: *They **all have the problems** that their parents had.*

Quick Practice
VII. Refaites les phrases suivantes en ajoutant "tout" à la forme correcte.

1. As-tu lu _____ l'histoire?

2. _____ les enfants se sont bien amusés.

3. _____ médaille a son revers.

4. Ils ont _____ étudié le chapitre précédent.

5. Mes soeurs sont _____ élégantes pour cette soirée.

6. Nous sommes _____ allées au cinéma hier.

7. _____ enfant aime jouer.

8. J'ai étudié _____ ce qui est important.

9. Le petit chien est _____ beau.

10. _____ les réponses étaient fausses.

MOTS CROISÉS
Adjectifs et adverbes

Across

6. J'ai un _____ appartement (new)

7. Un examen final, des examens _____

9. C'est un _____ homme (handsome)

10. Il est heureux, elle est _____

11. Il est menteur, elle est _____

12. Le chemisier est blanc, la jupe est _____

13. Everywhere

Down

1. Un jardin public, une ecole _____

2. Adverbe de spontane

3. Outside

4. Il est vieux, elle est _____

5. Elle est naïve, il est _____

8. Adverbe de meilleur

9. Adverbe de bon

Culture Capsule 11

La Bande Dessinée dont l'acronyme est BD ou bédé est une forme artistique surnommée le 9ème art, très appréciée par le public français. Et il ne s'agit pas uniquement d'une création moderne! Certains considèrent même les peintures et gravures de la grotte de Lascaux qui datent d'il y a environ 15.000 ans avant Jesus-Christ comme étant des formes de bandes dessinées de l'homme des cavernes!

La fameuse Tapisserie de la Reine Mathilde, ou Tapisserie de Bayeux, qui représente la conquête de l'Angleterre par Guillaume le Conquérant en 1066, est aussi une sorte de BD moyenâgeuse! Dès le début du vingtième siècle, en 1905, les aventures de Bécassine (Bécassine au pensionnat, l'enfance de Bécassine, Bécassine maîtresse d'école, etc.) sont savourées par tous les francophones. Plus tard, ce sont les aventures de Tintin, crées en Belgique en 1929 par Hergé (de son vrai nom Georges Rémi, d'où R G), dont tous les amateurs de bandes dessinées se délectent. Dans ces albums aussi, nous trouvons des personages aux noms amusants tels que le capitaine Haddock et le professeur Halambique. Parmi les plus célèbres bédés, n'oublions surtout pas les aventures d'Astérix, le petit guerrier gaulois et sa bande d'amis aux noms inoubliables: Obélix, le barde Assurancetourix, etc. par Goscinny et Uderzo.

De nouvelles bandes dessinées naissent tous les jours. Depuis 1972, un festival international de la bande dessinée a lieu en janvier à Angoulême au sud-ouest de Paris. Des trophées sont décernés aux auteurs de BD français ou étrangers. Il existe des prix pour les différentes catégories: prix du meilleur album, prix du scénario, prix du premier album, etc. Vive la BD!

VOCABULAIRE

surnommée	*nicknamed*
il ne s'agit pas	*it isn't about*
gravures	*engravings*
l'homme des caverns	*the caveman*
tapisserie	*tapestry*
moyenâgeuse	*from the Middle Ages*
parmi	*among*
guerrier gaulois	*warrior from Gaul*
décernés	*awarded*

16

Personal Pronouns

Personal pronouns replace the nouns of people or things. These pronouns are divided into different categories: (a) subject pronouns, (b) direct object pronouns, (c) indirect object pronouns, (d) disjunctive pronouns, and (e) adverb.

SUBJECT	DIRECT OBJECT	INDIRECT OBJECT	DISJUNCTIVE	ADVERB OR PRONOUN
je	me, m'	me, m'	moi	y
tu	te, t'	te, t'	toi	en
il	le, l'	lui	lui	
elle	la, l'	lui	elle	
on	se, s'*	se, s'	soi**	
nous	nous	nous	nous	
vous	vous	vous	vous	
ils	les	leur	eux	
elles	les	leur	elles	

Direct Object Pronouns
Le pronom objet direct

A noun that is a direct object answers the question *what* or *whom?*

I buy the dress.	→	*I buy what? The dress.*
J'achète la robe.	→	**J'achète quoi? La robe.**

I see Michael.	→	*I see whom? Michael.*
Je vois Michel.	→	**Je vois qui? Michel.**

The direct object pronoun follows the same rule.

I buy it.	→	*I buy what? It. (the dress)*
Je l'achète.	→	**J'achète quoi? L'. (la robe)**

I see him.	→	*I see whom? (Michael)*
Je le vois.	→	**Je vois qui? (Michel)**

The direct object pronoun is placed **before** the verb. When, however, two verbs follow each other, the second one is always in the infinitive. In this case, the object pronoun is placed between the conjugated verb and the infinitive.

Nous regardons **les photos**.	*We look at **the pictures**.*
Nous **les** regardons.	*We look at **them**.*
Nous allons **les** regarder.	*We are going to look at **them**.*
Nous regardons **les enfants**.	*We look at **the children**.*
Nous **les** regardons.	*We look at **them**.*
Nous allons **les** regarder.	*We are going to look at **them**.*

*Se and s' are used in conjugating pronominal verbs (reflexive or reciprocal).
Soi means *oneself* but can also mean *himself* in expressions such as **chacun pour soi (each man for himself).

In the compound tenses, such as the **passé composé** and the **plus-que-parfait**, the object pronouns are placed **before** the auxiliary verb **avoir** or **être**.

Nous avons regardé les photos.	*We looked at the pictures.*
Nous **les** avons regardées.	*We looked at them.*
Nous avions regardé les photos.	*We had looked at the pictures.*
Nous **les** avions regardées.	*We had looked at them.*

TIP

When using the direct object pronoun with a verb conjugated in a compound tense such as the passé composé, the past participle will take the gender and number of the noun replaced by the direct object pronoun since it is placed before the verb.

J'ai vu **la** pièce hier.	*I saw the play yesterday.*
Je **l'**ai vue hier.	*I saw it yesterday.*
Il a vu Emma et Elise.	*He saw Emma and Elise.*
Il les a vues.	*He saw them.*

Le can also replace a phrase (**une proposition**).

Pensez-vous **qu'ils n'aiment pas voyager en hiver**.
Do you think that they don't like to travel in the winter.

Je **le** pense.
I think so.

Indirect Object Pronouns
Le pronom objet indirect

The indirect object pronouns for the first and second person singular and plural are the same as the direct object pronouns: **me, te, nous, vous.** For the third person, singular and plural, they are different: *lui* (masculine and feminine), *leur* (masculine and feminine). They all translate into: *to me, to you, to him, to her, to us, to you, to them.*

- **Verbs followed by à require an indirect object pronoun. These verbs are not necessarily followed by *to* in English**

appartenir à quelqu'un	→	*to belong to someone*
parler à quelqu'un	→	*to speak to someone*
montrer à quelqu'un	→	*to show to someone*
défendre à quelqu'un	→	*to forbid someone (to do something)*
dire à quelqu'un	→	*to tell someone*
conseiller à quelqu'un	→	*to advise someone (to do something)*
aller à quelqu'un	→	*to suit someone (to become/look good on someone)*

écrire à quelqu'un	→	to write someone
téléphoner à quelqu'un	→	to telephone someone
demander à quelqu'un	→	to ask someone (something)
prêter à quelqu'un	→	to loan to someone
emprunter à quelqu'un	→	to borrow from someone
répondre à quelqu'un	→	to answer someone
appartenir à quelqu'un	→	to belong to someone
obéir à quelqu'un	→	to obey someone
plaire à quelqu'un	→	to appeal to someone
ressembler à quelqu'un	→	to resemble (look like) someone
vendre à quelqu'un	→	to sell to someone

Elle a téléphoné à Caroline.	*She telephoned Caroline.*
Elle lui a téléphoné.	*She telephoned her.*
Il a parlé à ses copains.	*He spoke to his friends.*
Il leur a parlé.	*He spoke to them.*

SENTENCES WITH BOTH A DIRECT AND AN INDIRECT OBJECT PRONOUN

- If both pronouns begin with the letter l (le, la, les *and* lui, leur), their position in the sentence is alphabetical (le, la, and les come before lui or leur)

Je donne <u>la</u> salade à Pierre.	→	Je **la lui** donne.
Je raconte **les histoires** aux enfants.	→	Je **les leur** raconte.

- If one pronoun begins with m, t, n, or v (me, te, nous, vous) and the other begins with l (le, la, and les), the pronoun beginning with l is closest to the verb

Je **vous** donne **la salade**.	→	Je **vous la** donne.
Il **me** raconte **les histoires**.	→	Il **me les** raconte.

COMPOUND TENSES

J'ai donné **la salade** à Pierre.	→	Je **la lui** ai donnée.
J'ai raconté **les histoires** aux enfants.	→	Je **les leur** ai racontées.
Je **vous** ai donné **la salade**.	→	Je **vous l'**ai donnée.
Il **m'**a raconté **les histoires**.	→	Il **me les** a racontées.

Do not mistake the reflexive pronouns for the object pronouns. The reflexive pronouns are **me, m', te, t', se, s', nous, vous, se, s'.** They are used with reflexive verbs only.

QUICK PRACTICE

I. Refaites les phrases suivantes en vous servant de pronoms objet, soit direct, soit indirect. A vous de décider!

Modèle: Il a envoyé la lettre à Julie.—Il la lui a envoyée.

1. Elle a dit bonjour **au professeur**.

2. J'ai acheté **la jupe verte**.

3. Marc a oublié **les devoirs**.

4. Ils **me** dit **la vérité**.

5. Il a offert **le cadeau à ses parents**.

6. Louis et Colette **m'**ont demandé **mon adresse**.

7. Nous montrons **le dessin au professeur**.

8. Tu as parlé **à Corinne**.

9. Nous étudions **la géométrie et l'algèbre**.

10. Il m'a montré **la voiture verte**.

II. Traduisez les phrases suivantes.

1. The book belongs to me.

2. The flowers? He gave them to her.

3. They received it (the letter) yesterday.

4. They obeyed them (their parents).

5. Henriette telephoned him.

Y and En
Y et En

- **The pronoun y replaces names of places and locations that are preceded by: à, dans, en, sur, sous, au-dessus, au-dessous, etc.**

  Ils sont à la bibliothèque. → Ils y sont.
  They are at the library.   *They are there.*

  Elle est en France. → Elle y est.
  She is in France.   *She is there.*

  Le livre est sur le bureau. → Le livre y est.
  The book is on the desk.   *The book is there.*

- **The pronoun y replaces à (à la, au, aux) + the name of a thing**

  Nous obéissons à la loi. → Nous y obéissons.
  We obey the law.   *We obey it.*

- **The pronoun en replaces de + the name of a thing or de + an infinitive**

  Elle a l'habitude de se lever à 6 heures. → Elle en a l'habitude.
  She is used to getting up at 6 o'clock.   *She is used to it.*

- **The pronoun en replaces the partitives du and des**

  Je bois du lait. → J'en bois.
  I drink milk.   *I drink (some of) it.*

  Je mange des bananes. → J'en mange.
  I eat bananas.   *I eat some.*

- **The pronoun en is used after verbs and expressions that are followed by de + an infinitive or a noun: avoir envie de, avoir besoin de, avoir peur de, parler de, profiter de, etc.**

  J'ai besoin de dormir. → J'en ai besoin.
  I need to sleep.   *I need it.*

  Ils parlent de leur problème. → Ils en parlent.
  They talk about their problem.   *They talk about it.*

- **The pronoun en is used with an expression of quantity, weights, and measures: assez de, plusieurs, beaucoup de, un kilo de, une livre de, une douzaine de, un, deux, trois, etc. mètres (kilomètres), grammes, un, une, deux, etc.**

NOTE: When **en** is used with an expression of quantity, weight or measure, the expression of quantity must follow.

Elle chante **beaucoup de** chansons. → Elle **en** chante **beaucoup**.
She sings a lot of songs. → *She sings a lot of them.*

J'ai reçu **plusieurs** lettres. → J'**en** ai reçu **plusieurs**.
I received several letters. → *I received several (of them).*

En is used mainly for things. However, it can be used for groups of people:

Nous avons vu plusieurs copains au café. →
Nous en avons vu plusieurs ... →
We saw several friends at the café. →
We saw several of them ...

Il parle des fermiers américains. →
Il en parle.
He talks about American farmers. →
He talks about them.

ORDER OF PRONOUNS WHEN Y AND EN ARE INCLUDED

me, m'				
te, t'	le	lui		
nous	la	leur	y	en
vous	le			

Il **me le** donne.   *He gives it to me.*
Il **la leur** donne.   *He gives it to them.*
Il **lui en** donne.   *He gives him (her) some.*
Nous **y** allons.   *We go there.*
Il **y en** a.   *There is (are) some.*

- **Y always precedes en. Both y and en are placed before the verb and after the direct and indirect object pronouns**

Il **les y** rencontre.   *He meets them there.*
Il **leur en** envoie.   *He sends them some.*

QUICK PRACTICE

III. Mme Dubois pose des questions à son fils Thierry. Il lui répond en se servant de pronoms objets. Ecrivez les réponses de Thierry.

Modèle: As-tu étudié le poème?—Oui, je l'ai étudié.

1. As-tu acheté **deux livres à la librairie**?

2. As-tu pris **des vitamines**?

3. Vas-tu **au cinéma** samedi?

4. As-tu peur de ne pas réussir **à l'examen**?

5. As-tu étudié plusieurs **chapitres**?

6. Est-ce que tu as passé la journée **à la plage**?

7. Est-ce que tu t'es occupé **du jardin**?

8. As-tu envoyé **une lettre à tante Louise**?

9. As-tu mangé **des pommes** ce matin?

10. Tes copains ont-ils chanté beaucoup **de chansons**?

Interrogative and Negative Forms
Les formes interrogative et négative

INTERROGATIVE FORM

- **Direct object pronoun (direct OP) + indirect object pronoun (indirect OP) + verb/subject inversion**

  Donnez-vous **les lettres à Lise**?   *Do you give the letters to Lise?*
  Les lui donnez-vous?   *Do you give them to her?*

- **Est-ce que + subject + direct OP + indirect OP + verb**

  Est-ce que vous donnez **les lettres à Lise**?
  Est-ce que vous **les lui** donnez?

NEGATIVE FORM

- **Subject + ne + direct OP + indirect OP + verb + pas**

Nous **ne** donnons **pas** les lettres à Lise.　　*We don't give the letters to Lise.*

Nous **ne** les lui donnons **pas**.　　*We don't give them to her.*

INTERROGATIVE AND NEGATIVE FORMS FOR COMPOUND TENSES

- **Direct OP + indirect OP + auxiliary verb/subject inversion + past participle**

Les lui avez-vous données?*　　*Did you give them to her?*

- **Est-ce que + subject + direct OP + indirect OP + compound tense**

Est-ce que **vous les lui** avez données?　*Did you give them to her?*

- **Subject + ne + direct OP + indirect OP + auxiliary verb + pas + past participle**

Nous **ne les lui** avons **pas** données.　　*We did not give them to her.*

INTERROGATIVE-NEGATIVE FORM

- **Ne + direct OP + indirect OP + inversion verb/subject + pas**

Ne les lui donne-t-il **pas**?　　*Doesn't he give them to her?*

- **Est-ce que + subject + direct OP + indirect OP + verb + pas**

Est-ce qu'il **ne les lui** donne **pas**?　*Doesn't he give them to her?*

- **Ne + direct OP + indirect OP + inversion aux. verb/subject + pas + past participle**

Ne les lui a-t-il **pas** données?　　*Didn't he give them to her?*

VERBS THAT ARE FOLLOWED BY AN INFINITIVE

- **Subject + ne + conjugated verb + pas + direct OP + indirect OP + infinitive**

Il **ne** va **pas** les lui donner.　　*He is not going to give them to her.*

- **Verb/subject inversion + direct OP + indirect OP + infinitive**

Va-t-il **les lui** donner?　　*Will he give them to her?*

---

*In this case, the past participle must agree with the direct object since it is placed before.

- Ne + verb/subject inversion + pas + direct OP + indirect OP + infinitive

Ne va-t-il **pas les lui** donner?   *Won't he give them to her?*

IV. Posez des questions pour les réponses suivantes en vous servant de pronoms objets:

Modèle: Il a donné **le cadeau à Colette**.—Il **le lui** a donné.

1. Je **les** ai vus **à la place de la Concorde.**

2. Je vais prêter **ma voiture à mon fils.**

3. Nous avons raconté **notre aventure au professeur.**

4. Il donne **la clef à sa soeur.**

5. Elle a étudié **les poèmes.**

Disjunctive Pronouns
Les pronoms disjoints

DISJUNCTIVE OR STRESS PRONOUNS			
moi	*me*	nous	*us*
toi	*you*	vous	*you*
lui	*him*	eux	*them*
elle	*her*	elles	*them*
soi	*oneself*		

They are used:

- **After a preposition to replace the name of a person or an animal only: devant, derrière, avec, pour, chez, etc.**

    J'habite **avec eux**.   *I live with them.*
    Ils viennent **chez moi**.   *They are coming to my house.*

- After certain verbs that are followed by à plus the name of **a person**. For these verbs, the indirect object pronoun cannot be used. They are:

penser à	*to think about, of*
s'intéresser à	*to be interested in*
s'adresser à	*to approach someone*
s'habituer à	*to be used to*
tenir à	*to hold dear, value*
se fier à	*to trust*
rêver à	*to dream about*
songer à	*to think of*
être à	*to belong to*
venir à	*to come to*

Ce livre est **à moi.**	→	*This book belongs to me.*
Je m'intéresse **à lui.**	→	*I am interested in him.*
Elle pense **à eux.**	→	*She thinks about (of) them.*
Elle s'est habituée **à lui.**	→	*She got used to him.*

TIP

When these verbs are used with a thing, the pronoun y is used instead.

Je m'habitue **à ma nouvelle maison.**	→	Je m'**y** habitue.
Elle a pensé **à ses vacances.**	→	Elle **y a pensé.**

- **When there are many subjects**

  Moi, j'aime la natation tandis que lui, il aime le foot.
  I like swimming whereas he likes soccer.

- **When there is a comparison**

  Mon frère est plus grand que moi.
  My brother is taller than I am.

- **After c'est or just as an elliptical answer**

  Qui est-ce? C'est moi.
  Who is it? It's me.

  C'est lui qui a ouvert la fenêtre.
  It is he who opened the window.

  Qui a vu ce film? Moi.
  Who saw this movie? Me (or I did).

- **Before même, meaning *self* (*myself, yourself*, etc.)**

    Je veux le faire moi-même.
    I want to do it myself.

- **With ni...ni**

    Ni elle ni moi n'avons vu ce film.
    Neither she nor I saw this movie.

- **Before aussi and non plus**

    J'aime beaucoup cette histoire! Moi aussi.
    I like this story a lot! Me too.

    Je ne vais pas en Europe cet été. Moi non plus.
    I am not going to Europe this summer. Me neither.

Placement of Pronouns in the Imperative
Où placer les pronoms à l'impératif

	le	moi (m')		
verb	la	toi (t')		
	les	lui	y	en
		nous		
		vous		
		leur		

Donne-le-lui.	*Give it to him.*	**Parle-lui-en.**	*Speak of it to him.*
Vas-y.	*Go ahead.*	**Allons-y.**	*Let's go.*
Raconte-la-leur.	*Tell it to them.*	**Dis-le-moi.**	*Tell it to me.*

- **In the negative, the order changes to ne + direct OP + indirect OP + verb + pas**

    Ne le lui donne **pas.**   *Don't give it to him.*
    Ne lui en parle **pas.**   *Don't speak of it to him.*
    Ne me* le dis **pas.**   *Don't tell it to me.*
    N'y allez **pas.**   *Don't go there.*

*In the negative imperative, **moi** becomes **me**.

QUICK PRACTICE

V. Refaites les phrases suivantes en utilisant des pronoms objets et des pronoms disjoints:

Modèle: Je m'adresse à/ils/pour demander/ils/leur opinion.
Je m'adresse à eux pour leur demander leur opinion.

1. Ils viennent chez/je/et ensuite ils vont chez/tu.

2. Elle a préparé un repas special pour/il.

3. Il écrit/elle/pour demander/elle/ si elle aimerait sortir avec/il.

4. Asseyez-vous derrière/je.

5. Je parle/elle/parce que je me fie/elle.

6. Nous pensons/il.

7. Je me suis habituée/ils/ car je connais/ils/depuis longtemps.

8. Cette voiture n'appartient pas/ils/elle appartient/je.

9. Je ne m'intéresse pas/cette histoire.

10. C'est/tu/qu'il aime.

VI. Traduisez

1. It is you that I saw yesterday.

2. I cannot live without you.

3. Neither he nor I.

4. I think of them.

5. I am not used to it.

6. I am not used to her.

7. Send it to her

8. He works with me.

9. Come to my house.

10. I don't want to go out! Me neither.

LES PRONOMS PERSONNELS

```
P I Y B S X D Z W D Z A L E J
A K C N J I Q S O P T Y L K E
R A T P S U D N I C Z L K U L
L Y F X F N N I D O E G X V E
E N O W T E O X U L B M E Y S
Z E D Y L K Q L E L N N Z B Y
L N N E Z F Z U L X E F E A V
U Y L T I K R N Z A H J W J O
I U J X E R G D B U Y K X I I
I N A D E T H Z S V N S V O S
I F E P Z B U R U H O Y U F K
K F O B C V Q E W H G S J O O
F N I L L U I E N P A R L E N
D M I I I M R R P Y R K G N T
F Z J F Z J D G Y O S K I G H
```

DONNE-LE-LUI   JE LES Y VOIS   NOUS Y ALLONS

ELLE LEUR REPOND   JE LUI DIS   PARLEZ-LUI

IL LUI EN PARLE   J'EN BOIS

212 Complete French Grammar Review

Culture Capsule 12

Le mot restaurant vient du verbe "restaurer". Jusqu'au 18ème siècle, le "restaurant" était un bouillon de viande qui réconfortait ceux qui le buvaient soit "restaurait" la bonne santé! A l'époque, les établissements qui servaient ce breuvage s'appelaient aussi "restaurants" ou "maisons de santé".

Petit à petit, ces établissements diversifient ce qu'ils offrent et composent même un menu. Déjà, en 1686, l'Italien Francesco Procopio (qui plus tard francise son nom en Procope) ouvre un café où les hommes de lettres viennent discuter de philosophie et de littérature. Au 18ème siècle, Voltaire, Rousseau et Diderot viennent échanger leurs idées au café Procope. Benjamin Franklin fréquente aussi cet établissement. Cependant, ce n'est qu'après la révolution que les restaurants tels que nous les connaissons commencent à se multiplier. Les grands cuisiniers qui jusque là avaient servi l'aristocratie se trouvent au chômage et décident de cultiver leur talent au profit de la classe bourgeoise et des hommes et femmes de lettres. Ces derniers se retrouvent dans des restaurants pour discuter mais aussi pour déguster leurs plats préférés. Le nombre de restaurants passe d'une cinquantaine avant la révolution à plus de 3000 trente ans plus tard. L'ancien café Procope existe toujours, et c'est aujourd'hui un des meilleurs restaurants de Paris.

En 1825, le célèbre gastronome Brillat-Savarin écrit, dans sa "Physiologie du goût": Les animaux se repaissent, l'homme mange, l'homme d'esprit seul sait manger. (Animals get fed, man eats, but only the thinking—or cultured—man knows how to eat.)

VOCABULAIRE

restaurer	*to restore (health in this case)*
réconfortait	*comforted*
breuvage	*beverage*
tels que	*such as*
chômage	*unemployment*
l'essor	*soaring*
déguster	*savor, eat with relish*

17

Possessive and Demonstrative Adjectives and Pronouns

Que savez-vous déjà?
What Do You Know Already?

(?)

Fill in the blanks with the correct possessive adjectives.

1. (*my*) _____ amie s'appelle Jenny.

2. (*your*/fam.) _____ enfants sont très intelligents.

3. (*their*) _____ famille vit au Canada.

4. (*our*) _____ directeur est en Afrique maintenant.

5. (*your*/formal) _____ examens sont difficiles.

Fill in the blanks with the correct demonstrative adjectives.

6. (*this*) _____ avion est un 747.

7. (*this*) _____ jeune fille vient d'arriver.

8. (*these*) _____ jeunes filles sont françaises.

9. (*these*) _____ chapitres sont très importants.

10. (*this*) _____ problème n'est pas facile.

The Possessive Adjectives
Les adjectifs possessifs

- In French, unlike English, the possessive adjectives (*my, your,* etc.) vary in gender and number according to the thing owned or the person belonging to someone

my book	➜	**mon** livre
my books	➜	**mes** livres
my uncle	➜	**mon** oncle
my aunt	➜	**ma** tante

PERSONAL PRONOUN	POSSESSIVE ADJECTIVE (one thing owned) masculine	feminine	POSSESSIVE ADJECTIVE (more than one thing owned)
je	mon	ma	mes
tu	ton	ta	tes
il/elle/on	son	sa	ses
nous	notre	notre	nos
vous	votre	votre	vos
ils/elles	leur	leur	leurs

NOTE: When a feminine noun begins with a vowel, use the masculine possessive adjective mon, ton, or son:

Mon amie Pierrette.   *My friend Pierrette.*

Ma cousine joue du piano.   *My cousin plays the piano.*
Son livre est sur la table.   *His (her) book is on the table.*
Leurs enfants jouent avec nos enfants.   *Their children play with our children.*

- **In English, possession is also expressed by adding 's after the noun or name. In French it is expressed by putting a form of de plus the name of the owner**

  La voiture du professeur (sa voiture)
  The teacher's car (his or her car)

  Les chausssures de Josette (ses chaussures)
  Josette's shoes (her shoes)

- **After the verb être possession is expressed by adding à plus the name of the owner (or the noun that represents the owner, or the disjunctive pronoun)**

  La voiture bleue est à Marie.   *The blue car is Marie's.*
  Le dictionnaire est à moi.   *The dictionary belongs to me (is mine).*

- **The possessive adjective is not used when referring to parts of the body when the owner is known. It is replaced by the definite article**

  Il a mal à **la** tête.   ***His** head hurts.*

I. Say the following in French.

1. Her house.

2. His friend Marie.

3. Your (formal) teachers.

4. Our family.

5. Their books.

6. Laure's vacation.

7. The umbrella is Laure's.

8. My friend Alain.

9. The book is mine.

10. I did not see your friends.

The Possessive Pronouns
Les pronoms possessifs

The possessive pronoun agrees in gender and number with the noun it replaces.

	MASCULINE		**FEMININE**	
	singular	*plural*	*singular*	*plural*
mine	le mien	les miens	la mienne	les miennes
yours	le tien	les tiens	la tienne	les tiennes
his/hers	le sien	les siens	la sienne	les siennes
ours	le nôtre	les nôtres	la nôtre	les nôtres
yours	le vôtre	les vôtres	la vôtre	les vôtres
theirs	le leur	les leurs	la leur	les leurs

For indefinite words such as **on, chacun, quelqu'un, personne, tout le monde,** the possessive adjectives or pronouns are **son, sa, ses,** and **le sien, la sienne, les siens, les siennes.**

Chacun a ses problèmes.
Chacun a les siens.

- When an article precedes the possessive pronoun, such as *to mine,* you just contract à + le or les, (au, aux) and de + le or les (du, des)

    Je parle **à mon père** et toi, tu parles **au tien.**
    *I speak to **my father** and you speak **to yours.***

- **Les miens, les tiens, les siens, les nôtres, les vôtres, les leurs used idiomatically means:** *my family, your family,* **etc.**

    Dis bonjour de ma part **aux tiens.**
    Say hello for me to your family.

QUICK PRACTICE
II. Traduisez les mots entre parenthèses.

Modèle: Son frère et (mine) ont dix ans.—Son frère et le mien ont dix ans.

1. Voilà tes crayons et voici (mine).

2. Sa réponse est moins bonne que (yours/fam).

3. Nos enfants sont moins sages que (theirs).

4. Que pensez-vous de son problème et (of mine)?

5. Ma soeur est actuellement au Japon. Et (yours/formal)?

6. Il a parlé à mon professeur et (to theirs).

7. J'ai écrit à mes parents, mais Colette n'a pas écrit (to hers).

8. Tu as oublié ton livre, emprunte (mine).

9. Mon mariage a eu lieu au bord de la mer, et (yours/formal)?

10. Il a rangé ses affaires et (yours/fam.).

The Demonstrative Adjectives
Les adjectifs demonstratifs

The demonstrative adjectives correspond to *this, that, these, those.*

	MASCULINE	FEMININE
Singular	ce, cet*	cette
Plural	ces**	ces**

*cet is used before a **masculine noun** that begins with a vowel or a mute h.
**ces is used for the masculine and the feminine plurals.

Ce tableau	*this painting*	**Cette maison**	*this house*
Ces tableaux	*these paintings*	**Ces maisons**	*these houses*
Cet ami	*this friend (masc.)*	**Cette amie**	*this friend (fem.)*
Cet homme	*this man*	**Cette habitude**	*this habit*

- To express **the idea of** *that* and *those*, **là** is added after the noun:

Ce tableau-**là**	*that painting*
Ces tableaux-**là**	*those paintings*

- **When comparing two things, one of which is close, and one is far, -ci is used for the item that is close and -là for the item that is far**

    Cette maison-ci et cette maison-là.
    This house and that house.

    Ces chocolats-ci et ces chocolats-là.
    These chocolates and those chocolates.

    Ce livre-ci et ce livre-là.
    This book and that book.

QUICK PRACTICE

III. Mettez les adjectifs démonstratifs qui conviennent:

Modèle: _____ école est excellente.—Cette école est excellente.

1. _____ magasin est plus grand que _____ boutique.

2. _____ chien est très mignon.

3. J'aime beaucoup _____ robe; elle est ravissante.

4. Elle n'a pas encore étudié _____ chapitres.

5. Je ne comprends pas _____ leçon; elle est difficile.

6. _____ gâteau-ci est meilleur que _____ gâteau-là.

7. Est-ce que tu connais _____ homme?

8. _____ animal est dangereux.

The Demonstrative Pronouns
Les pronoms demonstratifs

- **Demonstrative pronouns are used to replace a noun preceded by a demonstrative adjective. They are usually followed by -ci and -là**

  Il y a deux livres sur mon bureau; j'aime celui-ci mais je n'aime pas celui-là.
  There are two books on my desk; I like this one but I don't like that one.

  Quelle réponse est correcte? Celle-ci ou celle-là?

- **When followed by de the demonstrative pronoun indicates possession**

  Ma voiture et **celle de** mon père sont devant la maison.
  My car and my father's are in front of the house.

MASC. SING.	FEMININE SING.	MASC. PL.	FEM. PL.
celui	celle	ceux	celles
celui-ci	celle-ci	ceux-ci	celles-ci
celui-là	celle-là	ceux-là	celles-là

- **Celui-ci/celle-ci** = **the latter** (it is closest to the noun to which it refers)

- **Celui-là/celle-là** = **the former** (it is farthest from that noun)

   Bizet et Puccini ont écrit des opéras; celui-ci vivait en Italie, et celui-là vivait en France.
   Bizet and Puccini wrote operas; the latter lived in Italy and the former lived in France.

- **Ceci and Cela** = *This* **and** *That*
   Ceci and **cela** are used to replace a sentence or an idea.

   Ceci m'a beaucoup fait plaisir.   *This made me very happy.*
   Cela m'a beaucoup fait plaisir.   *That made me very happy.*

- **What about ça?**
   Ça is used in the familiar language as well as in the spoken language. You can say **Donne-moi ça** instead of **Donne-moi cela.**

   Expressions with ça:

Comment ça va?	*How are you?*
Ça va?	*Are you OK?*
Ça va bien.	*I am OK.*
Ça va mal.	*Things are going badly.*
Ça suffit.	*That is enough.*
Ça m'arrange.	*That's fine with me.*

QUICK PRACTICE

IV. **Complétez les phrases suivantes avec des pronoms démonstratifs:**

Modèle: Ce chapeau? C'est _____ de maman.—C'est celui de maman.

1. La soeur de Pierre est blonde; _____ de Claudine est brune.

2. Ce livre-là est ancien mais _____ est moderne.

3. Voici deux jeunes filles; _____ est grande, mais _____ est petite.

4. J'ai visité le Sénégal et le Bénin; _____ est plus petit que _____ .

5. J'aime ton parfum et _____ de ta mère.

6. Ces enfants? Ce sont _____ de ma tante.

7. Ces élèves sont sages mais _____ de Mme Deschamps sont bruyantes.

8. Ceci m'intéresse beaucoup mais _____ ne m'intéresse pas du tout.

How to Write a Letter in French
Comment ecrire une lettre en français

Formulas for letter writing vary from country to country. It is therefore important to know how to communicate by letter while being culturally correct.

Addressing the person

- **To friends**

  Cher Philippe, Chère Emma, Chers amis, Chères amies,

- **To someone who is an acquaintance**

  Cher Monsieur, Chère Madame, Chère Mademoiselle,

- **For a business letter**

  Monsieur, Madame, Mademoiselle,

- **For a business letter to someone with a title**

  Monsieur le Directeur, Madame la Directrice,

- **To friends**

  Je vous embrasse, je t'embrasse, avec toute mon amitié, grosses bises, avec toute mon affection, affectueusement, bisous.

- **To someone who is an acquaintance**

  Cordialement, Amical souvenir, Avec mes pensées les plus cordiales,

- **For a business letter**

  Avec mes sentiments distingués, Je vous prie d'agréer, Monsieur, l'assurance de mes sentiments distingués, *ou* Je vous prie d'agréer, Monsieur (Madame, Mademoiselle) mes salutations distinguées, *ou* Veuillez agréer, Monsieur (Madame, Mademoiselle) l'expression de mes sentiments distingués,

E-MAIL

COURRIER ÉLECTRONIQUE

For e-mail messages, just like in English, there is less formality.

- **For a friend**

  Cher (Chère) + name, Mon cher (ma chère) + name *or*
  Bonjour + name.

- **For business e-mail**

  The same greeting formula as that in normal letters is used. However, the end of the message can be less formal: **Meilleurs sentiments,** *or* **Cordialement, Très cordialement, Bien cordialement,**

SPECIALIZED VOCABULARY

the web	=	**la toile (or le web)**
ampersand	=	**arrobase, arrobas, arrobe, arobe, arobase**
e-mail address	=	**adresse électronique, adresse courriel, adresse e-mail, adresse mél**
mailbox	=	**BAL (boîte aux lettres)**
underscore	=	**tiret bas**
hyphen	=	**tiret**
slash	=	**barre oblique**
server	=	**serveur**
on line	=	**en ligne**
home page	=	**page d'accueil** *ou* **accueil**
password	=	**mot de passe**
link	=	**lien**
curser	=	**pointeur**

QUICK PRACTICE

V. Écrivez une lettre aux parents d'un ami pour les remercier de vous avoir invité à diner.

VI. Envoyez un message par courriel à l'ami qui vous a invité.

Possessifs et demonstratifs

Across

3. Yours (masc. sing.)

4. This

8. My parents (2 words)

9. This table (2 words)

Down

1. The one (masc.)

2. This man (2 words)

5. It is mine (4 words)

6. The ones (masc. pl.)

7. The one (fem.)

18

Relative Pronouns

A relative pronoun is a pronoun that links to clauses.

Who/Which and Whom/Which
Qui et que

*The student **who** is tall is going to Belgium.*
L'étudiant **qui** est grand va en Belgique.

The student is going to Belgium	→ principal clause: it can stand alone.
***who** is tall*	→ relative clause: it cannot stand alone.

L'étudiant va en Belgique	→ proposition principale.
qui est grand	→ proposition relative.

L'étudiant is the subject of **va**, therefore **qui** must be used.

*The student **that(whom)** I saw is tall.**
L'étudiant **que** j'ai vu est grand.

L'étudiant is the object of **j'ai vu**. The subject of the verb is **j'**. The relative pronoun that must be used is **que**.

*The garden **which (that)** is near the house has beautiful flowers.*
Le jardin **qui** est près de la maison a de belles fleurs.

The garden has beautiful flowers	→ principal clause: it can stand alone.
***which** is near the house*	→ relative clause: it cannot stand alone.

Le jardin is the subject of **a**, therefore **qui** must be used.

*The garden **which (that)** I admire is near the house.*
Le jardin **que** j'admire est près de la maison.

The garden is near the house	→ principal clause: it can stand alone.
***which** I admire*	→ relative clause: it cannot stand alone.

Le jardin is the object of **j'admire**. The subject of the verb is **j'**. The relative pronoun that must be used is **que**.

*In English, the relative pronoun is sometimes omitted (*the student I saw*) but never in French.

NOTE: In a fill-in sentence, if the space is directly followed by the verb, then use **qui**. If the space is followed by a noun or a personal pronoun and then the verb, use **que**.

QUICK PRACTICE

I. Complétez les phrases suivantes avec le pronom relatif qui convient.

Modèle: La salade _____ j'ai mangée était délicieuse.
La salade que j'ai mangée était délicieuse.

1. Les gens _____ étaient dans le bateau attendaient le départ avec impatience.

2. Geneviève, _____ n'avait jamais voyagé, avait peur de prendre l'avion.

3. Je ne connais pas la jeune fille _____ est assise devant vous.

4. J'ai oublié d'apporter les livres _____ tu m'avais prêtés.

5. Le professeur _____ j'admire n'est pas ici.

6. Où est la soupe _____ elle a préparée?

7. Donne-moi l'assiette _____ est sur la table.

8. Martin ne sait pas _____ Arlette va venir à la soirée.

9. Est-ce que tu connais la femme _____ a téléphoné?

10. J'aime beaucoup la bague _____ il m'a donnée.

Of Whom, of Which, Whose, That
Dont

The relative pronoun **dont** replaces de (du, de la, des) + noun (person or thing). It corresponds to the English *of whom, of which, whose, that.*

- **Some expressions and verbs followed by** de

avoir envie de	*to want, to feel like having something*
avoir peur de	*to be afraid of*
parler de	*to speak of, about*
manquer de	*to lack*
avoir besoin de	*to need*
être content de	*to be happy about*
douter de	*to doubt*
être fier de	*to be proud of*
être amoureux de	*to be in love with*
se servir de	*to use (utilize) something*
se souvenir de	*to remember*
rêver de	*to dream about*

- **Dont is used after a verb or an expression followed by** de **+ noun**

Où est le CD? Tu as **parlé du** CD. → Où est le CD **dont** tu as parlé?

Where is the CD? You spoke of the CD. → *Where is the CD of which you spoke?*

Où est le stylo? J'ai **besoin du** stylo. → Où est le stylo **dont** j'ai besoin?

Where is the pen? I need the pen. → *Where is the pen that I need?*

- **Dont is used to express possession for people and things**

Voici Paul; **sa** soeur est actrice. → Voici Paul **dont la** soeur est actrice.*

*Here is Paul; **his** sister is an actress.* → *Here is Paul **whose** sister is an actress.*

Voici le livre; son titre est drôle. → Voici le livre dont **le** titre est drôle.

Here is the book; its title is funny. → *Here is the book whose title is funny.*

*When **dont** is used to express possession, the possessive adjective is replaced by the definite article.

QUICK PRACTICE

II. Complétez les phrases suivantes avec qui, que, dont, selon le cas:

Modèle: Je ne connais pas l'homme _____ tu parles.
Je ne connais pas l'homme dont tu parles.

1. La voiture _____ il rêve coûte trop cher.

2. Je n'ai pas encore rencontré l'homme _____ tu m'as parlé.

3. Les enfants _____ jouent dans le parc sont mes élèves.

4. La robe _____ Suzanne a achetée est très élégante.

5. C'est le professeur _____ la femme a reçu le prix Nobel.

6. J'ai oublié le dictionnaire _____ j'avais besoin.

7. C'est un film _____ les enfants ont très peur.

8. Sébastien, _____ habite en banlieue, voudrait déménager.

9. Je ne me souviens pas du titre du film _____ j'ai vu samedi.

10. La femme _____ il aime s'appelle Sylvie.

Preposition + Qui (for People Only)
Préposition + Qui (pour les personnes seulement)

Examples
à qui = *to whom*
pour qui = *for whom*
de qui = *of whom*
avec qui = *with whom*
chez qui = *at whose place*

Le sénateur pour qui elle travaille est célèbre.
The senator for whom she works is famous.

Le boulanger chez qui j'achète mon pain est près de chez moi.
The baker at whose place I buy my bread is near my house (literal translation).
The bakery where I buy my bread is near my house (better translation).

Laure est la jeune fille avec qui je travaille.
Laure is the young woman with whom I work.

- When do you use **de qui** and when do you use **dont**?
  Both can be used, but **dont** is preferred. However, to indicate possession (*whose*), only **dont** is used.

> **L'étudiant de qui je parle = L'étudiant dont je parle**
> *The student of whom I speak*
>
> **Gérard est l'étudiant dont le père est sénateur.**
> *Gérard is the student whose father is a senator.*

Preposition + Lequel, Laquelle, Lesquels, Lesquelles (for Things and People)
Préposition + Lequel, Laquelle, Lesquels, Lesquelles (pour les choses et les personnes)

Prepositions precede the pronoun **lequel**, or one of its variations. For people, they can be used instead of **qui**.

Examples
pour lequel = *for which/whom*
avec lequel = *with which/whom*
sans lequel = *without which/whom*
d'après lequel = *according to which/whom*
chez lequel = *at whose place (people only)*
sur lequel = *on which/whom*
parmi lesquels = *among which/whom*
entre lesquels = *between which/whom*
autour de laquelle = *around which*

La société **pour laquelle** il travaille est énorme.
The company for which he works is enormous.

La femme **chez laquelle** nous avons vu ce beau tableau est antiquaire.
The woman at whose place we saw this beautiful painting is an antique dealer.

- **When do you use a preposition + qui and when do you use a preposition + a form of lequel for people?**
  They are interchangeable but **qui** is more commonly used for people.

> La femme **chez laquelle** nous avons vu ce beau tableau est antiquaire.
> La femme **chez qui** nous avons vu ce beau tableau est antiquaire.

However, when using **parmi** and **entre** for people, the prepositions **lesquels** or **lesquelles** have to be used instead of **qui**.

The Prepositions A and De + Lequel, Laquelle, Lesquels, Lesquelles (for Things and People)

Les prépositions A et De + Lequel, Laquelle, Lesquels, Lesquelles (pour les choses et les personnes)

When the prepositions à and de are used with **lequel, laquelle, lesquels,** and **lesquelles** they contract to form the following:

To Which or To Whom	**Of Which or Of Whom**
à + lequel = auquel	de + lequel = duquel
à + laquelle = à laquelle → *(no contraction)* ← de + laquelle = de laquelle	
à + lesquels = auxquels	de + lesquels = desquels
à + lesquelles = auxquelles	de + lesquelles = desquelles

Expressions and Verbs followed by à:

assister à	*to attend*
écrire à	*to write someone*
penser à	*to think about*
parler à	*to speak to*
aller à	*to go to*
raconter à	*to tell (a story) to*
dire à	*to tell (something) to*
mentir à	*to lie to*
faire face à	*to face*
s'adresser à	*to address someone, to apply*
envoyer à	*to send to*
tenir à	*to value*

J'ai des amis auxquels j'écris souvent. *ou* **J'ai des amis à qui j'écris souvent.**
I have friends to whom I write often.

Le concert auquel nous avons assisté était excellent.
The concert that we attended was excellent.

La personne à laquelle je pense n'est pas ici. *ou* **La personne à qui je pense n'est pas ici.**
The person of whom I am thinking is not here.

Les histoires auxquelles nous pensons seraient excellentes pour les enfants.
The stories of which we are thinking would be excellent for children.

QUICK PRACTICE

III. Mettez une forme de "qui" ou "lequel" dans les phrases suivantes.

1. La femme avec _____ il travaille parle quatre langues.

2. Le collier (*necklace*) _____ je tiens me vient de ma grand-mère.

3. Les problèmes _____ j'ai fait face n'étaient pas sérieux.

4. Il habite dans l'immeuble (*building*) à côté _____ se trouve ton école.

5. Le fait-divers (*news item*) _____ je pense est à la deuxième page.

6. Voici les élèves parmi _____ j'ai plusieurs amis.

7. L'année pendant _____ ils ont voyagé a semblé trop courte.

8. L'arbre sur _____ ils ont inscrit leurs noms est un chêne.

9. Voici l'élève derrière _____ je suis assise.

10. C'est la tante chez _____ il habite.

IV. Traduisez les phrases suivantes.

1. The girl with whom he is going to get married (*se marier*).

2. The house around which there is a big garden.

3. The performance (*le spectacle*) that we attended was excellent.

4. The woman to whom I spoke was very nice.

5. The movie of which I am thinking is very long.

Where
Où

- **Où (*where*) often replaces the relative expressions** sur lequel, dans lequel, devant lequel, derrière lequel. **It indicates location in space.**

  Le quartier **où** (dans lequel) ils habitent n'est pas loin d'ici.
  The part of town where (in which) they live is not far from here.

  La table **où** (sur laquelle) j'ai mis mes livres est dans la salle à manger.
  The table where (on which) I put my books is in the dining room.

- **Où** is used after expressions of time to indicate location in time.

Le jour où ils sont arrivés, il pleuvait des cordes.*
The day (that) they arrived, it was raining cats and dogs.

Le téléphone a sonné **au moment où** ils sont arrivés.
The telephone rang at the moment (that) they arrived.

- **D'où (De + où) = from where.**

Je ne sais pas **d'où** ils viennent.
I don't know from where they are coming.

QUICK PRACTICE

V. Choisissez entre "où", "d'où", et "que".

1. Je n'aime pas la maison _____ elle a achetée.

2. Voici les monuments _____ nous avons visités.

3. As-tu visité la ville _____ ils viennent?

4. Je ne sais pas encore _____ nous irons cet été.

5. J'ai beaucoup apprécié le parc _____ j'ai visité.

6. Le jour _____ j'ai vu Jeanne, elle était malade.

7. La salle de classe _____ nous allons n'est pas climatisée.

8. Pouvez-vous nous dire _____ cet avion va atterrir.

9. Peux-tu me dire _____ vient ce chemisier.

10. La librairie _____ j'aime est en face de l'école.

*The expression **pleuvoir des cordes** is idiomatic; it literally means *raining ropes* and is the equivalent of *raining cats and dogs.*

Ce + the Relative Pronoun
Ce + Le pronom relatif

When the relative pronoun has no antecedent, that is to say when the noun it refers to is not known or does not precede it, or when it refers to a clause, **ce** replaces that noun or that clause.

Subject	ce qui	*that which, what, which*
Direct object	ce que	*that which, what, which*
Object of à	ce à quoi	*that to which, what*
Object of de	ce dont	*that of which, what*

Ils n'ont pas pu partir, ce qui est dommage.
They were unable to leave, which is a pity.

Il est encore arrivé en retard, ce que je ne comprends pas.
He arrived late again, which I don't understand.

Ce que j'aime, c'est la tarte aux pommes.
What I like is apple pie.

Ce dont tu parles est très intéressant.
That of which (what) you are speaking (of) is very interesting.

Ce à quoi elle pense, c'est d'acheter une maison.
That of which (what) she is thinking (of), is to buy a house.

• **Tout ce qui, tout ce que, tout ce dont = *All that, everything that***

J'ai mangé tout ce qui était devant moi.
I ate all (everything) that was before me.

Tout ce que j'aime coûte cher.
Everything (that) I like is expensive.

Tout ce dont j'ai besoin, c'est de me reposer.
All (that) I need is to rest.

The One(s) + the Relative Pronoun
Celui, Celle, Ceux, Celles + Le pronom relatif

CELUI (masc.)   CELLE (fem.)   CEUX (masc. pl.)   CELLES (fem. pl.)

Never use the literal translation of *the one* → ~~L'ON~~

Il y a trois jeunes filles dans la salle à manger; **celle qui** a les cheveux roux est ma soeur.
*There are three young women in the dining room; **the one whose** hair is red is my sister.*

Est-ce que ces livres sont **ceux dont** le professeur a parlé?
*Are these books **the ones of which** the teacher spoke?*

Cet élève est **celui qui** arrive toujours en retard.
*This student is **the one who** always arrives late.*

Ces pommes sont celles que je préfère.
*These apples are **the ones that** I prefer.*

QUICK PRACTICE
VI. Complétez les phrases suivantes avec ce qui, ce que, ce dont, ce à quoi.

Modèle: Je ne comprends pas _____ vous dites.
       Je ne comprends pas **ce que** vous dites.

1. Il ne sait pas _____ il veut.

2. _____ vous avez besoin, c'est d'acheter un bon dictionnaire.

3. _____ m'ennuie, c'est que je n'ai pas le temps d'aller la voir.

4. Tout _____ est important n'est pas toujours facile à accomplir.

5. Elle ne m'a pas dit _____ est arrivé.

6. Tout _____ nous pensons, c'est les vacances!

7. Les élèves n'ont pas écrit_____ le professeur a dit.

8. _____ intéresse surtout mon frère, c'est la chimie.

VII. Complétez avec celui, celle, ceux, ou celles et le pronom relatif.

Modèle: _____ a répondu est ma soeur.—**Celle qui** a répondu est ma soeur.

1. Monique est _____ nous aimerions inviter.

2. Ces gâteaux sont bons, mais _____ ma mère prépare sont meilleurs.

3. Je ne veux pas d'un stylo vert. _____ j'ai besoin doit être bleu.

4. Est-ce que ces femmes sont _____ nous avons rencontrées hier?

5. _____ il parle est mon ami.

MOTS CROISÉS
Les pronoms relatifs

Across

2. To use something (3 words)

4. L'homme _____ je parle

7. Les choses _____ il pense

8. La maison devant _____
   il y a un jardin est petite.

9. Among

Down

1. L'homme _____ parle

3. Without which/whom

5. For whom (2 words)

6. Je ne sais pas _____ vous
   parlez (of whom—2 words)

19

Prepositions

Que savez-vous déjà?
What Do You Know Already?

The following sentences are incorrect. Can you correct them?

1. Elle cherche pour son livre.

2. Je vais chez la boulangerie.

3. Tu finis faire tes devoirs.

4. Ils vont à l'école dans voiture.

5. Nous faisons nos devoirs pendant nous écoutons la radio.

6. Ils entrent la salle de classe.

7. je téléphone mes parents.

8. Elle a fait ses devoirs dans une heures.

Preposition Categories
Catégories de prépositiones

Prepositions in French fall into several categories: prepositions following certain verbs, prepositions that precede an infinitive, prepositions that precede a noun, prepositions that reflect possession, prepositions of time, as well as prepositions of location.

- **Verbs that are followed by the preposition à before an infinitive**

apprendre à	*to learn to*	**renoncer à**	*to give up*
chercher à	*to try to*	**réussir à**	*to succeed in*
commencer à	*to begin to*	**servir à**	*to be used for*
consentir à	*to consent to*	**s'amuser à**	*to have fun doing*
continuer à	*to continue to*	**s'habituer à**	*to get used to*
obliger à	*to oblige, force to*	**songer à**	*to think about*
parvenir à	*to succeed in*	**tenir à**	*to insist upon*

J'apprends à nager depuis deux semaines.
I have been learning to swim for two weeks.

Je commence à comprendre.
I am beginning to understand.

Il a obligé son fils à prendre un parapluie.
He forced his son to take an umbrella.

- **Verbs that are followed by the preposition de before an infinitive**

cesser de	*to stop, cease*	interdire de	*to forbid*
choisir de	*to choose*	mériter de	*to deserve*
conseiller de	*to advise*	offrir de	*to offer*
craindre de	*to fear*	oublier de	*to forget*
décider de	*to decide*	parler de	*to talk about*
demander de	*to ask*	permettre de	*to allow*
défendre de	*to forbid*	promettre de	*to promise*
dire de	*to tell*	refuser de	*to refuse*
essayer de	*to try*	se dépêcher de	*to hurry*
éviter de	*to avoid*	se souvenir de	*to remember*
finir de	*to finish*	tâcher de	*to try to*

Elle a oublié de lire ce chapitre.
She forgot to read this chapter.

J'ai décidé d'acheter une nouvelle voiture.
I decided to buy a new car.

Tâche d'écrire une lettre à Colette.
Try to write Colette a letter.

- **Prepositions that precede a noun**

à	*to*	derrière	*behind*
avant	*before*	devant*	*in front of, before*
après	*after*	en*	*in, within a period of*
avec	*with*	envers*	*toward (abstract)*
chez*	*at the home of*	par	*by*
dans*	*in/inside of*	pendant	*for, during (time)*
de	*from/ of*	pour	*to, in order to*
depuis	*for, since*	vers*	*around, toward (concrete)*
dès	*since, as of*		

Chez means *at the home of, in the place of business of, in the country of, in the group of, in the works of*: **Chez ma tante, chez le boulanger (never *chez la boulangerie*), chez les américains, chez les soldats, chez les étudiants, chez Shakespeare.** It is always used with the names of people, *never of places.*

Dans means *in* or *inside (dans la rue, dans la maison)*. When pertaining to time, it refers to a period of time that begins in the present and ends in the future: **Il va finir ses devoirs dans une heure.** (*He will finish his homework in an hour from now.*) *En* refers to something that was completed within a period of time: **Il a fait tous ses devoirs en une heure.** (*He did all of his homework in an hour.*)

Devant means *in front of*: **Il joue du piano devant ses amis.** (*He plays the piano in front of his friends.*) It may also mean *before* in a concrete sense, not *before in time*: **Il est debout devant le tableau.** (*He is standing before the blackboard.*)

Envers refers to an abstract event: **Il est gentil envers ses élèves.** (*He is kind toward his students.*) *Vers* refers to a concrete event: **Il se dirige vers la porte.** (*He is walking toward the door.*) **Nous sommes arrivés vers dix heures.** (*We arrived around ten o'clock.*)

- **Contractions of prepositions**
When followed by the object pronouns **le** and **les**, the prepositions **à** and **de** change.

à + le	= au		de + le	= du
à + la	= à la		de + la	= de la
à + l'	= à l'		de + l'	= de l'
à + les	= aux		de + les	= des

Je parle **au** directeur.
Je parle **du** directeur.
Je parle **des** enfants.

- **Verbs that are followed by à or de before a noun**

aller à	*to go to, to suit**	Nous sommes allés à l'école.
assister à	*to attend (an event)*	Ils ont assisté à la pièce.
changer de	*to change*	J'ai changé de robe.
dire à	*to tell (something to someone)*	Dis la vérité à ton père.
écrire à	*to write to*	Elle écrit à sa soeur.
échouer à	*to fail*	J'ai échoué à l'examen.
jouer à	*to play a sport, a game*	Paul joue au tennis.
jouer de	*to play an instrument*	Francine joue du violon.
manquer à	*to be missed by*	Elle manque à ses parents.
manquer de	*to lack, to be lacking in*	Tu manques de patience.
obéir à	*to obey*	Il obéit à son professeur.
parler à	*to speak to*	Nous parlons aux élèves.
parler de	*to speak of (about)*	Elle parle toujours de Paul.
penser à	*to think about*	Je pense à mon fiancé.
penser de	*to think of (opinion)*	Que pensez-vous de Carole?

plaire à	*to appeal to, to be liked by*	Ce garçon plaît à Claire.
ressembler à	*to resemble, look like*	Tu ressembles à ta mère.
réussir à	*to succeed, to pass (a test)*	Elle a réussi à son examen.
s'habituer à	*to get used to*	Je m'habitue à ma classe.
s'inscrire à	*to register, to enroll*	Il s'est inscrit à l'université.
servir de	*to be used as*	Ma chambre sert de chambre d'amisse.
se servir de	*to use*	Le prof se sert d'un stylo rouge.
tenir à	*to value*	Je tiens à ce vieux livre.
tenir de	*to take after*	Il tient de son père.

aller à + *a person* has a second meaning: *to suit or look good on a person.*

Le chapeau gris **va** bien **à** Marie-Christine.
The gray hat suits (looks good on) Marie-Christine.

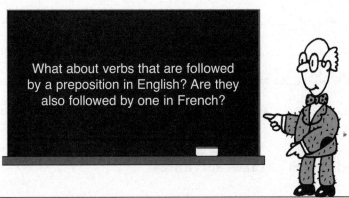

What about verbs that are followed by a preposition in English? Are they also followed by one in French?

SOME ARE, SOME AREN'T!

parler **à** → *to speak **to***   se moquer **de** → *to make fun **of***

but

*to wait **for***	→	attendre	J'attends le train.
*to look **for***	→	chercher	Elle cherche la réponse.
*to ask **for***	→	demander	Je demande une explication.
*to listen **to***	→	écouter	Nous écoutons le professeur.
*to pay **for***	→	payer	Elle paie les billets.
*to look **at***	→	regarder	Je regarde le tableau.

however

to attend	→	assister **à**	Elle assiste **à la** conference.
to change	→	changer **de**	J'ai changé **de** coiffure.
to enter	→	entrer **dans**	Il est entré **dans** le salon.
to telephone	→	téléphoner **à**	Je téléphone **au** directeur.

QUICK PRACTICE

I. Guy revient de l'université, il raconte à ses parents comment s'est passé son premier semestre, mais, comme il est surexcité et qu'il parle très vite, il oublie de mettre les prépositions dans ses phrases. Corrigez-le en mettant la préposition qui manque:

1. Le directeur était très gentil _____ moi!

2. _____ quelques jours, je connaissais déjà beaucoup de monde.

3. Je crois que mon premier essai a beaucoup plu _____ prof d'anglais.

4. En français, j'ai réussi _____la première interrogation.

5. J'ai immédiatement commencé _____ parler français en classe.

6. Je crois que je manque _____ maman parce qu'elle m'écrit beaucoup.

7. Hier, j'ai fini _____ faire ma recherche pour mon prochain essai.

8. J'ai décidé _____ suivre un cours de philosophie le semestre prochain.

9. On m'a aussi conseillé _____ faire de la psychologie.

10. Je songe _____ passer mes prochaines vacances en France.

II. Traduisez les phrases suivantes.

1. Did you finish doing your homework?

2. I wrote this essay in four hours.

3. I miss you a lot.

4. He told his students to write a poem.

5. I went to the dentist's.

- **The prepositions that reflect possession are à and de**

La robe **de** Justine.	*Justine's dress.*
La maison **de** Christophe.	*Christopher's house.*

After the verbs **être** (*to be*) and **appartenir** (*to belong*), the preposition **à** reflects the possessive.

La voiture est **à** mes parents.	*The car belongs to my parents.*
but	
C'est la voiture **de** mes parents.	*This is my parents' car.*
La voiture appartient **à** mes parents.	*The car belongs to my parents.*

- **Prepositions of time**

après	*after*	Je me repose après le dîner.
au	*in (the spring)*	Je compte voyager au printemps.
au début de	*at the beginning of*	Je les ai vus au début de l'hiver.
avant	*before*	Il est parti avant minuit.
dans	*in*	Je vais partir dans une heure.
depuis*	*since, for*	Elle travaille depuis lundi.
dès	*as of, from*	Dès demain, je te promets d'étudier.
en	*in (within)*	Il fait ce voyage en deux heures.
jusqu'à	*until*	Tu dois pratiquer jusqu'à 3 heures.
pendant**	*for, during*	J'ai travaillé pendant dix ans.
pour***	*for*	Il part pour deux semaines.

It is important to differentiate between **depuis**, **pendant**, and **pour**.

***depuis** is used when something begins in the past and continues in the present.

Elle travaille depuis deux semaines.
She has been working for two weeks.

Elle travaille depuis l'âge de seize ans.
She has been working since the age of sixteen.

****pendant** is used when something begins and ends within a certain period of time.

Il a beaucoup voyagé pendant qu'il étudiait en France.
He traveled a lot while he was studying in France.

Je n'aime pas travailler pendant mes vacances.
I don't like to work during my vacation.

J'ai l'intention d'aller au Sénégal pendant mes vacances.
I intend to go to Senegal during my vacation.

J'ai étudié pendant trois heures hier.
I studied for three hours yesterday.

***pour is used to indicate a completed period of time in the past, or a period of time in the future. It usually follows the verbs **aller**, **partir**, **venir**.

Ils sont partis pour trois jours chez leur grand-mère le mois dernier.
They went to their grandmother's for three days last month.

Nous allons à Québec pour dix jours l'été prochain.
We are going to Quebec for ten days next month.

- **Prepositions of manner (the manner in which something is done)**

à bicyclette	*on a bike*	par écrit	*in writing*
à pied	*on foot*	par avion	*by plane*
à haute voix	*in a loud voice*	par train	*by train*
à voix basse	*in a low voice*	par coeur	*by heart*
en train	*by train*	par exemple	*as an example*
en avion	*by plane*	avec joie	*with joy*
en voiture	*by car*	avec plaisir	*with pleasure*

- **Prepositions of description or quality**
  As their name indicates, they help to describe an object or a person.

Une jeune fille **aux** yeux verts	*A young woman **with** green eyes*
Une glace **à** la vanille	*A vanilla ice cream. (**with** vanilla)*
Un homme **à** la barbe grise	*A man **with** a gray beard*
La chambre **à** coucher	*The bedroom (the room **in which** to sleep)*
Le pull **à** col roulé	*The sweater **with** a rolled collar*
La robe **à** manches courtes	*The dress **with** short sleeves*
Le professeur **de** mathématiques	*The math teacher (**of** mathematics)*
La salade **de** pommes de terre	*The potato salad (**with** potatoes)*

NOTE: **de** or **en** can be used for objects that are *made of* a certain material.

une robe **de** coton	*or*	une robe **en** coton
a cotton dress		*a cotton dress*
un verre **de** cristal		un verre **en** cristal
a crystal glass		*a crystal glass*
un plateau **de** cuivre		un plateau **en** cuivre
a copper platter		*a copper platter*
un pull **de** laine		un pull **en** laine
a wool sweater		*a wool sweater*

When certain objects are used to serve or to contain something . . .

à is used to reflect the purpose of that object

                une tasse **à** café   *a coffee cup (meant for serving coffee)*

de is used to indicate that the container is filled

                une tasse **de** café   *a cup of coffee (with coffee in it)*

QUICK PRACTICE

III. Choisissez entre "depuis", "pendant" et "pour".

1. Elle habite ici _____ dix ans.

2. Nous comptons partir en France _____ une semaine.

3. _____ toute l'année scolaire, j'ai eu de bonnes notes.

4. Je ne vais pas travailler _____ le week-end.

5. _____ l'âge de six ans, ma soeur chante très bien.

IV. Mettez la préposition qui convient.

1. Je crois que _____ une semaine, je vais venir vous rendre visite.

2. Il fait très beau _____ printemps.

3. Donne-moi un verre _____ lait.

4. Je me sers _____ un stylo bleu pour écrire une lettre.

5. C'est un garçon _____ cheveux blonds.

6. J'ai lu ce livre _____ deux jours.

7. Ils ont voyagé _____ train pour venir ici.

8. J'admire ta nouvelle robe _____ satin.

9. J'ai appris à jouer _____ piano lorsque j'avais sept ans.

10. Elle parle toujours _____ voix basse, et je ne la comprends pas.

V. Traduisez les phrases suivantes.

1. I am looking for a car.

2. These tea cups are beautiful.

3. He speaks in a loud voice.

4. I have been traveling since yesterday.

5. The English teacher is not here today.

Conjunctions
Conjonctions

Conjunctions are words that connect two parts of a sentence. They fall into two categories: conjunctions of coordination and conjunctions of subordination.

- **Principal conjunctions of coordination**
  Conjunctions of coordination are used to reflect addition or explanation: **et, aussi, car**. Their function is to connect

  - elements that have the same purpose: **Le médecin et le patient sont ici.**
  - phrases that are similar in nature: **Le médecin est pressé et le patient veut partir.**

or	*now, but*	**mais**	*but*	**ou**	*or*
donc	*therefore*	**et**	*and*	**ni**	*neither/nor*
car*	*because*				
cependant, toutefois	*however*				
néanmoins	*however, nevertheless*				
parce que	*because*				

***Car** is never placed at the beginning of a sentence.

Jean **et** Margot aiment lire.	*Jean and Margot like to read.*
Je veux voyager, **or** je n'ai pas d'argent.	*I want to travel but I don't have money.*
Il aime voyager **mais** il est trop occupé.	*He likes to travel but he is too busy.*
Nous allons à la plage **ou** au parc.	*We go to the beach or the park.*
Je pense **donc** je suis.	*I think, therefore I am.*
Elle n'aime **ni** le thé **ni** le café.	*She likes neither tea nor coffee.*
Elle n'est pas ici **car** elle est malade.	*She isn't here because she is ill.*
Elle aime chanter; **cependant** elle n'est pas célèbre.	*She likes to sing; however she isn't famous.*

- **Principal conjunctions of subordination**

   Conjunctions of subordination often reflect comparison, cause, opposition, or time: **comme, puisque, bien que, lorsque.**

   Their function is to connect a principal clause to a subordinate clause.

comme	*as, like*	**quand***	*when*
pendant que	*while, during*	**dès que***	*as soon as*
lorsque*	*when*	**aussitôt que***	*as soon as*
avant que*	*before*	**après que**	*after*
ainsi que	*as well as*	**puisque**	*seeing that*
tandis que	*whereas*	**à moins que***	*unless*
bien que*	*although*	**quoique***	*although*
malgré que*	*although*		

   - **bien que, quoique, malgré que, avant que, à moins que** are followed by the subjunctive mood. (See Chapter 11.)
   - when using **quand, lorsque, aussitôt que,** and **dès que,** both sides of the sentence are conjugated in the same tense, except in the future when both the future tense and the future perfect can be used. (See Chapter 10.)

QUICK PRACTICE

VI. Refaites les phrases suivantes au passé composé ou à l'imparfait en ajoutant *lorsque, quand, puisque, tandis que, après que*:

1. (*tandis que*)   Delphine/aller/au cinéma/Paulette/aller/chez ses amis.

2. (*après que*)   Je/voir/le film/maman/m'offrir le livre.

3. (*lorsque*)   Patrick/venir/il/apporter/un dessert.

4. (*puisque*)   Elle/manger/elle/avoir faim.

5. (*quand*)   Le train/arriver/l'horloge/sonner.

Les prépositions

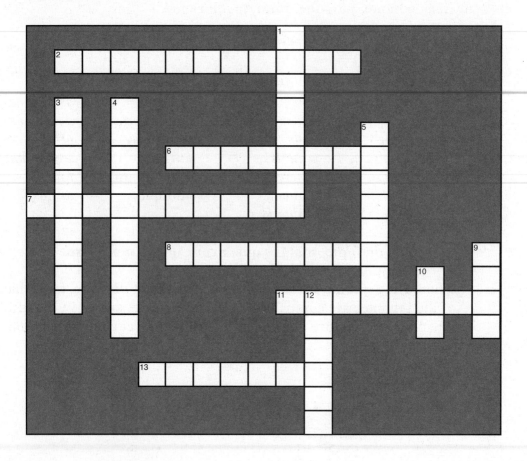

Across

2. I miss you (3 words)

6. Il _____ lire (apprendre—2 words)

7. Vous _____ lire (2 words)

8. To wait for

11. Behind

13. Je _____ parler (2 words)

Down

1. Il _____ fermer la porte (oublier)

3. By car (2 words)

4. Vous _____ travailler (continuer)

5. By heart (2 words)

9. At the home of

10. As of

12. Toward (abstract)

Culture Capsule 13

L'ancêtre du tennis moderne est le jeu de paume. Ce dernier était considéré comme "le jeu des rois et le roi des jeux". Il a été inventé en France pendant le Moyen Âge. Au début, il se jouait avec une balle et la paume de la main, d'où son nom. Plus tard, on envoie la balle toujours avec la paume de la main mais celle-ci est couverte d'un gant qui la protège. Une raquette de bois est introduite mais ce n'est qu'au XVIème siècle que l'on joue avec une raquette de bois et de cordage. Par contre, le filet est introduit dès le XVème siècle pour remplacer la corde qui divisait la salle de jeux en deux parties. La corde provoquait beaucoup de discussions car il était difficile de voir si la balle avait passé au-dessus ou au-dessous. Au début du XVème siècle, il y avait près de 2000 salles de jeu de paume à Paris.

Le premier championnat de France de tennis a lieu à Paris en 1801. En 1928, le stade Roland-Garros est inauguré. Aujourd'hui, Roland-Garros est l'un des tournois les plus prestigieux de la saison.

Le mot *tennis* lui-même vient du vieux français *tenetz* (aujourd'hui *tenez*). A l'époque, avant d'envoyer la balle, on prévenait son adversaire en criant *tenetz*. Ce mot fut déformé en passant en Angleterre pour devenir finalement *tennis*.

Les Points:

zéro (*love* en anglais).	On dit que le mot anglais *love* viendrait du français *l'oeuf* qui a la forme d'un zéro.
quinze	fifteen
trente	thirty
quarante	forty

VOCABULAIRE

l'ancêtre	*the ancestor*
une corde	*a rope*
un tas de	*a lot of*
le filet	*the net*
à l'époque	*at that time*
prévenait	*warned*

20

Comparative and Superlative

The Comparative
Le comparatif

As its name indicates, the comparative is used to compare the quality of two things. It is used with an adjective and with some adverbs. There are three categories of comparatives:

- **Comparative of equality/Comparatif d'égalité** ➔ (=) aussi

> **Subject + verb être + AUSSI + adjective + que + noun**

Sébastien est aussi grand que toi.

> **Subject + any verb + AUSSI + adverb + que + noun**

Sébastien parle aussi intelligemment que toi.

248

- **Comparative of superiority/Comparatif de supériorité** → (=) plus

> **Subject + verb être + PLUS + adjective + que + noun**

Simone est plus petite que Pierre.

> **Subject + any verb + PLUS + adverb + que + noun**

Simone court plus vite que Pierre.

- **Comparative of inferiority/Comparatif d'infériorité** → (=) moins

> **Subject + verb être + MOINS + adjective + que + noun**

Vous êtes moins curieux que moi.

> **Subject + any verb + MOINS + adverb + que + noun**

Vous sortez moins souvent que moi.

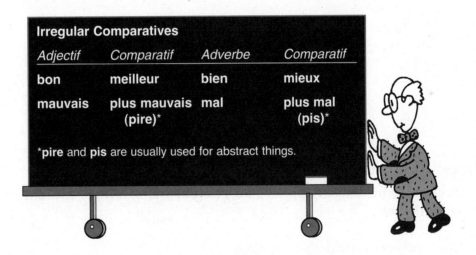

Irregular Comparatives

Adjectif	Comparatif	Adverbe	Comparatif
bon	meilleur	bien	mieux
mauvais	plus mauvais (pire)*	mal	plus mal (pis)*

*pire and pis are usually used for abstract things.

Colette est bonne en chimie, mais Julie est meilleure.
Colette is good in chemistry, but Julie is better.

André écrit mieux que Paul.
André writes better than Paul.

Elle est mauvaise en calcul, mais son frère est pire.
She is bad in calculus, but her brother is worse.

- **Quantities** → autant de—plus de—moins de—autant que

Subject + verb + AUTANT + DE + noun + que + noun *or* pronoun

Nous avons autant de livres que vous.
We have as many books as you.

Didier a autant d'argent que Claire.
Didier has as much money as Claire

Subject + verb + PLUS + DE + noun + que + noun *or* pronoun

Josette a plus de patience que Charles.
Josette has more patience than Charles.

Subject + verb + MOINS + DE + noun + que + noun *or* pronoun

Ils ont moins de devoirs que nous.
They have less homework than we do.

Subject + verb + AUTANT + que + noun *or* pronoun

Je voyage autant que lui.
I travel as much as he does.

QUICK PRACTICE

I. Mettez les phrases suivantes au comparatif selon les indications entre parenthèses:

1. (+) Elizabeth danse /bien/Céline.

2. (=) Je suis /élégante/toi.

3. (=) Le professeur de français a/patience/le professeur de biologie.

4. (–) Maman n'est pas/fatiguée/papa.

5. (=) Nous mangeons/lui.

II. Conversation: avec un copain ou une copine, comparez ce que vous avez ou ce que vos n'avez pas.

Modèle: crayons—Tu as plus de crayons que moi *ou* Tu as moins de crayons que moi. *ou* Tu as autant de crayons que moi. (Possibilités: livres, amis, professeurs, devoirs, etc.)

III. Choisissez entre "aussi" et "autant":

Modèle: Il est _____ intelligent que sa soeur.—Il est aussi intelligent que sa soeur.
J'étudie _____ que toi.—J'étudie autant que toi.

1. Il a _____ de livres que moi.

2. Catherine est _____ jolie que Suzanne.

3. Nous voyageons _____ souvent que vous.

4. Nous aimons l'opéra _____ que le ballet.

5. Rolande travaille _____ que Pierre.

The Superlative
Le superlatif

The superlative is formed by adding the definite articles (**le**, **la**, or **les**) before the adverbs of comparison **plus** or **moins**. If there is a complement that follows, the preposition **de** precedes the complement.

• **When the superlative demonstrates superiority**

definite article + **plus** + adjective + noun + DE (du, etc.) + complement
(most)

la	plus	belle maison		
la	plus	belle maison	du	village

• **When the superlative demonstrates inferiority**

definite article + **moins** + adjective + noun + DE (du, etc.) + complement
(least)

la	moins	grande maison		
la	moins	grande maison	du	village

- **If the adjective comes after the noun, the definite article must be repeated**

> Le garcon le plus intelligent de la classe
> *The most intelligent boy in the class*

- **There are adjectives that precede the noun when using a superlative**

Adjectives that are usually placed before the noun, such as **grand**, **beau**, **petit**, **bon**, **nouveau**, **long**, can be placed before the noun in a superlative sentence.

Compare		
	La plus **belle** maison	*The most beautiful house*
	La maison la plus **moderne**	*The most modern house*
	Le plus **long** discours	*The longest speech*
	Le discours le plus **ennuyeux**	*The most boring speech*

- **The superlative can be used after a verb**

> Denise travaille le moins ici.
> *Denise works the least here.*

> Denise a le moins de travail ici.
> *Denise has the least amount of work here.*

Irregular Superlatives

Adjectif	Superlatif	Adverbe	Superlatif
bon	le meilleur	bien	le mieux
	la meilleure		la mieux
	les meilleurs(es)		les mieux
mauvais	le (les) plus mauvais		
	la (les) plus mauvaise(s)		
	le (la) pire*		
	les pires		
petit	le(s) plus petit(s)		
	la plus petite		
	les plus petites		
	le, la (les) moindre(s)*		

*pire and moindre are used in the abstract sense only.

Ma mère fait la meilleure tarte aux pommes!	My mother makes the best apple pie!
C'est Lucie qui cuisine le mieux.	It is Lucie who cooks the best.
Paul est le mieux préparé pour l'examen.	Paul is the best prepared for the test.
C'est la pire des idées.	It is the worst of all ideas. (abstract)
Carole est la plus mauvaise élève.	Carole is the worst student. (concrete)
Je suis la plus petite de la famille.	I am the smallest in the family. (concrete)
C'est le moindre de mes soucis.	It's the least of my worries.

QUICK PRACTICE

IV. Vous discutez avec un copain ou une copine au sujet de votre voyage à Tahiti. Il ou elle vous répond en se servant de superlatifs:

Modèle: Comment était le taxi de l'aéroport à l'hôtel? (chauffeur/imprudent)
C'était le chauffeur le plus imprudent de l'île!

1. Est-ce que tu as aimé ton agence de voyage? (bonne)

   C'était la _____ de la ville.

2. Comment était le dîner en avion? (mauvais)

   C'était le _____ de mes vacances.

3. Quand tu es arrivé(e), qui t'a accueilli(e) à l'aéroport? (hôtesse/belle)

   C'était la _____ de l'aéroport.

4. Comment était ton hôtel? (élégant)

   C'était l'_____ de la ville.

5. Comment était la plage de l'hôtel? (calme)

   C'était la _____ de l'île.

V. Répondez aux questions suivantes en vous servant d'un superlatif:

Modèle: Ce musée est intéressant? Oui, c'est le musée le plus intéressant de la ville.
Cette fille est belle? Oui, c'est la plus belle fille de l'école.

1. Ce dessert est bon? Oui, c'est_____ du restaurant.

2. Ce garçon est sportif? Non , c'est _____ du lycée.

3. Ce professeur est intéressant? Oui, c'est _____du lycée.

4. Cette actrice est célèbre? Oui, c'est _____de Hollywood.

5. Ce livre est long? Non, c'est _____ de cet auteur.

More, Even More, As/Like/Since
Plus, Davantage, Comme

PLUS—MORE (ADVERB)

- **Pronunciation**

  In math, the s is pronounced: **3 plus 4 font sept.**

  In front of a name, the s is not pronounced: **Je ne vois plus Annie.**

  In the name of the verb plus-que-parfait, the s is pronounced.

  In the negative expression **ne ... plus**, the s is pronounced as a z to apply the liaison before a mute **h** or a vowel, but not before a consonant: **Il n'est plus ici.**

  At the end of a sentence, the s is not pronounced: **Il ne l'aime plus.**

  When the meaning is *even more* or **davantage**, and when **plus** is placed before pausing or as a last word, the s is pronounced: **Tu m'aimes? Eh bien, moi je t'aime encore plus.**
  In the expression **non plus** the s is not pronounced: **Elle n'aime pas le café, lui non plus.**

- **Expressions with plus (when the s is in boldface, it is pronounced)**

de plus	*moreover*	ni plus ni moins	*no more no less*
plu**s** ou moins	*more or less*	de plus en plus*	*more and more*
plus . . . plus*	*the more . . . the more*	d'autant plus . . . que	*all the more*

*The opposite of **plus . . . plus** is **moins . . . moins** (*the less . . . the less*) and the opposite of **de plus en plus** is **de moins en moins** (*less and less*).

DAVANTAGE—MORE/EVEN MORE (ADVERB)

- **Davantage is usually placed at the end of a sentence instead of plus. It can be used only with a verb.**

> **Il est riche, mais elle l'est davantage.**
> *He is rich, but she is even more rich.*

> **Tu m'aimes? Mais moi, je t'aime davantage.**
> *You love me, but I love you more.*

> **Vous devez travailler davantage.**
> *You must work more.*

- **Davantage de is used before a noun. It is the same as plus de.**

> **Mettez davantage de sel dans la soupe.** *Put more salt in the soup.*

- **With an adjective or an adverb, use plus.**

> **Cette histoire est plus intéressante** *(adj). This story is more interesting.*

> *Not* → ~~Cette histoire est davantage intéressante.~~

> **Bernard court plus vite** *(adv.).*

> *Not* → ~~Bernard court davantage vite.~~

COMME—AS/LIKE/SINCE (ADVERB OR CONJUNCTION)

- **When comme means *like***

> **Hélène, comme son frère, n'aime pas la tarte au citron.**
> *Hélène, like her brother, doesn't like lemon pie.*

> **Elle sourit comme La Joconde.**
> *She smiles like the Mona Lisa.*

- **When comme means *as* or *since***

> **Comme elle était en retard, elle n'a pas dîné avec nous.**
> *As (since) she was late, she didn't have dinner with us.*

- **Expressions with comme**

comme on peut s'y attendre	*as can be expected*
comme quoi	*this proves that*

Comme on pouvait s'y attendre, elle est arrivée en retard.
As could be expected, she arrived late.

Elle passe ses journées à jouer au golf. Comme quoi le travail ne l'intéresse pas.
She spends her days playing golf. This proves that working doesn't interest her.

QUICK PRACTICE

VI. Mettez plus, davantage, comme, ou l'une des expressions idiomatiques dans le passage suivant:

La petite Corinne ne veut _____ aller à l'école. Elle a décidé que les études, ce n'était pas pour elle! Elle pense que, _____ elle a déjà sept ans, cela suffit. _____ l'école, c'est bien pour son petit frère Denis qui a six ans, mais elle est trop grande pour ça! _____ Madame Desrosiers lui a dit de se taire, Corinne s'est mise en colère. Elle aime bien lire, mais elle aime jouer _____. Papa et maman, bien entendu, ne sont pas d'accord. Ils lui ont dit qu'il n'était pas question de quitter l'école et que _____ elle étudierait, _____ elle apprendrait, et _____ elle aimerait l'école. Ils lui ont aussi dit que, si elle insistait, elle ne pourrait _____ jouer avec ses amis. Maintenant, Corinne n'ose _____ demander de ne _____ aller en classe.

VII. Traduction

1. Nicole talks like a child.

2. As I was tired, I did not go out.

3. I travel a lot, but you travel more.

4. I have more patience than you do.

5. He doesn't play tennis. Me neither.

```
K  D  N  D  S  B  K  W  Z  I  O  E  U  C  K
L  E  M  E  I  L  L  E  U  R  J  U  L  N  T
E  U  Q  T  N  A  T  U  A  G  U  Q  E  R  J
O  M  W  E  U  Q  X  U  E  I  M  S  P  H  M
Z  A  C  F  G  U  I  J  N  C  H  U  I  B  E
I  F  O  B  L  R  G  D  H  G  L  L  R  A  N
I  Z  C  L  K  Q  V  E  G  A  I  P  E  H  E
S  P  V  F  Q  B  D  M  U  L  S  O  J  R  G
S  U  L  P  N  E  S  U  L  P  E  D  D  G  I
D  A  V  A  N  T  A  G  E  E  V  N  T  M  G
K  B  O  A  J  R  P  L  T  Y  I  V  X  B  X
M  T  I  C  B  P  G  B  O  O  M  T  J  G  Q
V  T  N  A  N  S  Z  T  M  B  Y  X  D  O  S
X  N  S  O  Q  T  V  E  F  F  S  Y  V  K  F
Q  N  H  Y  N  X  L  G  X  J  F  Z  A  K  J
```

AUTANT QUE   LE MEILLEUR   MIEUX QUE

DAVANTAGE   LE MOINDRE   PLUS QUE

DE PLUS EN PLUS   LE PIRE

Culture Capsule 14

Lorsque l'on offre des fleurs en France, il faut qu'il y en ait un nombre impair . . . sauf 13 qui a la réputation de porter malheur, comme dans plusieurs autres pays! Et attention, certaines fleurs sont associées aux funérailles: les chrysanthèmes et les lis. Eviter aussi les fleurs blanches car celles-ci font partie de la cérémonie nuptiale.

Lorsque l'on va au restaurant, on dit au garçon ou à la serveuse "bonjour/bonsoir Monsieur, bonjour/bonsoir Madame". Et quand on appelle ces derniers, on dit "Monsieur/Madame, s'il vous plaît". Bien entendu, si la serveuse est très jeune, on dit "Mademoiselle".

A table, on tient la fourchette dans la main gauche et le couteau dans la main droite, et on les garde en main pendant que l'on mange. On ne met jamais les mains sur les genoux car elles doivent demeurer visibles pendant tout le repas. Cependant, il ne faut pas mettre les coudes sur la table.

En France, on ne téléphone pas après 22 heures, sauf à la famille ou aux amis intimes.

En général, à la fin d'un repas au restaurant, on partage l'addition, sauf si l'un des convives insiste pour payer. Par contre, un homme invite toujours la femme qui l'accompagne, à moins qu'il ne s'agisse d'un groupe d'adolescents. Dans ce cas, tout le monde partage l'addition.

VOCABULAIRE

porter malheur	*to bring bad luck*
nombre impair	*uneven number*
lis	*lily*
les genoux	*the knees*
demeurer	*to remain*
les coudes	*the elbows*

21

The Negative

Que savez-vous déjà?
What Do You Know Already?

Each of the following sentences is incorrect. Can you correct them?

1. Elle n'a étudié pas.

2. Nous nous ne réveillons pas avant dix heures.

3. Ne pas courez; c'est dangereux.

4. Je ne vais finir pas avant six heures.

5. Ils n'ont pas des devoirs.

6. Tu ne jamais écoutes le professeur.

7. Il ne rien fait!

8. Ne personne est arrivé en retard.

The Simple Negative
La négation simple

SIMPLE TENSE				
Affirmative	**subject**	ne	**verb**	pas*
	Ils	ne	dansent	pas.
Negative interrogative	ne	**verb**	**subject**	pas
inversion**	Ne	dansent-	ils	pas?

*The other form of **ne . . . pas** is **ne . . . point**. It is usually used in literature. Another more insistent form is **ne . . . pas du tout**, which means *not at all.*
For the interrogative with **est-ce que use **est-ce qu'** before the negative affirmative.

COMPOUND TENSE

Affirmative	subject	ne/n'	auxiliary verb	pas	past participle
	Ils	n'	ont	pas	dansé.
	Nous	ne	sommes	pas	allés.

Negative	n'/ne	auxiliary verb	subject	pas	past participle
interrogative	N'	avons	nous	pas	dansé?
inversion*	Ne	sommes	nous	pas	allés?

*For the negative/interrogative with **est-ce que**, use **est-ce qu'** before the negative affirmative.

REFLEXIVE VERBS—SIMPLE TENSES

Affirmative	subject	ne	reflexive pronoun	verb		pas
	Ils	ne	se	dépêchent		pas.

Negative						
interrogative	ne	reflexive pronoun	verb	subject		pas
inversion*	Ne	se	dépêchent-	ils		pas?

*For the interrogative with **est-ce que** use **est-ce qu'** before the negative affirmative.

REFLEXIVE VERBS—COMPOUND TENSES

Affirmative	subject	ne	reflexive pronoun	auxiliary verb	pas	past participle
	Ils	ne	se	sont	pas	dépêchés.

Negative		reflexive pronoun	auxiliary verb			past participle
interrogative	ne	pronoun	verb	subject		participle
inversion*	Ne	se	sont-	ils	pas	dépêchés?

*For the interrogative with **est-ce que** use **est-ce qu'** before the negative affirmative.

When answering a question posed in the negative-interrogative, the positive answer is **si** instead of **oui**.

N'as-tu pas vu ce film? Si, je l'ai vu!
Didn't you see this movie? Yes, I did.

Where do you place the negative when two verbs follow each other, as in **Je pense acheter ce livre?** (*I think that I will buy this book.*) The two parts of the negative surround the conjugated verb: **Je ne pense pas acheter ce livre.** (*I don't think I will buy this book*)

And what happens to the negative in the infinitive form? **Ne** and **pas** are not separated, they are placed together before the infinitive.

Il m'a dit de **ne pas** oublier notre rendez-vous.
*He told me **not to** forget our date.*

In the negative form, **un, une**, and **des** become **de:**

J'ai **des** pommes. → Je n'ai pas **de** pommes.

Ils ont **un** bateau. → Ils n'ont pas **de** bateau.

> **TIP**
> **When is pas omitted? After the verbs** cesser, pouvoir, oser, **and** savoir **and before an infinitive,** pas **may be omitted, but not necessarily.**
>
> Il n'ose répondre.
> or   *He dares not answer.*
> Il n'ose pas répondre.

QUICK PRACTICE

I. Mettez les phrases suivantes à la forme négative:

1. Elle a acheté des bijoux.

2. Il écrit une lettre à sa fiancée.

3. As-tu vu les voisins?

4. Etaient-ils fatigués après le voyage?

5. Elle veut voyager en été.

6. Nous aimons la salade.

7. J'ai rencontré Maurice au café.

8. Il travaille dans un supermarché.

9. Ont-ils passé un examen hier?

10. Je peux conduire.

II. Le petit Rémi refuse d'obéir à ses parents. Il répond négativement aux questions que lui pose sa mère.

1. Vas-tu finir ta soupe?

2. As-tu appris ta leçon?

3. Tu veux m'aider à faire la vaisselle?

4. As-tu téléphoné à tante Lucie pour la remercier?

5. Vas-tu te dépêcher?

III. Traduisez:

1. He says not to answer.

2. She told me not to go to the movies.

3. We can't see the screen (*l'écran*).

4. Didn't they go out?

5. Aren't you coming? Yes!

Negative Expressions
Expressions négatives

Remember that negative expressions always contain two components. If **ne pas** is not used, **pas** must be omitted.

AFFIRMATIVE	NEGATIVE
OUI	NON
↓	↓

- **Tout/quelque chose**
  (*Everything/something*)

  Elle comprend tout.
  She understands everything.

  Elle a tout compris.
  She understood everything.

Ne … rien/rien … ne*
(*Nothing*)

Elle ne comprend rien.
She doesn't understand anything.

Elle n'a rien compris.
She didn't understand anything.

*All asterisks: see *Special Cases*, page 265.

- **Toujours/souvent/parfois/**
  Quelquefois/de temps en temps
  (Still or always/often/sometimes/
  from time to time)

  Ne ... jamais*
  (Never)

  Nous allons souvent au ciné.
  We often go to the movies.

  Nous n'allons jamais au ciné.
  We never go to the movies.

  Ils ont toujours voyagé en hiver.
  They have always traveled in winter.

  Ils n'ont jamais voyagé en hiver.
  They have never traveled in winter.

- **Quelqu'un/tout le monde**
  (Someone/everybody or everyone)

  Ne ... personne/personne ... ne/
  nul(le) ne*
  (No one/nobody/not ... anyone)

  Il y a quelqu'un ici.
  There is someone here.

  Il n'y a personne ici.
  There is no one here.

  J'ai vu quelqu'un chez eux.
  I saw someone at their house.

  Je n'ai vu personne chez eux.
  I didn't see anyone at their house.

- **Encore/toujours**
  (Again/still)

  Ne ... plus
  (No more, no longer, not ... anymore)

  Il est encore en France.
  He is still in France.

  Il n'est plus en France.
  He is no longer in France.

  Nous avons toujours correspondu.
  We have always corresponded.

  Nous n'avons plus correspondu.
  We didn't correspond anymore.

- **Dèjá**
  (Already)

  Ne ... pas encore
  (Not yet)

  Il est déjà 9 heures.
  It is already 9 o'clock.

  Il n'est pas encore 9 heures.
  It isn't yet 9 o'clock.

  Tu as déjà fini.
  You have already finished.

  Tu n'as pas encore fini.
  You have not finished yet.

- **Très/beaucoup**
  (Very/ a lot/much)

  Ne ... guère
  (Hardly/barely)

  Ils voyagent beaucoup.
  They travel a lot.

  Ils ne voyagent guère.
  They hardly travel.

- **Chacun(e)/chaque/plusieurs/ quelques**
  (Each/ every/several/ some)

Aucun(e) ... ne
(No/none)

Chaque enfant aime jouer ici.
Every child likes to play here.

Aucun enfant n'aime jouer ici.
No child likes to play here.

Chaque élève a étudié.
Every student studied.

Aucun élève n'a étudié.
No student studied.

Quelques enfants jouent ici.
Some children play here.

Aucun enfant ne joue ici.
No child plays here.

Quelques livres sont intéressants.
Some books are interesting.

Aucun livre n'est intéressant.
No book is interesting.

- **Quelques-uns (unes)/ Quelques-uns (unes) de**
  (Some /some of the)

Aucun(e) ... ne* Aucun(e) de ... ne
(None/none of the)

Quelques-uns de ces films sont bons.
Some of these movies are good.

Aucun de ces films n'est bon.
None of these movies is good.

Quelques-uns des élèves sont venus.
Some of the students came.

Aucun des élèves n'est venu.
None of the students came.

- **Partout**
  (Everywhere)

Ne ... nulle part
(Anywhere/nowhere)

Il cherche partout.
He searches everywhere.

Il ne cherche nulle part.
He doesn't search anywhere.

J'ai balayé partout.
I swept everywhere.

Je n'ai balayé nulle part.
I didn't sweep anywhere.

- **Et/ou ... ou**
  (And/or)

Ne ... ni ... ni*
(Either ... or/neither ... nor)

Ils aiment le café et le thé.
They like coffee and tea.

Ils n'aiment ni le café ni le thé.
They like neither coffee nor tea.

- **Aussi**
  (Also/too)

Non plus
(Neither)

Elle étudie trop. Moi aussi.
She studies too much. Me too.

Elle n'étudie pas trop. Moi non plus.
She doesn't study too much. Me neither.

SPECIAL CASES

* **Rien ne** is used as the subject of a sentence.

    Rien ne m'intéresse. *Nothing interests me.*

* **Jamais** by itself also means *never*.

    Es-tu allé à l'opéra? Jamais. *Did you go to the opera? Never.*

    Jamais can also be translated into *ever*.

    As-tu jamais vu cet opéra? *Did you ever see this opera?*

* **Personne ne** is used as the subject of a sentence.

    Personne n'est arrivé à l'heure. *No one came on time.*

* **Aucun** is always used in the third person singular.

* **Ne ... ni ... ni:** Whenever the negative expression **Ne ... ni ... ni** is used with verbs that indicate likes or dislikes such as **aimer, préférer, détester,** the article must be used before the noun, as in the example. However, when another verb is used, the article is *not* used before the noun.

    Compare: **Je n'aime ni le café ni le thé.** → **Je ne veux ni café ni thé.**

    When the expression **Ne ... ni ... ni** is used with two verbs, the order of the negatives is different.

    Elle **ne chante ni ne danse** devant ses copains parce qu'elle est timide. *She neither sings nor dances in front of her friends because she is shy.*

    In compound tenses, the placement of **Ne ... ni ... ni** is as follows:

Subject + N'+ aux. verb + past participle + Ni + noun + Ni + noun

    Il   n'a   vu   ni Pierre ni   Edmond.

Subject + N' + aux. verb + Ni + past participle + Ni + past participle

    Je   n'ai   **ni**   chanté   **ni**   dansé.

TIP

Ne ... que *(only)* is an expression that indicates a restriction. It is not a true negative.

Je n'aime que toi. *I love only you.*
Je n'ai vu que Monique. *I saw only Monique.*

IV. Eliane et Simone sont deux soeurs. Chaque fois qu'Eliane dit quelque chose, Simone dit exactement le contraire. Vous êtes Simone!

Modèle: Je prends toujours le métro. ➔ Moi, je ne prends jamais le métro.

1. Je perds toujours quelque chose.

2. J'ai rencontré quelqu'un au supermarché.

3. J'ai acheté un cahier et un livre.

4. J'aime le poisson et le poulet.

5. J'étudie beaucoup.

6. Je regarde parfois la télévision.

7. J'ai encore de l'argent.

8. Tout me plaît ici.

9. J'ai toujours aimé la musique rock.

10. J'ai quelques chapeaux.

V. Traduisez les phrases suivantes.

1. Nothing is interesting in this book.

2. Did you ever go to Alaska?

3. I did not buy a new car. Me neither.

4. They met only Sara.

5. No one saw Jean-Claude yesterday.

6. She doesn't understand anything.

7. We neither bought pencils nor pens.

8. I hardly see the director.

9. I didn't go anywhere yesterday.

10. I have not yet received the flowers.

Multiple Negatives
Négations multiples

It is important to remember that **pas** is not used in a multiple negative.

- **jamais + plus, personne, rien**

  Je **ne** l'ai **jamais plus** rencontré à la plage.
  I never met him again at the beach.

  Elle **ne** voit **jamais personne**.
  She never sees anyone.

  Il **ne** fait **jamais rien** en classe.
  He never does anything in class.

- **rien + personne**

  Elle **n'a rien** offert à **personne**.
  She didn't offer anything to anyone.

- **plus + rien**

  Je **n'ai plus rien** acheté dans ce magasin.
  I no longer bought anything in this store.

- **plus + personne**

  Ils **n'**invitent **plus personne.**
  They no longer invite anyone.

- **plus + jamais**

  Je te promets de **ne plus jamais** mentir.
  I promise you that I will never lie again.

- **jamais + plus + personne**

  Je ne veux **jamais plus** voir **personne.**
  I never want to see anyone again.

- **jamais + plus + rien**

  Ils **ne** font **jamais plus rien**.
  They never do anything anymore.

VI. Mettez à la forme négative:

Modèle: Il veut toujours inviter quelqu'un.—Il ne veut jamais inviter personne.

1. Elle offre toujours du café à tout le monde.

2. Nous voyons toujours quelqu'un chez les voisins.

3. Il y a toujours quelque chose d'intéressant à la télé.

4. Paul fait toujours quelque chose en classe.

5. Quelqu'un est toujours absent.

Someone, Something, No One, Nothing
Quelqu'un de, Quelque chose de, Personne de, Rien de

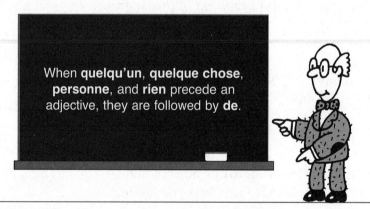

When **quelqu'un**, **quelque chose**, **personne**, and **rien** precede an adjective, they are followed by **de**.

Quelqu'un de + adjectif	→	*someone + adjective*
Quelque chose de + adjectif	→	*something + adjective*
Personne de + adjectif	→	*no one + adjective*
Rien de + adjectif	→	*nothing + adjective*

Elle connaît **quelqu'un d'**important.	*She knows someone important.*
J'ai vu **quelque chose de** drôle.	*I saw something funny.*
Il n'y a **personne de** libre maintenant.	*There is no one (who is) free now.*
Nous n'avons **rien** vu **d'**intéressant.	*We didn't see anything interesting.*

After **quelqu'un de, quelque chose de, personne de,** and **rien de,** the adjective is always in the *masculine singular* form.

In the compound tenses, **quelqu'un, quelque chose, personne,** and **rien** precede the auxiliary verb, and **de** comes between the auxiliary verb and the past participle.

QUICK PRACTICE

VII. Mettez "quelque chose de", "quelqu'un de", "personne de" ou "rien de".

Modèle: Il ne fait _____ de difficile.—Il ne fait rien de difficile.

1. Elle a vu _____ très beau à la soirée.

2. As-tu rencontré _____ intéressant?

3. Nous ne faisons _____ important cette semaine.

4. Je ne connais _____ très riche.

5. Françoise est _____ célèbre dans cette ville.

La négation

```
N X I C T R A P E L L U N S M
E P L J H S E B D X Z C C Q O
P D M M D R R Z E G T O X G I
A B H K E S W U S U Q M I T N
S Y P U P E R S O N N E N E O
Z F G I Q V Q T H J H F A U N
Z E Y S T U U W C Y U Q I R P
N D M S T D E S E J E O V D L
K K K U S Z L L U P W Q T T U
E X L A M R R U Q W L U G R S
N O P I O A Y J L U S C I K C
Q E Q O L O Q H E I U E H P P
N I Q M U A U C U N N N T K J
S H B U W X T R Q E U Z D P V
T O U J O U R S F O T W Y E P
```

AUCUN	NE PAS	QUELQUE CHOSE DE
MOI AUSSI	NE PAS DU TOUT	QUELQU'UN DE
MOI NON PLUS	NULLE PART	RIEN
NE GUERE	PERSONNE NE	TOUJOURS

Culture Capsule 15

La Bretagne, région de l'ouest de la France, s'appelait à l'origine l'Armorique. Vers 850 avant Jésus-Christ, des Celtes viennent s'y établir. Leur religion est le druidisme. Lorsque les romains envahissent la Gaule, ils interdisent le druidisme et plus tard, à l'avènement de l'ère chrétienne, cette interdiction continue car la religion celte est traitée de barbare. Cependant le druidisme continue clandestinement. Au Vème siècle après Jésus-Christ, les Bretons d'Angleterre, chassés de leur île par la guerre, s'établissent en Armorique.

Aujourd'hui, le Breton (*Brezhoneg* en Breton) est la troisième langue celtique parlée dans le monde, après le gallois et l'irlandais. En 1805, Napoléon Premier crée l'Académie Celtique qui associe la langue et la culture bretonnes. En 1864, le grand-oncle du futur Général de Gaulle publie un "Appel aux Celtes" qui encourage la renaissance linguistique de la Bretagne. Le 17 décembre 2004, le conseil régional de Bretagne reconnait officiellement le breton et le gallo comme *«langues de la Bretagne, au côté de la langue française »*.

Une personne qui parle Breton est dite "bretonnante" ou "brittophone". Quoique le nombre de locuteurs ait diminué, beaucoup de Bretons aujourd'hui parlent toujours, avec le français, leur langue maternelle. La plupart de ceux qui parlent Breton se trouvent dans la région de Basse-Bretagne. Il existe d'ailleurs un certain nombre d'écoles bilingues où l'on apprend les deux langues. Ceux qui étudient le breton sont ravis de savoir qu'il n'existe que cinq verbes irréguliers: aller, avoir, être, faire et savoir!

Breton	Français
da	ton
mor	mer
penn	tête, extrémité
Breizh	Bretagne
danteg	dents
demat	bonjour

Finalement, à l'intérieur des alliances bretonnes on trouve l'inscription "atao feal da viken" qui veut dire "toujours fidèle à jamais".

VOCABULAIRE

alliance	*wedding band*
s'établissent	*settle*
le gallois	*gaelic*
ravis	*delighted*
qui veut dire	*which means*
fidèle à jamais	*forever faithful*

22

Interrogatives

Que savez-vous déjà?
What Do You Know Already?

Change the following sentences into the interrogative using (a) Est-ce que, and (b) the inverted form.

1. Ils travaillent beaucoup.

   (a) _____

   (b) _____

2. Nous avons faim.

   (a) _____

   (b) _____

3. Tu es allé au cinéma.

   (a) _____

   (b) _____

4. Il a vendu sa voiture.

   (a) _____

   (b) _____

5. Elle parle à ses amis.

   (a) _____

   (b) _____

The Simple Interrogative
La forme interrogatif
• Simple tenses

Est-ce que + affirmative	ou	Inversion verb + subject
Est-ce que vous avez un imper? *Do you have a raincoat?*		Avez-vous un imper? *Do you have a raincoat?*

For the third person singular (**elle** or **il**), if the verb ends with a vowel, a **t** is used between two hyphens before the personal pronoun:

Est-ce qu'elle aime le soufflé?   **Aime-t-elle le soufflé?**
Does she like the soufflé?

Est-ce qu'il parle chinois?   **Parle-t-il chinois?**
Does he speak Chinese?

When a noun or a name precedes the verb, the question will be:

Est-ce que Colette aime soufflé?   **Colette aime-t-elle le soufflé?**
Does Colette like the soufflé?

Est-ce qu'Antoine parle chinois?   **Antoine parle-t-il chinois?**
Does Antoine speak Chinese?

The inversion is usually not used with the first person singular **je** *except* for the verbs **avoir**, **être**, **pouvoir**, and **devoir**.

Est-ce que j'ai le temps de finir?   **Ai-je le temps de finir?**
Do I have time to finish?

Est-ce que je suis en retard?   **Suis-je en retard?**
Am I late?

Est-ce que je peux ouvrir la porte?   **Puis-je* ouvrir la porte?**
Can I open the door?

Est-ce que je dois écrire un message?   **Dois-je écrire un message?**
Must I write a message?

*In the inverted form **je peux** becomes **puis-je**.

- **Compound tenses**

Affirmative

subject	auxiliary verb/past participle	object
Il	a vendu	le parapluie.
He	*sold*	*the umbrella.*

Interrogative

aux.verb/subject	past participle	object
A-t-il	vendu	le parapluie?
Did he	*sell*	*the umbrella?*

noun/aux.verb/subject	past participle	object
Le marchand a-t-il	vendu	le parapluie?
Did the merchant	*sell*	*the umbrella?*

What happens when there are two verbs in a row?

Elle veut acheter une robe.	→	**Veut-elle** acheter une robe?
She wants to buy a dress.		*Does she want to buy a dress?*
Elle a voulu acheter une robe.	→	**A-t-elle voulu** acheter une robe?
She wanted to buy a dress.		*Did she want to buy a dress?*
Claire a voulu acheter une robe.	→	Claire **a-t-elle voulu** acheter une robe?
Claire wanted to buy a dress.		*Did Claire want to buy a dress?*

- **Reflexive verbs**

Affirmative	*Interrogative*
Elle se couche à minuit.	**Se couche-t-elle** à minuit?
She goes to bed at midnight.	**Est-ce qu'elle** se couche à minuit?
	Does she go to bed at midnight?
Elle s'est couchée à minuit.	**S'est-elle couchée** à minuit?
She went to bed at midnight.	**Est-ce qu'elle s'est couchée à minuit?**
	Did she go to bed at midnight?

QUICK PRACTICE

I. Monsieur Duhamel est professeur de math. Imaginez les questions qu'il pose à son élève Jean-Paul d'après les réponses de ce dernier (*according to the answers of the latter*). **Utilisez l'inversion.**

Modèle: Non, je n'ai pas vu l'explication.—As-tu vu l'explication?

1. – Oui, j'ai étudié hier soir.

2. – Non, je n'ai pas compris la troisième partie.

3. – Oui, ma mère est professeur de math.

4. – Non, elle n'enseigne pas la trigonométrie.

5. – Non, elle ne m'a pas aidé.

6. – Vous voulez bien me l'expliquer? Oh, merci beaucoup monsieur!

II. Mettez à la forme interrogative.

Modèle: Elle sort souvent   (a) Est-ce qu'elle sort souvent?
                                (b) Sort-elle souvent?

1. Nous aimons les chocolats aux amandes.

2. Ils se sont réveillés à huit heures.

3. Alain a oublié le livre de biologie.

4. Jacqueline se couche tard.

5. Les enfants se sont dépêchés.

6. Elles veulent écouter les informations (*the news*).

7. Je peux sortir après le déjeuner.

8. Il a fait ses devoirs.

9. Elle achète des livres d'occasion.

10. Caroline a fait un beau voyage.

The Interrogative Adjective
L'adjectif interrogatif

The interrogative adjectives always agree in gender and number with the noun they modify.

MASCULINE SINGULAR	MASCULINE PLURAL	FEMININE SINGULAR	FEMININE PLURAL
Quel	Quels	Quelle	Quelles
Quel livre? *What book?*	**Quels livres?** *What books?*	**Quelle élève?** *What student?*	**Quelles élèves?** *What students?*

- In some cases, the interrogative adjective is separated from the noun by the verb **être**. However, this applies to things, not to people.

  Quel est ce bruit?   *What is this noise?*
  Qui est ce garçon?   *Who is this boy?*

- **Quel, Quels, Quelle, Quelles** also mean *what (a) + noun and/or adjective + exclamation point.*

  What a story!   **Quelle** histoire!
  What a pretty girl!   **Quelle** jolie fille!
  What problems!   **Quels** problèmes!

QUICK PRACTICE
III. Mettez l'adjectif interrogatif qui manque:

1. _____ maison est la plus chère?

2. _____ est votre nom?

3. A _____ élèves voulez-vous parler?

4. _____ problème est sérieux?

5. _____ livres allez-vous acheter?

The Interrogative Pronoun
Le pronom interrogatif

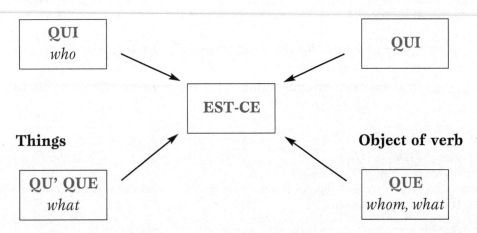

People

QUI
who

Things

QU' QUE
what

EST-CE

Subject of verb

QUI

Object of verb

QUE
whom, what

- When the question is about the identity of a **person**, and that person is the subject of the verb, the following are used

> Qui + verb   *or*   Qui est-ce qui + verb

Qui a vu ce film?
Who saw this movie?

Qui est-ce qui a vu ce film?
Who saw this movie?

- When the person is the object of the verb, the following are used

> Qui + inversion subject/verb   *or*   Qui est-ce que + subject + verb

Qui aimez-vous?
Whom do you love?

Qui est-ce que vous aimez?
Whom do you love?

- When the question is about the identity of a thing, and that thing is the subject of the verb, the following is used

> Qu' + est-ce qui + verb

Qu'est-ce qui est sur la table? Le livre est sur la table.
What is on the table? The book is on the table.

- When the thing is the object of the verb, the following are used

| Qu'/Que + inversion subject/verb *or* Qu'est-ce que + subject + verb |

Qu'est-ce que vous recommandez?   **Le soufflé au citron.**
What do you recommend?   *The lemon soufflé.*
Que recommandez-vous?   **Le soufflé au citron.**

TIP

Qui est-ce? *(Who is it?)*
Qu'est-ce que c'est? *(What is it?)*
Qu'est-ce que c'est que + noun? is an interrogative expression used to ask for a definition or an explanation.

> Qu'est-ce que c'est que "le tour de France"? Le tour de France est une compétition de cyclisme.
> *What is the Tour de France? The Tour de France is a cycling competition.*

Qu'est-ce qu'il y a? *(What's the matter?)*

> Qu'est-ce qu'il y a?   →   J'ai mal à la tête.
> *What is the matter?*   *I have a headache.*

Qui and Quoi
Qui et Quoi

After a preposition (**de, à, pour, avec, dans, derrière, devant,** etc.), **qui** is used for **people**, and **quoi** is used for **things**.

Avec qui allez-vous au Sénégal? Avec mes camarades de classe.
With whom are you going to Senegal? With my classmates.

Pour qui préparez-vous ce dessert? Pour mes amis.
For whom do you prepare this dessert? For my friends.

De qui parlez-vous? Du directeur.
Of whom are you speaking? Of the director.

Avec quoi peut-on se protéger de la pluie? Avec un parapluie.
With what can one be protected from the rain? With an umbrella.

Dans quoi avez vous mis les clés? Dans le tiroir.
In what did you put the keys? In the drawer.

A quoi pensez-vous? Je pense aux grandes vacances.
What are you thinking of? I think of summer vacation.

QUICK PRACTICE

IV. Choisissez *qui, que, qu'est-ce qui, qui est-ce qui, qu'* **ou** *quoi* **pour compléter les phrases suivantes:**

Modèle: _____ a écrit cette lettre? Valérie.

Qui/qui est-ce qui a écrit cette lettre?—Valérie (*in this case, both are applicable*).

_____ raconte ce film? Une aventure en Chine. *Réponse:* Que.

_____ ce film raconte? *Réponse:* Qu'est-ce que.

1. _____ tu as fait hier? J'ai joué au tennis.

2. _____ a ouvert la fenêtre? Le professeur.

3. _____ la journaliste a dit? Elle n'a rien dit.

4. _____ voulez-vous voir? Un film de science fiction.

5. _____ tu as rencontré à la soirée? Une vieille amie.

6. Avec _____ avez-vous voyagé? Avec Dorothée.

7. _____ ce tableau représente? Une scène de chasse.

8. De _____ parlez-vous? Des objets électroniques.

9. _____ veut aller en France en été? Jeanne.

10. _____ désirez-vous? un café s'il vous plait.

V. Posez les questions pour les réponses suivantes en remplaçant les mots en italiques par un pronom interrogatif:

Modèle: J'entends *quelqu'un.* Qui entendez-vous?

1. Nous mangeons *de la salade.*

2. *Le professeur* a posé la question.

3. Elle m'a offert *un livre* pour mon anniversaire.

4. J'ai rencontré *mes amis* au café.

5. *Le Sahara* est un désert.

The Interrogative Pronouns of Choice
Le pronoms interrogatifs de choix

MASCULINE SINGULAR	MASCULINE PLURAL	FEMININE SINGULAR	FEMININE PLURAL
Lequel *which one*	Lesquels *which ones*	Laquelle *which one*	Lesquelles *which ones*

Lequel des films avez-vous vu?	*Which one of the movies have you seen?*
Lesquels des films préférez-vous?	*Which ones of the movies do you prefer?*
Laquelle des questions est facile?	*Which one of the questions is easy?*
Lesquelles des villes sont grandes?	*Which ones of the cities are large?*

- **When lequel, laquelle, lesquels, lesquelles are preceded by the preposition à or de, the following changes occur**

à + lequel	= auquel	de + lequel	= duquel
à + laquelle	= à laquelle	de + laquelle	= de laquelle
à + lesquels	= auxquels	de + lesquels	= desquels
à + lesquelles	= auxquelles	de + lesquelles	= desquelles

  Il y a cinq étudiants ici; auquel voulez-vous parler?
  (parler **à** = *to speak to*)
  There are five students here; to which one do you want to speak?

  Il y a plusieurs jeunes filles ici; desquelles parlez-vous?
  (parler **de** = *to speak of*)
  There are several young women here; of which ones are you speaking?

- **With prepositions such as avec, pour, etc. there is no contraction**

  Il y a deux stylos ici; **avec** lequel vas-tu écrire?
  There are two pens here; with which one are you going to write?

  Les étudiants sont dans la salle de classe. Dans laquelle?
  The students are in the classroom. In which one?

QUICK PRACTICE

VI. Posez la question qui convient en vous servant d'une des formes de "lequel".

Modèle: Aimes-tu le livre?—Lequel?

1. Voici plusieurs chapeaux, madame, _____ préférez-vous?

2. La vendeuse montre quatre colliers à Julie, _____ des quatre veut-elle acheter?

3. De tous les colliers qu'elle a vus, _____ sont les moins chers?

4. Marc, regarde ces fleurs! _____ ?

5. Les robes sont originales. _____ ?

VII. Posez la question qui convient en vous servant d'une forme de "lequel" avec la préposition.

Modèle: Elle a envie d'un dessert.—Duquel?

1. Nous parlons à la jeune fille. _____ parlez-vous?

2. Nous parlons au professeur. _____ parlez-vous?

3. J'ai besoin d'un de ces stylos. _____ ?

4. L'enfant parle à l'oncle. _____ des oncles parle-t-il?

5. Elle se souvient des élèves. _____ ?

The Interrogative Adverbs
Le adverbes interrogatifs

The interrogative adverbs are **combien** (*how much, how many*), **comment** (*how*), **pourquoi** (*why*), **où** (*where*), and **quand** (*when*). They can either be followed by the inversion of the subject and the verb, or by the long form, using **est-ce que**.

Answers	Questions
Je vais au cinéma.	**Où allez-vous?**
	Où est-ce que vous allez?
I am going to the movies.	*Where are you going?*
J'ai acheté trois cartes.	**Combien de cartes avez-vous achetées?**
	Combien de cartes est-ce que vous avez achetées?
I bought three cards.	*How many cards did you buy?*
Les cartes coûtent un euro.	**Combien coûtent les cartes?**
	Combien est-ce que les cartes coûtent?
The cards cost one euro.	*How much do the cards cost?*
Claire conduit très bien.	**Comment Claire conduit-elle?**
	Comment est-ce que Claire conduit?
Claire drives very well.	*How does Claire drive?*
Il bâille parce qu'il a sommeil.	**Pourquoi bâille-t-il?**
	Pourquoi est-ce qu'il bâille?
He yawns because he is sleepy.	*Why is he yawning?*
Nous partons en janvier.	**Quand partez-vous?**
	Quand est-ce que vous partez?
We are leaving in January.	*When are you leaving?*

QUICK PRACTICE

VIII. Madame Vivier s'intéresse à ce que font les amis de sa fille Véronique. Elle pose beaucoup de questions!

1. Véronique: Oh, maman, tu sais, Michel part en Espagne.
   Mme Vivier: _____ part-il?
   V: Il part au mois de juillet.

2. M: _____ en Espagne va-t-il aller?
   V: À Madrid et à Barcelone.

3. M: _____ va-t-il y aller, en avion ou en voiture?
   V: En avion.

4. M: Avec _____ va-t-il y aller?
   V: Avec Pierre.

5. M: _____ de temps comptent-ils rester en Espagne?
   V: Trois semaines.

6. M: Trois semaines, c'est beaucoup. _____ ne vont-ils qu'à Madrid
   et Barcelone?
   V: Parce qu'ils ont des amis dans les deux villes.

7. M: _____ sont les amis espagnols de Michel et de Pierre?
   V: Je ne sais pas, je ne les connais pas.

8. M: _____ jour en juin partent-ils?
   V: Le premier juin, je crois.

9. M: _____ vont-ils revenir?
   V: Le 21 ou le 22 juin.

10. M: _____ va les accompagner à l'aéroport?
    V: Eh bien, maman, j'allais justement te demander de le faire!

MOTS CROISÉS
Les interrogatifs

Across
   6. Who (4 words)
   8. Where
   9. Which ones (masc.)
   10. With whom (2 words)

Down
   1. How
   2. How much
   3. Who is it (3 words)
   4. With what (2 words)
   5. When
   7. Of which one (masc.)

Culture Capsule 16

Quarante pour cent environ des mots anglais sont d'origine française, du moins, c'est ce que l'on dit! En voici quelques-uns qui font partie du vocabulaire de tous les jours:

- I am going to the **barber** to get a haircut.

  Oui, *barber* fait reference à la barbe (*beard*) et vient de l'ancien français: barbier!

- I'd like a bowl of clam **chowder**, please.

  Chowder vient du français *chaudron* ou *chaudière*. A l'origine, c'est dans un chaudron (*a soup kettle*) que l'on faisait cuire le poisson en Normandie.

- I love my **denim** skirt.

  Denim vient de *toile de Nîmes* car c'est dans la ville de Nîmes que ce tissu durable et populaire a vu naissance!

- I'd like two **tickets**, please.

  Oui, même *tickets* vient du français *étiquette* (*label*).

  Et nous ne devons pas oublier *etiquette* qui veut dire la même chose en français!

- To observe the rules of **etiquette**—Observer *l'étiquette*.

VOCABULAIRE

font partie	*are part*
faisait cuire	*cooked*
a vu naissance	*was born*

23

Numbers, Dates, Time

Numbers
Les nombres

CARDINAL NUMBERS (*LES NOMBRES CARDINAUX*)

1 un*	11 onze	21 vingt et un
2 deux	12 douze	22 vingt-deux
3 trois	13 treize	23 vingt-trois
4 quatre	14 quatorze	24 vingt-quatre
5 cinq	15 quinze	25 vingt-cinq
6 six	16 seize	26 vingt-six
7 sept	17 dix-sept	27 vingt-sept
8 huit	18 dix-huit	28 vingt-huit
9 neuf	19 dix-neuf	29 vingt-neuf
10 dix	20 vingt	30 trente

*If the number **un** is followed by a feminine noun, it becomes **une**.

285

31	trente et un	60	soixante	81	quatre-vingt-un
40	quarante	61	soixante et un	90	quatre-vingt-dix
41	quarante et un	70	soixante-dix	91	quatre-vingt-onze
50	cinquante	71	soixante et onze	100	cent
51	cinquante et un	80	quatre-vingts	101	cent un

After 71 and 91, the numbers are as follows:

72	soixante-douze	92	quatre-vingt-douze
73	soixante-treize	93	quatre-vingt-treize
74	soixante-quatorze	94	quatre-vingt-quatorze
75	soixante-quinze	95	quatre-vingt-quinze
76	soixante-seize	96	quatre-vingt-seize
77	soixante-dix-sept	97	quatre-vingt-dix-sept
78	soixante-dix-huit	98	quatre-vingt-dix-huit
79	soixante-dix-neuf	99	quatre-vingt-dix-neuf

After 100, the numbers start over from 101 to 199, 201 to 299, etc.

| 200 | deux cents | 300 | trois cents | 400 | quatre cents |
| 201 | deux cent un | 301 | trois cent un | 401 | quatre cent un |

- **When there is a third number, the second number does not have an s**

| quatre-vingts | → | quatre-vingt-un |
| deux cents | | deux cent un |

1.000	mille
1.001	mille un
1.011	mille onze
1.100	mille cent
1.200	mille deux cents

2.000	deux mille
2.001	deux mille un
2.011	deux mille onze
2.100	deux mille cent
2.200	deux mille deux cents

3.000	trois mille
3.001	trois mille un
3.011	trois mille onze
3.100	trois mille cent
3.200	trois mille deux cents

- Cent and mille are not preceded by the indefinite article un.
  The number mille, unlike cent, does not take an s in the plural.
  In French, a period is used to separate one thousand, whereas in
  English a comma is used. For decimals in French, it is the opposite:
  a comma is used to mark the decimal point

  English: 2.5 → French: 2,5

  100.000 **cent mille**   1.000.000 **un million**

- The indefinite article un always precedes million and de is always
  used after un million before a noun

  Il y a un million d'habitants dans cette ville.
  There are a million inhabitants in this city.

- The French word for *a billion* is un milliard (de), and the French
  word for *a trillion* is un billion de.

- Expressions with numbers

Une (deux, trois, etc.) fois	=	One time (once), two times (twice), three times, etc.
Cinq pour cent	=	Five **per** cent

QUICK PRACTICE

I. Écrivez les nombres en toutes lettres:

1. 11	6. 165	11. 1.151
2. 45	7. 390	12. 12.005
3. 72	8. 475	13. 159.000
4. 97	9. 918	14. 1.140.000
5. 102	10. 970	15. 4.100.000

II. Conversation à deux: Avec un(e) camarade, discutez du nombre de choses que vous faites chaque semaine.

Modèle: Moi, je fais la vaisselle sept fois par semaine. *(faire des sports, suivre un cours, prendre des leçons, téléphoner à une amie, etc.)*

ORDINAL NUMBERS (LES NOMBRES ORDINAUX)

- **To form an ordinal number in French, you add ième at the end of the cardinal number to all numbers except un, cinq, neuf.**

deuxième*	*second*
troisième	*third*
quatrième	*fourth*
sixième	*sixth*
septième	*seventh*
huitième	*eighth*
dixième	*tenth*
onzième	*eleventh*
douzième	*twelfth*
vingtième	*twentieth*
vingt et unième	*twenty first*
trente et unième	*thirty first*
centième	*hundredth*
cent unième	*hundred and first*
millième	*thousandth*
mille et unième	*thousand and first*

*The number **deuxième** is usually used in a series, when other numbers will follow it. If there are only two numbers, then **second, seconde** (pronounced "segond, segonde") is used. However, this rule is not always followed, especially in the spoken language.

un, une	→	premier, première**	*first*
cinq	→	cinquième	*fifth*
neuf	→	neuvième	*ninth*

In a train, one travels **en première or **en seconde**. In a high school (lycée), one goes from **la troisième** to **la seconde**, although there are more than two.

Ma soeur est en seconde cette année.
My sister is in the 10th grade this year.

In French, to express approximation, the suffix **aine** is added to certain numbers, sometimes requiring a change in the last letter. They are always preceded by the feminine indefinite article **une** or **des**.

une dizaine	*about ten*
une douzaine	*about twelve, or a dozen*
une quinzaine	*about fifteen*
une vingtaine	*about twenty*
une trentaine	*about thirty*
une quarantaine	*about forty*

Il y avait une dizaine d'enfants dans la cour.
There were about(around) ten children in the courtyard.

Il y avait environ (à peu près) deux cents personnes
dans la salle.
There were approximately (nearly) two hundred people in the room.

- **In French, cardinal numbers are used for titles, except for** premier **(*first*). No article precedes the number.**

François Premier   *Francis the first*
Henri IV (Quatre)   *Henri the fourth*

- **Other expressions**

The first three weeks	→	les trois premières semaines
The last two weeks	→	les deux dernières semaines

one fourth	un quart
half of	la moitié de
one third	un tiers
half a + noun	un(une) demi + noun
three fourths	trois quarts
nine tenths	neuf dixièmes

Il a mangé la moitié du gateau.   *He ate half the cake.*
Elle a bu un demi-verre de lait.   *She drank half a glass of milk.*
Donnez-moi un quart de litre.   *Give me a fourth of a liter.*

QUICK PRACTICE

III. Complétez les phrases suivantes avec le nombre ordinal indiqué:

1. Lundi est le _____ jour de la semaine.   (1)

2. Les deux _____ jours de mes vacances, j'étais malade.   (1)

3. Nous habitons au _____ étage de ce gratte-ciel.   (41)

4. C'est la _____ fois que je te dis cela.   (2)

5. Le _____ chapitre n'est pas intéressant.   (27)

6. Octobre est le _____ mois de l'année.   (10)

7. Charles est leur _____ enfant.   (5)

8. Le _____ étage a une vue magnifique.   (101)

9. Shéhérazade est un conte des _____ nuits.   (1001)

10. C'est le _____ jour de classe.   (30)

IV. Traduisez:

1. About 15 roses.

2. The fiftieth day.

3. About 30 students.

4. Hundreds of toys (**jouets**).

5. Henri the eighth.

Dates
Les dates

THE DAYS OF THE WEEK (*LES JOURS DE LA SEMAINE*)

- **In French, the first letter of the days of the week is *not* capitalized**

lundi	*Monday*	**vendredi**	*Friday*
mardi	*Tuesday*	**samedi**	*Saturday*
mercredi	*Wednesday*	**dimanche**	*Sunday*
jeudi	*Thursday*		

- **When referring to one specific day, *no article* precedes the day in French**

On Monday (Tuesday, etc.)	→	lundi, mardi, etc.
I will come on Monday.		Je viendrai lundi.

- **When referring to actions occurring regularly or repeatedly, the indefinite masculine article le is used before the name of the day**

On Mondays (Tuesdays, etc.)	→	**le** lundi, **le** mardi, etc.
I see them on Sundays.		Je les vois **le** dimanche.

- **Expressions**

Hier	*Yesterday*
Avant-hier*	*The day before yesterday*
Aujourd'hui	*Today*
Demain	*Tomorrow*
Après-demain*	*The day after tomorrow*
Quel jour sommes-nous?	*What day is it?*
C'est jeudi.	*It is Thursday.*
Nous sommes jeudi aujourd'hui.	*Today is Thursday.*
C'est aujourd'hui jeudi.	*Today is Thursday.*
La semaine dernière	*Last week*
La semaine passée	*Last week*
La semaine prochaine	*Next week*
La dernière semaine du mois	*The last week of the month*
Tous les jours	*Every day*
À demain.	*See you tomorrow.*
D'aujourd'hui en huit	*A week from today*
De jour en jour	*From day to day*

*Unlike English, nothing precedes **avant-hier** and **après-demain**.

NOTE: *The day before yesterday* → **avant-hier**

NOT ~~le jour avant-hier~~

I saw them the day before yesterday.
Je les ai vus avant-hier.

I will see them the day after tomorrow.
Je les verrai après-demain.

THE MONTHS OF THE YEAR (*LES MOIS DE L'ANNÉE*)

- In French, the first letter of the name of the month is *not* capitalized

janvier	*January*	juillet	*July*
février	*February*	août	*August*
mars	*March*	septembre	*September*
avril	*April*	octobre	*October*
mai	*May*	novembre	*November*
juin	*June*	décembre	*December*

- The months are all masculine, but no article precedes them. They are preceded by the preposition en

en février	*in February*
au mois de février	*in the month of February*

- The years before the 21st century (le vingt et unième siècle) are expressed in multiples of 10 or 1000. The 21st century is in thousands

1965	dix-neuf cent soixante-cinq
	ou mille neuf cent soixante-cinq
2006	deux mille six

- For the twentieth century, when referring to a decade, the first two numbers of the year are dropped, as in English, but les années is added

The sixties
Les années soixante

La carrière des Beatles a commencé pendant les années soixante.
The Beatles' career began during the sixties.

- When writing the date, the first of the month is an ordinal number, but the rest of the days are cardinal numbers

The first of November	Le premier novembre
The second of November	Le deux novembre

NOT ~~Le deux de novembre~~

Ils se sont mariés le vingt décembre deux mille cinq.
They got married on the twentieth of December two thousand and five.

- **When writing the date in its abbreviated form, the day comes first, then the month, then the year**

English	December 20, 2005	→	12/20/05
French	**le 20 décembre 2005**	→	**20/12/05**

- **Writing the full date, including the day of the week, does not require an article before the number**

  mardi 18 juillet 2006 *ou* **le 18 juillet 2006**

- **Expressions**

Le mois dernier	*Last month*
Le mois passé	*Last month*
Le mois prochain	*Next month*
Tous les mois	*Every month*
La mi-août	*The middle of August*
Au début du mois	*In the beginning of the month*
À la fin du mois	*At the end of the month*
Dans un mois	*A month from now (in a month)*
En un mois	*Within (the period of) a month*

Ils sont allés à Lyon le mois dernier.
They went to Lyon last month.

Ils ont visité tous les monuments en un mois.
They visited all the monuments in one month.

Nous allons partir dans un mois.
We are leaving in a month.

Nous partons dans un mois.
We are leaving a month from now.

Je les ai vus au début du mois dernier.
I saw them at the end of last month.

THE SEASONS (LES SAISONS)

- **The seasons in French are all masculine**

Le printemps	*spring*	au printemps	*in the spring*
L'été	*summer*	en été	*in the summer*
L'automne	*autumn/fall*	en automne	*in autumn*
L'hiver	*winter*	en hiver	*in winter*

NOTE: **automne** is pronounced "auto**nn**e."

QUICK PRACTICE

V. Madame Leblanc a demandé à ses élèves d'écrire leur biographie en écrivant les dates en français. Voici le brouillon (*the rough draft*) de John qu'il va traduire à la maison ce soir:

Modèle: January 1st, 2006   Le premier janvier deux mille six.

1. April 18, 1991   La date de ma naissance.

2. August 20, 1994   Mon premier jour au jardin d'enfants.

3. August 22, 1996   Mon premier jour d'école.

4. July 5, 2004   Mon premier voyage en France.

5. July 10, 2004   Ma visite au Louvre.

6. July 14, 2004   Fête de la Bastille à Paris.

7. July 18, 2004   Voyage de Paris à Nice.

8. August 5, 2004   Retour aux Etats-Unis.

9. September 6, 2005   J'ai rencontré Cassie, ma petite amie.

10. December 25, 2005   Mon premier Noël avec Cassie.

VI. Choisissez la réponse correcte.

1. Un mois d'hiver
   a. septembre
   b. janvier

2. Nous partons en vacances
   a. en août
   b. au août

3. Le mois de la Saint Valentin
   a. janvier
   b. février

4. Nous allons partir _____ un mois.
   a. dans
   b. en

5. Nous avons vu Colette la semaine _____ .
   a. dernière
   b. prochaine

6. _____ janvier, nous aurons un examen.
   a. le
   b. en

7. Le mois d'avril est
   a. en hiver
   b. au printemps

8. Je compte les voir pendant le mois _____ juin.
   a. de
   b. du

VII. **Et maintenant, écrivez votre biographie avec toutes les dates importantes.**

The Time
Les heures

THE HOURS (LES HEURES)

- **The word *time* in French is** heure. **The word** temps **has different meanings**

Quel temps fait-il?	*What's the weather like?*
As-tu le temps d'aller au café?	*Do you have time to go to the café?*
Le temps passe vite.	*Time flies.*

- **The hours are feminine in French**

Quelle heure est-il?	*What time is it?*
À quelle heure?	*At what time?*
Il est une heure.	*It is one o'clock.*
Il est deux heures.	*It is two o'clock.*
Il est trois heures.	*It is three o'clock.*
Il est quatre heures.	*It is four o'clock.*
Il est cinq heures.	*It is five o'clock.*
Il est midi.	*It is twelve noon.*
Il est minuit.	*It is midnight.*

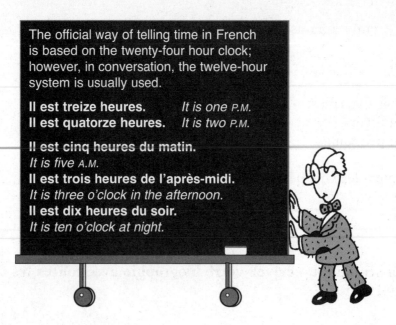

The official way of telling time in French is based on the twenty-four hour clock; however, in conversation, the twelve-hour system is usually used.

Il est treize heures.   *It is one P.M.*
Il est quatorze heures.   *It is two P.M.*

Il est cinq heures du matin.
It is five A.M.
Il est trois heures de l'après-midi.
It is three o'clock in the afternoon.
Il est dix heures du soir.
It is ten o'clock at night.

THE MINUTES (LES MINUTES)

Il est deux heures cinq.	*It is five after two.*
Il est trois heures dix.	*It is ten past three.*
Il est quatre heures et quart.	*It is a quarter past four.*
Il est cinq heures vingt.	*It is twenty past five.*
Il est six heures vingt-cinq.	*It is six twenty-five.*
Il est sept heures trente **(ou)**	
Il est sept heures et demie.	*It is seven thirty.*
Il est huit heures trente-cinq **(ou)**	*It is eight thirty-five (or)*
Il est neuf heures moins vingt-cinq.	*It is twenty-five to nine.*
Il est dix heures moins vingt.	*It is twenty to ten.*
Il est onze heures moins le quart.	*It is a quarter to eleven.*
Il est midi moins dix.	*It is ten to twelve.*
Il est une heure moins cinq.	*It is five to one.*

- **Heure is a feminine word; therefore, when following the noun heure demie has to be in the feminine. Midi and minuit are masculine words; demi will have to be in the masculine. When demi is placed before the hour, even though the word heure is feminine, the e is omitted**

  Une heure et demie *but* **une demi-heure**
  an hour and a half—a half hour

  Midi et demi—Minuit et demi
  Half past noon—Half past midnight

- **Minute and seconde are also feminine words**

- In the twenty-four hour system, douze heures **and** vingt-quatre heures **are used instead of** midi **and** minuit.

- **Expressions**

L'horaire des trains (des vols).	*The train (or flight) schedule.*
Il est à l'heure.	*He(it) is on time.*
Il est trois heures pile.	*It is three o'clock on the dot.*
Il est trois heures précises.	*It is exactly three o'clock.*
Il est tard.	*It is late (i.e., after 10.00 P.M.)*
Il est tôt.	*It is early (i.e., 5 A.M.).*
Je me suis couché tard (tôt).	*I went to bed late (early).*
Nous sommes en retard.	*We are late.*
Nous sommes en avance.	*We are early.*
Elle se lève de bonne heure (tôt).	*She gets up early.*
Une montre	*A watch*
Ta montre avance de deux minutes.	*Your watch is 2 minutes fast.*
Ta montre retarde de deux minutes.	*Your watch is 2 minutes slow.*
Une horloge	*A clock*
Un réveille-matin (réveil-matin)	*An alarm clock*
L'aube	*Dawn*
Le crépuscule	*Twilight*
Le coucher du soleil	*Sunset*
La nuit	*Night*

Quick Practice

VIII. Écrivez en toutes lettres:

1. 2:15 A.M.

2. 7:10 A.M.

3. 6:35 A.M.

4. 11:20 A.M.

5. 12:00 noon

6. 13:45

7. 17:30

8. 19:07

9. 23:18

10. Midnight

IX. Dites en français:

1. We are late.

2. It is exactly five o'clock.

3. My watch is five minutes fast.

4. She woke up early on Sunday.

5. It is midnight.

6. At what time do you go to bed?

7. Your watch is slow.

8. The train is on time.

LA NOMBRES, LES DATES ET LES HEURES

```
G  J  M  Z  B  X  C  P  B  U  M  Y  Q  K  T
H  Q  E  O  V  L  I  D  K  N  Y  C  I  R  B
I  E  R  V  Z  T  P  S  T  Z  M  R  T  T  N
T  F  C  Q  J  T  Y  G  E  R  V  T  W  F  U
U  K  R  W  Y  G  N  N  C  T  U  E  P  Q  Z
E  B  E  J  V  I  Z  X  H  Y  N  F  Q  A  K
H  I  D  F  V  X  P  F  O  J  Y  E  A  R  R
J  D  I  M  I  N  U  I  T  O  Q  Y  R  O  D
H  A  N  C  L  T  J  U  X  K  V  V  G  T  B
F  Y  M  A  O  L  P  A  G  P  M  D  S  V  X
D  R  A  T  E  R  N  E  N  T  P  M  J  M  J
R  S  V  H  Z  Q  T  L  Z  V  Q  A  K  J  Z
Q  S  B  H  Y  J  P  B  L  P  I  B  Q  G  U
T  F  T  U  P  L  F  M  N  U  A  E  O  D  T
E  T  N  A  X  I  O  S  I  D  I  M  R  Y  K
```

EN RETARD	MIDI	TRENTE SIX
JANVIER	MINUIT	VINGT
MERCREDI	SOIXANTE	

Culture Capsule 17

Le calendrier, tel que nous le connaissons, avait été remplacé pendant la Révolution française pour rompre avec l'ordre ancien. Le calendrier révolutionnaire, appelé aussi calendrier républicain, a été adopté le 24 octobre 1793. Cependant, le début de la nouvelle ère a été fixé au jour où la République a été proclamée, soit le 22 septembre 1792 qui est devenu le 1er vendémiaire, an I.

Selon le calendrier républicain, le début de chaque année correspond au jour de l'équinoxe d'automne où la durée est la même pour le jour et pour la nuit. Chaque année est divisée en douze mois de trente jours … ce qui laisse cinq jours à la fin de l'année, appelés sans-culotides.*

Les noms des mois ont été changés de façon à refléter les saisons ou bien les produits agricoles.

Vendémiaire	(septembre/octobre)	le mois des vendanges
Brumaire	(octobre/novembre)	le mois où le temps est brumeux
Frimaire	(novembre/décembre)	le mois où il fait froid
Nivôse	(décembre/janvier)	le mois où il neige
Pluviôse	(janvier/février)	le mois où il pleut beaucoup
Ventôse	(février/mars)	le mois où il y a beaucoup de vent
Germinal	(mars/avril)	le mois de la germination
Floréal	(avril/mai)	le mois des fleurs
Prairial	(mai/juin)	le mois où les prairies sont vertes
Messidor	(juin/juillet)	le mois des moissons
Thermidor	(juillet/août)	le mois où il fait très chaud
Fructidor	(août/septembre)	le mois des fruits

Ce calendrier a été aboli sous Napoléon Premier, le 11 nivôse de l'an quatorze, soit le 1er janvier 1806.

VOCABULAIRE

rompre	to break
ère	era
de façon à	so as to
ou bien	or else
produits agricoles	agricultural products
vendanges	grape harvest
brumeux	foggy
moissons	harvest
aboli	abolished

*Sans-culotides comes from the name sans-culottes, name of the revolutionaries who had chosen to wear pants (often striped) instead of the short culotte and silk stockings worn by the aristocracy.

PART IV:
Appendices

Frequently Used Idiomatic Expressions and Vocabulary

Some French idioms translate literally into English, but most can only be interpreted.

A

à	*at*
à bientôt	*see you soon*
à cause de	*because of*
à deux pas d'ici	*very close to here*
à droite	*to the right*
à gauche	*to the left*
à l'avance	*in advance*
à moins de	*unless + infinitive*
à moins que	*unless + subjunctive*
à mon avis	*in my opinion*
à partir d'aujourd'hui	*as of today*
à peine	*barely*
à peu près	*approximately*
à plus tard	*see you later*
à propos	*by the way*
actuel(le)	*current*
actuellement	*currently, at the present time*
aéroport *(m.)*	*airport*
afin de	*in order to + infinitive*
afin que	*in order to + subjunctive*
aider	*to help, assist*
ailleurs	*elsewhere*
aimer	*to like, love*
aller	*to go*
aller à	*to fit, to suit*
aller bien	*to be in good health, to feel well*
aller mal	*to be in bad health, to feel badly*
un aller simple	*a one-way ticket*
un aller-retour	*a round-trip ticket*
Allons donc!	*Come on! (I don't believe you)*
Allons-y!	*Let's go!*
alors	*then*

américain(e) *(adj.)*	*American*
Américain(e)[1]	*American man or woman*
ami, amie	*friend*
an *(m.)*, année *(f.)*	*year*
appartement *(m.)*	*apartment*
appétit *(m.)*	*appetite*
après	*after*
ascenseur *(m.)*	*elevator*
assez	*enough*
attention	*attention*
au fond	*deep down, basically*
au lieu de	*instead of*
au revoir	*goodbye*
aucun, aucune	*no, none*
aujourd'hui	*today*
aussi	*also*
aussitôt que	*as soon as*
auto(mobile) *(f.)*	*car*
autobus *(m.)*	*bus*
autre	*other*
avion *(m.)*	*airplane*
avoir . . . ans[2]	*to be . . . years old*
avoir besoin de	*to need*
avoir bon caractère	*to have a good temper*
avoir chaud[3]	*to feel warm*
avoir confiance en (quelqu'un)	*to trust (someone)*
avoir de la chance	*to be lucky*
avoir envie de (quelque chose)	*to feel like having (something)*
avoir faim	*to be hungry*
avoir froid	*to feel cold*
avoir hâte de	*to be in a hurry to*
avoir honte de	*to be ashamed of*
avoir horreur de	*to abhor*
avoir l'air + adjectif[4]	*to look + adjective*
avoir l'air de + nom ou infinitif du verbe être[5]	*to appear to be + noun or an infinitive*
avoir l'habitude de + infintif	*to be used to + gerund*
avoir l'intention de	*to intend to*
avoir l'occasion de	*to have the opportunity to*
avoir mal à (une partie du corps)[6]	*to have a pain (in a part of the body)*

[1]Américain(e)—the A is capitalized because it is a noun. In the previous line, it is not capitalized because it is an adjective. The same applies to all nationalities.

[2]avoir ... ans—refers to the age of a person.

[3]avoir chaud and avoir froid—only apply to people.

[4]avoir l'air—is followed by an adjective.

[5]avoir l'air de—is either followed by a noun or by the verb être in the infinitive, followed by an adjective.

[6]avoir mal à—is followed by the definite article + a part of the body. The possessive is never used in this case.

304 Complete French Grammar Review

avoir mauvais caractère	*to have a bad temper*
avoir peur de	*to be afraid of/to*
avoir pitié de (quelqu'un)	*to feel sorry for (someone)*
avoir raison	*to be right*
avoir soif	*to be thirsty*
avoir sommeil	*to feel sleepy*
avoir tort	*to be wrong*

B

bagages *(m.pl.)*	*luggage*
bain *(m.)*	*bath*
baiser *(m.)*	*a kiss*
banc *(m.)*	*bench*
banque *(f.)*	*bank*
bas, basse	*low*
bateau *(m.)*	*ship*
beau, belle	*handsome, beautiful*
bébé *(m.)*	*baby*
bien	*well*
bien entendu	*of course*
bien payé/mal payé	*well paid/badly paid*
bien sûr	*of course*
bise *(f.)*	*kiss (familiar language)*
blesser quelqu'un	*to hurt someone's feelings (fig.)*
blond, blonde	*blond*
bon, bonne	*good*
bonjour	*good morning, hello*
bonne nuit	*good night*
bonsoir	*good evening*
branché(e)	*with it, modern*
brancher	*to plug in*
briser le coeur de quelqu'un	*to break someone's heart*
broyer du noir	*to have sad thoughts*

C

Ça va!	*I'm fine!; All is well*
Ça va?	*Are you OK? How are things?*
cacher	*to hide something*
calendrier *(m.)*	*calendar*
casier *(m.)*	*locker*
casser les pieds à quelqu'un	*to annoy, bore someone*
c'est chouette	*that's great*
c'est dommage	*it's a pity*
c'est simple comme bonjour	*it's as easy as one, two, three*
Ce n'est pas la mer à boire	*It's not so bad*
certainement	*certainly*
chacun, chacune	*each one*
chanter comme une casserole	*to sing very badly*

chaud(e)	hot
chemise (f.)	shirt
chemisier (m.)	blouse
chose (f.)	thing
circulation (f.)	traffic
clavier (m.)	keyboard
client, cliente	client
climatisation, clim (f.)	air conditioning
construire	to build
un coup d'oeil	a glance
un coup de soleil	a sunstroke, a sunburn
couramment	fluently
courir à toutes jambes	to run very fast
course (f.)	the race
cousin, cousine	cousin
coûter	to cost
crier	to shout, yell
crier à tue-tête	to yell very loudly
critiquer	to criticize

D

d'abord	at first, first
d'ailleurs	beside
d'après (moi, lui, etc.)	according to (me, him, etc.)
de nouveau	again
de plus	moreover
de tout coeur	willingly, eagerly
de toute façon	in any case, anyway
debout	standing (up)
début (m.)	beginning
décider	to decide
déjà	already
demain	tomorrow
demoiselle	single woman
demoiselle d'honneur	maid of honor
dès aujourd'hui	as of today
dès demain	as of tomorrow
désordre (m.)	disorder, mess
désormais	from now on
dessiner	to draw
devenir	to become
dinde (f.)	turkey hen
dindon (m.)	turkey
un dîner de famille	a family dinner
dire des bêtises	to say stupid things
dire la vérité	to tell the truth
dire l'heure	to tell the time
dire ses quatres vérités à quelqu'un	to tell it as it is
disque dur (m.)	hard drive

donc	therefore
donner	to give
donner du courage	to give courage
donner envie	to make someone want something
donner un coup de fil	to telephone (call) someone
donner un coup de main	to lend a helping hand
donner un coup de téléphone	to telephone someone
dorénavant	from now on
dormir comme un loir	to sleep like a log (dormouse)
durée (f.)	duration
durer	to last

E

eau (f.)	water
éclairer	to light
éclater de rire	to burst out laughing
écran (m.)	screen
écriture (f.)	handwriting
effacer	to erase
efficace	efficient
embarquer	to embark
embrasser	to kiss
émission (f.)	TV show, emission
emploi (m.)	job
employé(e)	employee
emprunter	to borrow
ému(e)	moved
en avoir assez	to have had enough
en avoir marre	to have had enough
en direct	live show (TV)
en plein air	outdoors
en un clin d'oeil	in the wink of an eye
enchanté(e)	delighted
encore une fois	once more, once again
encore	again
enfin	finally
ennuyeux (se)	boring, annoying
entier, entière	entire, whole
envers	toward (abstract)
épuisé(e)	exhausted
escalier (m.)	staircase
espoir (m.)	hope
esprit d'équipe	team spirit
un essuie-glace	windshield wiper
un essuie-mains	a hand towel
étiquette (f.)	label, etiquette
être à bout[7]	to have had enough

[7]être à bout—*to have had enough, to be exhausted.*

être à bout de + nom[8]	not to have any more + noun
être à l'heure	to be on time
être à quelqu'un[9]	to belong to someone
être au courant de	to be aware of, to be informed about
être confus(e)[10]	to be embarassed
être d'accord	to be in agreement
être d'accord avec (quelqu'un)	to agree with (someone)
être dans les nuages	to be daydreaming
être de bonne humeur	to be in a good mood
être de mauvaise humeur	to be in a bad mood
être désolé(e)	to be sorry
être en avance[11]	to be early (for an appointment)
être en colère	to be angry
être en retard[12]	to be late (for an appointment)
être en train de faire quelque chose	to be in the process of doing
être en vacances	to be on vacation
être fauché(e)	to be broke (slang)
exiger	to require

F

face-à-face	face to face
facture (f.)	bill
faible	weak
faiblesse (f.)	weakness
faim (f.)	hunger
faire attention	to pay attention
faire de la natation	to practice swimming
faire des projets	to make plans
faire des sports	to play sports
faire du foot	to play soccer
faire du vélo	to practice bicycle riding
faire gaffe (argot)	to pay attention (slang)
faire l'appel	to take attendance
faire la moue	to pout
faire la tête[13]	to make a long face
faire la vaisselle	to do the dishes
faire le ménage	to clean the house
faire peur à quelqu'un	to scare someone
faire plaisir à quelqu'un	to make someone happy, to please

[8] être à bout de followed by a noun means *to have used up all of* or *not to have any more.*

[9] être à quelqu'un—*to belong to someone.*

[10] être confus(e) is a false cognate. In French, when pertaining to people, it means *to be embarassed* whereas ne pas comprendre means *to be confused.* When pertaining to things, however, confus(e) means *unclear, jumbled, blurred, nebulous.*

[11] être en avance is *to be early for something.* It does not pertain to time itself.

[12] être en retard is *to be late to something.*

[13] faire la tête is always used with the article la and not the possessive adjective.

faire sa toilette[14]	*to wash up and get ready*
faire un cadeau à quelqu'un	*to give a gift to someone*
faire voir	*to show*
fatigué(e)	*tired*
fauché(e)	*penniless*
faute de mieux	*for lack of a better thing to do*
faux, fausse	*false, untrue*
femme	*woman, wife*
fête *(f.)*	*party, celebration*
fêter	*to celebrate*
feuille *(f.)*	*leaf, sheet of paper*
fiancé(e)	*fiancé(e)*
fier, fière	*proud*
fièvre *(f.)*	*fever*
fillette	*little girl*
fin *(f.)*	*the end*
finalement	*finally*
foi *(f.)*	*faith*
foie *(m.)*	*liver*
football *(m.)*	*soccer*
four *(m.)*	*oven*
frais, fraîche	*fresh*
Français(e)	*Frenchman, Frenchwoman*
le français	*the French language*
frein *(m.)*	*brake*
frère	*brother*
fromage *(m.)*	*cheese*
froncer les sourcils	*to frown*
fumée *(f.)*	*smoke*
fumer	*to smoke*

G

gagner	*to win, to earn*
gant *(m.)*	*glove*
garçon	*boy*
garçon d'honneur	*best man*
garder rancune à quelqu'un	*to hold a grudge against someone*
gare *(f.)*	*railroad station*
garer la voiture	*to park the car*
gaucher(ère)	*left-handed*
génial(e)	*great, fantastic*
genou *(m.)*	*knee*
gens *(m. pl.)*	*people*
glace *(f.)*	*ice cream/mirror*
gorge *(f.)*	*throat*
goûter *(m.)*	*afternoon snack*
grâce à	*thanks to*

---

[14]faire sa toilette is always used with the possessive adjective.

grand-mère	*grandmother*
grand-père	*grandfather*
gratuit(e)	*free*
grève *(f.)*	*strike (workers)*
gros(se)	*fat, stout*
guérir	*to get cured*
guerre *(f.)*	*war*

H

habiter	*to live (in a place)*
habitude *(f.)*	*habit, custom*
hasard *(m.)*	*chance, luck*
hâte *(f.)*	*haste, hurry*
hausser les épaules	*to shrug one's shoulders*
haut(e)	*high*
héritage *(m.)*	*inheritance*
héroïne	*heroin*
héros	*hero*
heureusement	*happily, luckily*
heureux comme un poisson dans l'eau	*happy as a lark (fish in water)*
heureux(se)	*happy*
hôpital *(m.)*	*hospital*
hors de soi (moi, lui, etc.)	*beside oneself (myself, himself, etc.*
huile *(f.)*	*oil (edible)*
huile d'olive	*olive oil*

I

ici	*here*
idée *(f.)*	*idea*
ignorer	*not to know, to be unaware*
île *(f.)*	*island*
il est grand temps	*it's high time*
il était temps	*it's about time*
il fait un froid de canard	*it is very cold (fit for a duck)*
il n'y a pas de quoi	*you're welcome*
il paraît que	*it is rumored that*
il va sans dire que	*it goes without saying that*
immeuble *(m.)*	*high-rise building*
immobile	*motionless*
impôt *(m.)*	*tax*
inacceptable	*unacceptable*
incendie *(m.)*	*fire, burning of a building*
indépendant(e)	*independent*
informatique *(f.)*	*computer science*
ingénieur *(m.)*	*engineer*
insensible	*insensitive*
interrogation *(f.)*	*interrogation, quiz (school)*
interroger	*to question, interrogate*

interrompre	to interrupt
invité(e)	guest
issue (f.)	exit, end of something

J

jalousie (f.)	jealousy
jambon (m.)	ham
jardin (m.)	garden
jaune	yellow
jeu (m.)	game, gambling
jouer	to play
jouer au football	to play soccer
jouer du piano	to play the piano
jouer un tour	to play a trick
jouet (m.)	toy
jour (m.)	day, daylight
journée (f.)	daytime, the whole day
juger	to judge
jusqu'à	up to, as far as, until
jusqu'au bout	until the end

K

kilo, kilogramme (m.)	kilo, kilogram
kilomètre (m.)	kilometer
un klaxon	a car horn
klaxonner	to activate the horn

L

l'est	the East
l'occident (m.)	the west, occident
l'ouest (m.)	the West
là-bas	over there
laid(e)	ugly
laine (f.)	wool
laisser-aller	free and easy attitude
laisser-faire	policy of no interference
laisser tomber quelque chose ou quelqu'un	to drop something or someone
un laissez-passer	a pass; a permit
lait (m.)	milk
lampe (f.)	lamp
langue (f.)	language, tongue
large	wide
larme (f.)	tear
lecture (f.)	reading
léger, légère	light (adj.)
le lendemain	the following day
libérer	to free

liberté (f.)	freedom, liberty
lire couramment	to read fluently
lire entre les lignes	to read between the lines
le logiciel	the software
louange (f.)	praise
lumière (f.)	light
lune (f.)	moon
lunettes (f.pl.)	eyeglasses

M

maigre	skinny
maillot de bain (m.)	swimsuit
maïs (m.)	corn
malade	ill, sick
maladie (f.)	illness, sickness
malheur (m.)	misfortune
malheureusement	unfortunately
maman	mom, mommy
manquer	to miss
manquer à	to be missed by
manquer de	to be lacking in
mariage (m.)	wedding, marriage
marier	to marry off
matinée (f.)	the whole morning, afternoon performance
mauvais(e)	bad, wicked
mécanicien (m.)	mechanic
méchant(e)	mean
médecin (m.)	physician
medicament (m.)	medicine
même	same, even
mensonge (m.)	lie
mentir	to lie
mer (f.)	sea
mère	mother
mètre (m.)	meter
mettre au pied du mur	to corner someone
mettre le couvert, la table	to set the table
mettre ses vêtements	to put on one's clothes
meuble (m.)	piece of furniture
milieu (m.)	middle, social environment
mince	thin
mode (f.)	fashion
Mon oeil!	My foot! (expression of disbelief)
monde (m.)	world
mot (m.)	word
moteur (m.)	motor
musique (f.)	music

N

nager	to swim
naissance (f.)	birth
nappe (f.)	tablecloth
natation (f.)	swimming
navire (m.)	ship, vessel
ne pas être dans son assiette	to be out of sorts
ne pas fermer l'oeil	to be unable to sleep
ne pas savoir où donner de la tête	not to know what to do
ne pas savoir sur quel pied danser	to be at a loss of what to do
néanmoins	nevertheless
négliger	to neglect
nettoyer de fond en comble	to clean from top to bottom
nez (m.)	nose
niveau (m.)	level
noir(e)	black
nom (m.)	name, noun
le nord	the North
nouveau, nouvelle	new
nouveau-né (m.)	newborn
nuage (m.)	cloud
nuque (f.)	nape of the neck

O

obéir	to obey
obligatoire	compulsory
obscur(e)	dark, gloomy, dim
observateur(trice)	observer
obtenir	to obtain
occasion (f.)	occasion, opportunity
occupé(e)	busy, occupied
oeil (m.), yeux (pl.)	eye, eyes
oiseau (m.)	bird
un oiseau rare	a rare bird
ombragé(e)	shaded
ombre (f.)	shadow
on passe un film	a movie is showing
ordinateur (m.)	computer
ordonnance (f.)	prescription
orthographe (f.)	spelling, orthography
outre-mer	overseas
ouvre-boîte (m.)	can opener
ouvre-bouteille (m.)	bottle opener
ouvrir l'oeil	to watch out

P

pain (m.)	bread
panne (f.)	engine breakdown

papa	*dad, daddy*
par coeur	*by heart*
par contre	*on the other hand*
par terre	*on the floor*
parapluie *(m.)*	*umbrella*
parasol *(m.)*	*beach umbrella*
parce que	*because*
parent *(m.)*	*parent, relative*
parole *(f.)*	*spoken word*
passer à table	*to go to the table*
passer la nuit	*to spend the night*
passer le temps	*to pass the time*
passer outre à quelque chose	*to ignore, to overlook something*
passer un examen	*to take a test*
payer à l'heure/au mois	*to pay by the hour / by the month*
payer comptant	*to pay cash*
payer d'avance/à l'avance	*to pay in advance*
peigne *(m.)*	*comb*
perdre la tête	*to lose one's head*
perdre son temps	*to waste one's time*
père	*father*
personnage *(m.)*	*character in a play, novel, etc.*
peuple *(m.)*	*population, nation*
peur *(f.)*	*fear*
pièce *(f.)*	*room, play, piece*
piscine *(f.)*	*swimming pool*
plage *(f.)*	*beach*
plan *(m.)*	*plan, city map*
pleurer	*to cry*
pointure *(f.)*	*shoe size*
poser un lapin à quelqu'un	*to stand someone up*
prendre en main	*to take charge*
prendre froid	*to catch a cold*
prendre le petit-déjeuner, le déjeuner, le dîner	*to have breakfast, lunch, dinner*
prendre part à quelque chose	*to take part in something*
prendre un café	*to have a coffee*
prendre un dessert	*to have a dessert*
prix *(m.)*	*price, prize*
projet *(m.)*	*plan, project*
puis	*then, afterward, next*

Q

quand	*when*
quant à	*as for*
quart *(m.)*	*a quarter, a fourth*
Quel dommage!	*What a pity!*
Quelle chance!	*How lucky!*

Quelle mouche te pique?	*What's the problem?*
quelqu'un	*someone*
quelque chose	*something*
quelque part	*somewhere*
quelque	*some, any*
Qu'est-ce qui se passe?	*What's going on?*
quotidien *(m.)*	*daily paper*
quotidien(ne)	*daily occurrence*

R

racine *(f.)*	*root*
raconter	*to narrate, recount, tell (a story)*
radio *(f.)*	*radio*
raison *(f.)*	*reason*
ranger ses affaires	*to straighten up one's things*
râter un examen	*to fail a test*
reconnaître	*to recognize*
réduire	*to reduce*
réfrigérateur *(m.)*	*refrigerator*
rendez-vous *(m.)*	*date, appointment*
repos *(m.)*	*rest*
ressembler à	*to resemble, look like*
rester	*to remain, stay*
retard *(m.)*	*delay*
retour *(m.)*	*return*
réussir à un examen	*to pass a test*
Revenons à nos moutons	*Let's get back to the subject*
rêver	*to dream*
riche	*rich*
richesse *(f.)*	*wealth*
rire aux éclats	*laugh heartily*
roman *(m.)*	*novel*
roux, rousse	*redhead*

S

sable *(m.)*	*sand*
sac *(m.)*	*handbag, sack*
sage	*wise, well-behaved*
sain et sauf	*safe and sound*
sain(e)	*healthy*
saison *(f.)*	*season*
Salut!	*Hi!*
sanglot *(m.)*	*sob*
sangloter	*to sob*
Sans blague!	*No kidding!*
sans-logis *(m.)*	*homeless*
sauf	*except*
sauter du coq à l'âne	*to go from one subject to another*

sauvegarder	to save (in the computer)
sauver	to save (a person or a thing)
savoir sur le bout du doigt	to know very well (a subject)
savon (m.)	soap
scène (f.)	stage, scene
SDF (sans domicile fixe)	homeless
se cacher	to hide (oneself)
se détendre	to relax
se garer	to park
se laisser aller	to neglect oneself
se lever du pied gauche	to get up on the wrong side of the bed
se marier	to get married
se mettre à + infinitif	to begin to + infinitive
se mettre à table	to sit down to eat
se mettre en colère	to get angry
se mettre en route	to get on the road
se mordre les doigts	to be sorry
se passer	to happen
se reposer	to rest
sécher	to dry
sécher un cours	to skip a class
semblable	similar
sensible	sensitive
s'habituer à	to get used to
siècle (m.)	century
soi	oneself
sol (m.)	floor
soleil (m.)	sun
souci (m.)	worry
soudain	sudden, suddenly
souris (f.)	mouse, computer mouse
le sud	the South
super	super, fantastic
sûr(e)	sure, safe, secure
le surlendemain	two days later
un surligneur	a highlighter
surtout	particularly, above all
s'y mettre	to get into it/to start doing something
sympathique	likable

T

tache (f.)	stain
tâche (f.)	task
taille (f.)	size, height, waistline
tant	so much, so many
tant mieux	so much the better
tant pis	too bad
tapis (m.)	carpet

teinte *(f.)*	color, shade, hue
la télécommande	the television remote control
tellement	so much
témoin *(m.)*	witness
tête *(f.)*	head
thèse *(f.)*	thesis, proposition
timbre *(m.)*	stamp
timide	timid, shy
toilettes *(f.pl.)*	toilet
toit *(m.)*	roof
tomber amoureux de quelqu'un	to fall in love with someone
tomber des nues	to fall off one's chair (from surprise)
tomber malade	to become ill
la tonalité	the beep
toujours	always
tout à coup	all of a sudden
tout à l'heure	in a little while
tranche *(f.)*	slice
transpiration *(f.)*	perspiration
transpirer	to perspire
travailler d'arrache pied	to work very hard
trou *(m.)*	hole

U

ultrachic	extremely well dressed
ultramoderne	ultra modern
unique	unique, only
uniquement	solely, only
université *(f.)*	university, college
urgence *(f.)*	urgency, emergency
urgent(e)	urgent
usé(e)	worn, frayed
usine *(f.)*	factory
utile	useful

V

vacance *(f.)*	vacancy
vacances *(f.pl.)*	vacation
vache *(adj.)*	nasty, mean
vachement	very (slang)
vague *(adj.)*	vague
vague *(f.)*	wave
valoir la peine	to be worth the trouble
veille *(f.)*	eve, preceding day
vent *(m.)*	wind
vente *(f.)*	sale
ventilateur *(m.)*	floor or ceiling fan
vérité *(f.)*	truth

verre *(m.)*	*glass*
vers *(m.)*	*verse*
vers	*toward (concrete)*
veste *(f.)*	*jacket*
vêtement *(m.)*	*garment, (pl.) clothes*
vide	*empty*
vie *(f.)*	*life*
visage *(m.)*	*face*
vitesse *(f.)*	*speed*
voici, voilà	*here is (are), there is (are)*
voir de ses propres yeux	*to see with one's own eyes*
voir la vie en rose	*to see life through rose-colored glasses*
voir rouge	*to see red; to become angry*
voisin(e)	*neighbor*
voiture *(f.)*	*car*
vol *(m.)*	*flight, theft*
volant *(m.)*	*steering wheel*
voleur(se)	*thief*
voyage *(m.)*	*trip, journey*
Voyons!	*See here now!*
vraiment	*really, truly*
vue *(f.)*	*sight, view*

W

W.C. *(pl.)*	*toilet*
wagon *(m.)*	*railway car*
un wagon-lit	*sleeping car (in a train)*

Y

un yaourt	*a yoghurt*

Z

Zut!	*Darn!*

Proverbs

Some proverbs have their equivalent in English; some can only be interpreted.

FRANÇAIS	ANGLAIS
Après la pluie, le beau temps. *After the rain comes fair weather.*	*Bad things come to an end.*
Aide-toi le ciel t'aidera.	*God helps those who help themselves.*
L'argent ne fait pas le bonheur.	*Money does not make happiness.*
Bien faire et laisser dire. *Do what's right, let people talk.*	*Don't worry about the opinion of others.*
Ce que femme veut, Dieu le veut.	*Whatever woman wants, God wants.*
Chose promise, chose due.	*A promise is a promise.*
Comme on fait son lit, on se couche. *As you make your bed, you must sleep in it.*	*We reap what we sow.*
Dans le doute, abstiens-toi.	*When in doubt, abstain.*
Deux avis valent mieux qu'un. *Two opinions are better than one.*	*Two heads are better than one.*
La fin justifie les moyens.	*The end justifies the means.*
L'habit ne fait pas le moine. *The clothes don't make the monk.*	*You cannot judge by appearances.*
Loin des yeux, loin du coeur. *Far from the eyes, far from the heart.*	*Out of sight, out of mind.*
Mieux vaut tard que jamais.	*Better late than never.*
Les murs ont des oreilles.	*Walls have ears.*

La nuit porte conseil. *Night brings good advice.*	*Sleep on it.*
Oeil pour oeil, dent pour dent.	*An eye for an eye and a tooth for a tooth.*
Pauvreté n'est pas vice.	*Poverty is not a vice.*
Point de nouvelles, bonnes nouvelles.	*No news is good news.*
Qui se ressemble s'assemble. *Those who are alike get together.*	*Birds of a feather flock together.*
Rira bien qui rira le dernier.	*He will laugh best who will laugh last.*
Tout est bien qui finit bien.	*All is well that ends well.*
Un tiens vaut mieux que deux tu l'auras. *One "here it is" is better than two "you'll have it."*	*A bird in the hand is worth two in the bush.*
Vouloir c'est pouvoir. *To want is to be able to.*	*Where's a will there's a way.*

Synonyms, Antonyms, Cognates

SYNONYMS (SYNONYMES)

English	Français	Synonymes
after	après	ensuite
astonish	étonner	surprendre
before (in time)	avant	auparavant
besides	en outre	en plus
a bottle	une bouteille	un flacon (de parfum)
cafeteria	une caféteria	un libre-service
certain	certain(e)	sûr(e)
a claim	une demande	une réclamation
clothes	vêtements (m.)	habits (m.)
damage	dommages (m.pl)	dégat(s) (m.)
to deny	nier	démentir
drinkable	buvable	potable
effect	effet (m.)	influence (f.)
embarrassed	embarrassé(e)	gêné(e)
exhausted	épuisé(e)	exténué(e)
face	figure (f.)	visage (m.)
to finish	finir	terminer
flashy	voyant(e)	criard(e)
gift	cadeau (m.)	présent (m.)
to happen	arriver	se passer
help	aide (f.)	secours (m.)
immediate	immediate(e)	instantané(e)
to increase	augmenter	accroître
laughable	risible	ridicule
to let someone	permettre à quelqu'un	laisser quelqu'un
loyal	loyal(e)	dévoué(e)
to miss	manquer	râter
nonsense	absurdité (f.)	non-sens (m.)
notice	avis (m.)	notification (f.)
object	objet (m.)	chose (f.)
to occur	avoir lieu	survenir

English	Français	Synonymes
package	**paquet** (*m.*)	**colis** (*m.*)
paper (studies)	**essai** (*m.*)	**rédaction** (*f.*)
to remember	**se souvenir de**	**se rappeler**
to return (come back)	**retourner**	**revenir/rentrer**
safety	**sécurité** (*f.*)	**sureté** (*f.*)

As explained in Chapter 3, **connaître** and **savoir** both mean *to know*. However, they are used differently:

- **connaître**   *to know someone or something, to be familiar with*

  Je connais cette ville.   *I know this town.*
  Je connais ta cousine.   *I know your cousin.*

- **savoir**   *to know something by heart, to know a fact, to know how to do something*

  Elle sait danser.   *She knows how to dance.*
  Il sait le poème.   *He knows the poem (by heart).*
  Je sais où ils sont.   *I know where they are.*

ANTONYMS (ANTONYMES)

Français	English	Antonyme français	English Antonym
âgé(e)	*old*	jeune	*young*
ami(e)	*friend*	ennemi(e)	*enemy*
attacher	*to tie, unfasten*	détacher	*to untie, to unfasten*
beau, belle	*beautiful*	laid(e)	*ugly*
bon, bonne	*good (adj.)*	mauvais(e)	*bad (adj.)*
bien	*well (adv.)*	mal	*badly (adv.)*
chance (*f.*)	*luck*	malchance (*f.*)	*bad luck*
clair	*light*	foncé, sombre	*dark, somber*
le début	*the beginning*	la fin	*the end*
dedans	*inside*	dehors	*outside*
l'entrée (*f.*)	*the entrance*	la sortie	*the exit*
éteindre	*to turn off (light)*	allumer	*to light, turn on*
faux, fausse	*wrong*	correct(e), juste	*correct*
finir	*to finish*	commencer	*to begin*
généreux (se)	*generous*	mesquin(e), avare	*stingy*
gros, grosse	*fat*	mince	*thin*
s'habiller	*to get dressed*	se déshabiller	*to get undressed*
honnête	*honest*	malhonnête	*dishonest*
infidèle	*unfaithful*	fidèle	*faithful*
joie (*f.*)	*joy*	peine (*f.*)	*sorrow*

large	wide	étroit(e)	narrow
matin *(m.)*	*morning*	soir *(m.)*	*evening*
mouillé(e)	*wet*	sec, sèche	*dry*
nerveux(se)	*nervous*	calme	*calm*
ouvrir	*to open*	fermer	*to close*
pauvre	*poor*	riche	*rich*
petit(e)	*small*	grand(e)	*big, tall*
plaire	*to appeal to, please*	déplaire	*to dislike*
poli(e)	*polite*	impoli(e)	*impolite*
récompense *(f.)*	*reward*	punition *(f.)*	*punishment*
sympathique	*likeable, nice*	antipathique	*unpleasant*
trouver	*to find*	perdre	*to lose*
vieux, vieille	*old*	jeune	*young*
vendre	*to sell*	acheter	*to buy*
vide	*empty*	plein(e)	*full*

COGNATES *(MOTS APPARENTÉS)*

English Endings	Terminaisons Françaises
al	**al**
animal	**animal** *(m.)*
central	**central(e)**
social	**social(e)**
ary	**aire**
extraordinary	**extraordinaire**
ordinary	**ordinaire**
vocabulary	**vocabulaire**
ce	**ce**
difference	**différence** *(f.)*
importance	**importance** *(f.)*
ion	**ion**
admiration	**admiration** *(f.)*
conclusion	**conclusion** *(f.)*
conversation	**conversation** *(f.)*
division	**division** *(f.)*
nation	**nation** *(f.)*
multiplication	**multiplication** *(f.)*
operation	**opération** *(f.)*
pollution	**pollution** *(f.)*
tension	**tension** *(f.)*
tradition	**tradition** *(f.)*

English Endings	Terminaisons Françaises
ist	**iste**
artist	**artiste** *(m.f.)*
dentist	**dentiste** *(m.)*
pianist	**pianiste** *(m.f.)*
tourist	**touriste** *(m.f.)*
or	**eur**
actor	**acteur** *(m.)*
color	**couleur** *(f.)*
doctor	**docteur** *(m.)*
odor	**odeur** *(f.)*
professor	**professeur** *(m.)*
terror	**terreur** *(f.)*
valor	**valeur** *(f.)*

FALSE COGNATES (FAUX AMIS)

English word	Faux ami	Vrai ami
actually	**actuellement** *(at the present time)*	**en réalité**
to assist	**assister à** *(to attend)*	**aider**
to attend	**attendre** *(to wait for)*	**assister à**
to attend the university	attendre	**aller à l'université**
conductor	**conducteur** *(driver)*	**chef d'orchestre**
confidence	**confidence** *(secret)*	**confiance** *(f.)*
figure	**figure** *(face)*	**corps** *(m.)*
journey	**journée** *(day)*	**voyage** *(m.)*
library	**librairie** *(bookstore)*	**bibliothèque** *(f.)*
sensible	**sensible** *(sensitive)*	**raisonnable**
to support	**supporter** *(to bear)*	**appuyer, entretenir**
sympathetic	**sympathique** *(likeable, nice)*	**compatissant(e)**

Verb Charts

VERBES REGULIERS

- **Verbes en -er**

Accepter *to accept*

participe présent:	**acceptant**
participe passé:	**accepté**

Présent de l'indicatif	**accepte, acceptes, accepte, acceptons, acceptez, acceptent**
Passé Composé	**ai accepté, as accepté, a accepté, avons accepté, avez accepté, ont accepté**
Imparfait	**acceptais, acceptais, acceptait, acceptions, acceptiez, acceptaient**
Plus-que-parfait	**avais accepté, avais accepté, avait accepté, avions accepté, aviez accepté, avaient accepté**
Passé Simple	**acceptai, acceptas, accepta, acceptâmes, acceptâtes, acceptèrent**
Futur Simple	**accepterai, accepteras, acceptera, accepterons, accepterez, accepteront**
Futur Antérieur	**aurai accepté, auras accepté, aura accepté, aurons accepté, aurez accepté, auront accepté**
Conditionnel Présent	**accepterais, accepterais, accepterait, accepterions, accepteriez, accepteraient**
Conditionnel Passé	**aurais accepté, aurais accepté, aurait accepté, aurions accepté, auriez accepté, auraient accepté**
Subjonctif Présent	**accepte, acceptes, accepte, acceptions, acceptiez, acceptent**
Subjonctif Passé	**aie accepté, aies accepté, ait accepté, ayons accepté, ayez accepté, aient accepté**
Infinitif Passé	**avoir accepté**
Impératif	**accepte, acceptons, acceptez**

- **Verbes en -ir**

Finir *to finish*
participe présent: **finissant**
participe passé: **fini**

Présent de l'indicatif	**finis, finis, finit, finissons, finissez, finissent**
Passé Composé	**ai fini, as fini, a fini, avons fini, avez fini, ont fini**
Imparfait	**finissais, finissais, finissait, finissions, finissiez, finissaient**
Plus-que-parfait	**avais fini, avais fini, avait fini, avions fini, aviez fini, avaient fini**
Passé Simple	**finis, finis, finit, finîmes, finîtes, finirent**
Futur Simple	**finirai, finiras, finira, finirons, finirez, finiront**
Futur Antérieur	**aurai fini, auras fini, aura fini, aurons fini, aurez fini, auront fini**
Conditionnel Présent	**finirais, finirais, finirait, finirions, finiriez, finiraient**
Conditionnel Passé	**aurais fini, aurais fini, aurait fini, aurions fini, auriez fini, auraient fini**
Subjonctif Présent	**finisse, finisses, finisse, finissions, finissiez, finissent**
Subjonctif Passé	**aie fini, aies fini, ait fini, ayons fini, ayez fini, aient fini**
Infinitif Passé	**avoir fini**
Impératif	**finis, finissons, finissez**

- **Verbes en -re**

Attendre *to wait for*
participe présent: **attendant**
participe passé: **attendu**

Présent de l'indicatif	**attends, attends, attend, attendons, attendez, attendent**
Passé Composé	**ai attendu, as attendu, a attendu, avons attendu, avez attendu, ont attendu**
Imparfait	**attendais, attendais, attendait, attendions, attendiez, attendaient**
Plus-que-parfait	**avais attendu, avais attendu, avait attendu, avions attendu, aviez attendu, avaient attendu**
Passé Simple	**attendis, attendis, attendit, attendîmes, attendîtes, attendirent**
Futur Simple	**attendrai, attendras, attendra, attendrons, attendrez, attendront**
Futur Antérieur	**aurai attendu, auras attendu, aura attendu, aurons attendu, aurez attendu, auront attendu**
Conditionnel Présent	**attendrais, attendrais, attendrait, attendrions, attendriez, attendraient**
Conditionnel Passé	**aurais attendu, aurais attendu, aurait attendu, aurions attendu, auriez attendu, auraient attendu**

Subjonctif Présent	attende, attendes, attende, attendions, attendiez, attendent
Subjonctif Passé	aie attendu, aies attendu, ait attendu, ayons attendu, ayez attendu, aient attendu
Infinitif Passé	avoir attendu
Impératif	attends, attendons, attendez

VERBES IRREGULIERS

Aller to go

participe présent:	allant
participe passé:	allé(e)(s)

Présent de l'indicatif	vais, vas, va, allons, allez, vont
Passé Composé	suis allé(e), es allé(e), est allé(e), sommes allés(es), êtes allés(es), sont allés(es)
Imparfait	allais, allais, allait, allions, alliez, allaient
Plus-que-parfait	étais allé(e), étais allé(e), était allé(e), étions allés(es), étiez allés(es), étaient allés(es)
Passé Simple	allai, allas, alla, allâmes, allâtes, allèrent
Futur Simple	irai, iras, ira, irons, irez, iront
Futur Antérieur	serai allé(e), seras allé(e), sera allé(e), serons allés(es), serez allés(es), seront allés(es)
Conditionnel Présent	irais, irais, irait, irions, iriez, iraient
Conditionnel Passé	serais allé(e), serais allé(e), serait allé(e), serions allés(es), seriez allés(es), seraient allés(es)
Subjonctif Présent	aille, ailles, aille, allions, alliez, aillent
Subjonctif Passé	sois allé(e), sois allé(e), soit allé(e), soyons allés(es), soyez allés(es), soient allés(es)
Infinitif Passé	être allé(e)(s)(es)
Impératif	va, allons, allez

S'asseoir to sit down

participe présent:	s'asseyant
participe passé:	assis(e)(es)

Présent de l'indicatif	m'assieds, t'assieds, s'assied, nous asseyons, vous asseyez, s'asseyent
Passé Composé	me suis assis(e), t'es assis(e), s'est assis(e), nous sommes assis(es), vous êtes assis(es), se sont assis(es)
Imparfait	m'asseyais, t'asseyais, s'asseyait, nous asseyions, vous asseyiez, s'asseyaient
Plus-que-parfait	m'étais assis(e), t'étais assis(e), s'était assis(e), nous étions assis(es), vous étiez assis(es), s'étaient assis(es)
Passé Simple	m'assis, t'assis, s'assit, nous assîmes, vous assîtes, s'assirent

Futur Simple	m'assiérai, t'assiéras, s'assiéra, nous assiérons, vous assiérez, s'assiéront
Futur Antérieur	me serai assis(e), te seras assis(e), se sera assis(e), nous serons assis(es), vous serez assis(es), se seront assis(es)
Conditionnel Présent	m'assiérais, t'assiérais, s'assiérait, nous assiérions, vous assiériez, s'assiéraient
Conditionnel Passé	me serais assis(e), te serais assis(e), se serait assis(e), nous serions assis(es), vous seriez assis(es), se seraient assis(es)
Subjonctif Présent	m'asseye, t'asseyes, s'asseye, nous asseyions, vous asseyiez, s'asseyent
Subjonctif Passé	me sois assis(e), te sois assis(e), se soit assis(e), nous soyons assis(es), vous soyez assis(es), se soient assis(es)
Infinitif Passé	s'être assis(e)(s)(es)
Impératif	assieds-toi, asseyons-nous, asseyez-vous

Avoir *to have*

participe présent:	ayant
participe passé:	eu

Présent de l'indicatif	ai, as, a, avons, avez, ont
Passé Composé	ai vu, as vu, a vu, avons vu, avez vu, ont vu
Imparfait	avais, avais, avait, avions, aviez, avaient
Plus-que-parfait	avais eu, avais eu, avait eu, avions eu, aviez eu, avaient eu
Passé Simple	eus, eus, eut, eûmes, eûtes, eurent
Futur Simple	aurai, auras, aura, aurons, aurez, auront
Futur Antérieur	aurai eu, auras eu, aura eu, aurons eu, aurez eu, auront eu
Conditionnel Présent	aurais, aurais, aurait, aurions, auriez, auraient
Conditionnel Passé	aurais eu, aurais eu, aurait eu, aurions eu, auriez eu, auraient eu
Subjonctif Présent	aie, aies, ait, ayons, ayez, aient
Subjonctif Passé	aie eu, aies eu, ait eu, ayons eu, ayez eu, aient eu
Infinitif Passé	avoir eu
Impératif	aie, ayons, ayez

Boire *to drink*

participe présent:	buvant
participe passé:	bu

Présent de l'indicatif	bois, bois, boit, buvons, buvez, boivent
Passé Composé	ai bu, as bu, a bu, avons bu, avez bu, ont bu
Imparfait	buvais, buvais, buvait, buvions, buviez, buvaient
Plus-que-parfait	avais bu, avais bu, avait bu, avions bu, aviez bu, avaient bu
Passé Simple	bus, bus, but, bûmes, bûtes, burent
Futur Simple	boirai, boiras, boira, boirons, boirez, boiront
Futur Antérieur	aurai bu, auras bu, aura bu, aurons bu, aurez bu, auront bu

Conditionnel Présent	**boirais, boirais, boirait, boirions, boiriez, boiraient**
Conditionnel Passé	**aurais bu, aurais bu, aurait bu, aurions bu, auriez bu, auraient bu**
Subjonctif Présent	**boive, boives, boive, buvions, buviez, boivent**
Subjonctif Passé	**aie bu, aies bu, ait bu, ayons bu, ayez bu, aient bu**
Infinitif Passé	**avoir bu**
Impératif	**bois, buvons, buvez**

Conduire *to drive*

participe présent:	**conduisant**
participe passé:	**conduit**
Présent de l'indicatif	**conduis, conduis, conduit, conduisons, conduisez, conduisent**
Passé Composé	**ai conduit, as conduit, a conduit, avons conduit, avez conduit, ont conduit**
Imparfait	**conduisais, conduisais, conduisait, conduisions, conduisiez, conduisaient**
Plus-que-parfait	**avais conduit, avais conduit, avait conduit, avions conduit, aviez conduit, avaient conduit**
Passé Simple	**conduisis, conduisis, conduisit, conduisîmes, conduisîtes, conduisirent**
Futur Simple	**conduirai, conduiras, conduira, conduirons, conduirez, conduiront**
Futur Antérieur	**aurai conduit, auras conduit, aura conduit, aurons conduit, aurez conduit, auront conduit**
Conditionnel Présent	**conduirais, conduirais, conduirait, conduirions, conduiriez, conduiraient**
Conditionnel Passé	**aurais conduit, aurais conduit, aurait conduit, aurions conduit, auriez conduit, auraient conduit**
Subjonctif Présent	**conduise, conduises, conduise, conduisions, conduisiez, conduisent**
Subjonctif Passé	**aie conduit, aies conduit, ait conduit, ayons conduit, ayez conduit, aient conduit**
Infinitif Passé	**avoir conduit**
Impératif	**conduis, conduisons, conduisez**

Connaître *to know*

participe présent:	**connaissant**
participe passé:	**connu**
Présent de l'indicatif	**connais, connais, connait, connaissons, connaissez, connaissent**
Passé Composé	**ai connu, as connu, a connu, avons connu, avez connu, ont connu**
Imparfait	**connaissais, connaissais, connaissait, connaissions, connaissiez, connaissaient**

Plus-que-parfait	**avais connu, avais connu, avait connu, avions connu, aviez connu, avaient connu**
Passé Simple	**connus, connus, connut, connûmes, connûtes, connurent**
Futur Simple	**connaîtrai, connaîtras, connaîtra, connaîtrons, connaîtrez, connaîtront**
Futur Antérieur	**aurai connu, auras connu, aura connu, aurons connu, aurez connu, auront connu**
Conditionnel Présent	**connaîtrais, connaîtrais, connaîtrait, connaîtrions, connaîtriez, connaîtraient**
Conditionnel Passé	**aurais connu, aurais connu, aurait connu, aurions connu, auriez connu, auraient connu**
Subjonctif Présent	**connaisse, connaisses, connaisse, connaissions, connaissiez, connaissent**
Subjonctif Passé	**aie connu, aies connu, ait connu, ayons connu, ayez connu, aient connu**
Infinitif Passé	**avoir connu**
Impératif	**connais, connaissons, connaissez**

Courir *to run*

participe présent:	**courant**
participe passé:	**couru**

Présent de l'indicatif	**cours, cours, court, courons, courez, courent**
Passé Composé	**ai couru, as couru, a couru, avons couru, avez couru, ont couru**
Imparfait	**courais, courais, courait, courions, couriez, couraient**
Plus-que-parfait	**avais couru, avais couru, avait couru, avions couru, aviez couru, avaient couru**
Passé Simple	**courus, courus, courut, courûmes, courûtes, coururent**
Futur Simple	**courrai, courras, courra, courrons, courrez, courront**
Futur Antérieur	**aurai couru, auras couru, aura couru, aurons couru, aurez couru, auront couru**
Conditionnel Présent	**courrais, courrais, courrait, courrions, courriez, courraient**
Conditionnel Passé	**aurais couru, aurais couru, aurait couru, aurions couru, auriez couru, auraient couru**
Subjonctif Présent	**coure, coures, coure, courions, couriez, courent**
Subjonctif Passé	**aie couru, aies couru, ait couru, ayons couru, ayez couru, aient couru**
Infinitif Passé	**avoir couru**
Impératif	**cours, courons, courez**

Craindre *to fear*

participe présent:	**craignant**
participe passé:	**craint**

Présent de l'indicatif	**crains, crains, craint, craignons, craignez, craignent**
Passé Composé	**ai craint, as craint, a craint, avons craint, avez craint, ont craint**

Imparfait	craignais, craignais, craignait, craignions, craigniez, craignaient
Plus-que-parfait	avais craint, avais craint, avait craint, avions craint, aviez craint, avaient craint
Passé Simple	craignis, craignis, craignit, craignîmes, craignîtes, craignirent
Futur Simple	craindrai, craindras, craindra, craindrons, craindrez, craindront
Futur Antérieur	aurai craint, auras craint, aura craint, aurons craint, aurez craint, auront craint
Conditionnel Présent	craindrais, craindrais, craindrait, craindrions, craindriez, craindraient
Conditionnel Passé	aurais craint, aurais craint, aurait craint, aurions craint, auriez craint, auraient craint
Subjonctif Présent	craigne, craignes, craigne, craignions, craignies, craignent
Subjonctif Passé	aie craint, aies craint, ait craint, ayons craint, ayez craint, aient craint
Infinitif Passé	avoir craint
Impératif	crains, craignons, craignez

Croire *to believe*

participe présent:	croyant
participe passé:	cru

Présent de l'indicatif	crois, crois, croit, croyons, croyez, croient
Passé Composé	ai cru, as cru, a cru, avons cru, avez cru, ont cru
Imparfait	croyais, croyais, croyait, croyions, croyiez, croyaient
Plus-que-parfait	avais cru, avais cru, avait cru, avions cru, aviez cru, avaient cru
Passé Simple	crus, crus, crut, crûmes, crûtes, crurent
Futur Simple	croirai, croiras, croira, croirons, croirez, croiront
Futur Antérieur	aurai cru, auras cru, aura cru, aurons cru, aurez cru, auront cru
Conditionnel Présent	croirais, croirais, croirait, croirions, croiriez, croiraient
Conditionnel Passé	aurais cru, aurais cru, aurait cru, aurions cru, auriez cru, auraient cru
Subjonctif Présent	croie, croies, croie, croyions, croyiez, croient
Subjonctif Passé	aie cru, aies cru, ait cru, ayons cru, ayez cru, aient cru
Infinitif Passé	avoir cru
Impératif	crois, croyons, croyez

Devoir *to have to, to owe*

participe présent:	devant
participe passé:	dû

Présent de l'indicatif	dois, dois, doit, devons, devez, doivent
Passé Composé	ai dû, as dû, a dû, avons dû, avez dû, ont dû
Imparfait	devais, devais, devait, devions, deviez, devaient

Plus-que-parfait	**avais dû, avais dû, avait dû, avions dû, aviez dû, avaient dû**
Passé Simple	**dus, dus, dut, dûmes, dûtes, durent**
Futur Simple	**devrai, devras, devra, devrons, devrez, devront**
Futur Antérieur	**aurai dû, auras dû, aura dû, aurons dû, aurez dû, auront dû**
Conditionnel Présent	**devrais, devrais, devrait, devrions, devriez, devraient**
Conditionnel Passé	**aurais dû, aurais dû, aurait dû, aurions dû, auriez dû, auraient dû**
Subjonctif Présent	**doive, doives, doive, devions, deviez, doivent**
Subjonctif Passé	**aie dû, aies dû, ait dû, ayons dû, ayez dû, aient dû**
Infinitif Passé	**avoir dû**
Impératif	**dois, devons, devez**

Dire *to say, to tell*

participe présent:	**disant**
participe passé:	**dit**

Présent de l'indicatif	**dis, dis, dit, disons, dites, disent**
Passé Composé	**ai dit, as dit, a dit, avons dit, avez dit, ont dit**
Imparfait	**disais, disais, disait, disions, disiez, disaient**
Plus-que-parfait	**avais dit, avais dit, avait dit, avions dit, aviez dit, avaient dit**
Passé Simple	**dis, dis, dit, dîmes, dîtes, dirent**
Futur Simple	**dirai, diras, dira, dirons, direz, diront**
Futur Antérieur	**aurai dit, auras dit, aura dit, aurons dit, aurez dit, auront dit**
Conditionnel Présent	**dirais, dirais, dirait, dirions, diriez, diraient**
Conditionnel Passé	**aurais dit, aurais dit, aurait dit, aurions dit, auriez dit, auraient dit**
Subjonctif Présent	**dise, dises, dise, disions, disiez, disent**
Subjonctif Passé	**aie dit, aies dit, ait dit, ayons dit, ayez dit, aient dit**
Infinitif Passé	**avoir dit**
Impératif	**dis, disons, dites**

Dormir *to sleep*

participe présent:	**dormant**
participe passé:	**dormi**

Présent de l'indicatif	**dors, dors, dort, dormons, dormez, dorment**
Passé Composé	**ai dormi, as dormi, a dormi, avons dormi, avez dormi, ont dormi**
Imparfait	**dormais, dormais, dormait, dormions, dormiez, dormaient**
Plus-que-parfait	**avais dormi, avais dormi, avait dormi, avions dormi, aviez dormi, avaient dormi**
Passé Simple	**dormis, dormis, dormit, dormîmes, dormîtes, dormirent**
Futur Simple	**dormirai, dormiras, dormira, dormirons, dormirez, dormiront**

Futur Antérieur	**aurai dormi, auras dormi, aura dormi, aurons dormi, aurez dormi, auront dormi**
Conditionnel Présent	**dormirais, dormirais, dormirait, dormirions, dormiriez, dormiraient**
Conditionnel Passé	**aurais dormi, aurais dormi, aurait dormi, aurions dormi, auriez dormi, auraient dormi**
Subjonctif Présent	**dorme, dormes, dorme, dormions, dormiez, dorment**
Subjonctif Passé	**aie dormi, aies dormi, ait dormi, ayons dormi, ayez dormi, aient dormi**
Infinitif Passé	**avoir dormi**
Impératif	**dors, dormons, dormez**

Écrire *to write*

participe présent:	**écrivant**
participe passé:	**écrit**

Présent de l'indicatif	**écris, écris, écrit, écrivons, écrivez, écrivent**
Passé Composé	**ai écrit, as écrit, a écrit, avons écrit, avez écrit, ont écrit**
Imparfait	**écrivais, écrivais, écrivait, écrivions, écriviez, écrivaient**
Plus-que-parfait	**avais écrit, avais écrit, avait écrit, avions écrit, aviez écrit, avaient écrit**
Passé Simple	**écris, écris, écrit, écrivons, écrivez, écrivent**
Futur Simple	**écrirai, écriras, écrira, écrirons, écrirez, écriront**
Futur Antérieur	**aurai écrit, auras écrit, aura écrit, aurons écrit, aurez écrit, auront écrit**
Conditionnel Présent	**écrirais, écrirais, écrirait, écririons, écririez, écriraient**
Conditionnel Passé	**aurais écrit, aurais écrit, aurait écrit, aurions écrit, auriez écrit, auraient écrit**
Subjonctif Présent	**écrive, écrives, écrive, écrivions, écriviez, écrivent**
Subjonctif Passé	**aie écrit, aies écrit, ait écrit, ayons écrit, ayez écrit, aient écrit**
Infinitif Passé	**avoir écrit**
Impératif	**écris, écrivons, écrivez**

Être *to be*

participe présent:	**étant**
participe passé:	**été**

Présent de l'indicatif	**suis, es, est, sommes, êtes, sont**
Passé Composé	**ai été, as été, a été, avons été, avez été, ont été**
Imparfait	**étais, étais, était, étions, étiez, étaient**
Plus-que-parfait	**avais été, avais été, avait été, avions été, aviez été, avaient été**
Passé Simple	**fus, fus, fut, fûmes, fûtes, furent**
Futur Simple	**serai, seras, sera, serons, serez, seront**
Futur Antérieur	**aurai été, auras été, aura été, aurons été, aurez été, auront été**

Conditionnel Présent	**serais, serais, serait, serions, seriez, seraient**
Conditionnel Passé	**aurais été, aurais été, aurait été, aurions été, auriez été, auraient été**
Subjonctif Présent	**sois, sois, soit, soyons, soyez, soient**
Subjonctif Passé	**aie été, aies été, ait été, ayons été, ayez été, aient été**
Infinitif Passé	**avoir été**
Impératif	**sois, soyons, soyez**

Faire *to do, to make*

participe présent:	**faisant**
participe passé:	**fait**

Présent de l'indicatif	**fais, fais, fait, faisons, faites, font**
Passé Composé	**ai fait, as fait, a fait, avons fait, avez fait, ont fait**
Imparfait	**faisais, faisais, faisait, faisions, faisiez, faisaient**
Plus-que-parfait	**avais fait, avais fait, avait fait, avions fait, aviez fait, avaient fait**
Passé Simple	**fis, fis, fit, fîmes, fîtes, firent**
Futur Simple	**ferai, feras, fera, ferons, ferez, feront**
Futur Antérieur	**aurai fait, auras fait, aura fait, aurons fait, aurez fait, auront fait**
Conditionnel Présent	**ferais, ferais, ferait, ferions, feriez, feraient**
Conditionnel Passé	**aurais fait, aurais fait, aurait fait, aurions fait, auriez fait, auraient fait**
Subjonctif Présent	**fasse, fasses, fasse, fassions, fassiez, fassent**
Subjonctif Passé	**aie fait, aies fait, ait fait, ayons fait, ayez fait, aient fait**
Infinitif Passé	**avoir fait**
Impératif	**fais, faisons, faites**

Falloir *to be necessary*

participe présent:	[not in use]
participe passé:	**fallu**

Présent de l'indicatif	**il faut**
Passé Composé	**il a fallu**
Imparfait	**il fallait**
Plus-que-parfait	**il avait fallu**
Passé Simple	**il fallut**
Futur Simple	**il faudra**
Futur Antérieur	**il aura fallu**
Conditionnel Présent	**il faudrait**
Conditionnel Passé	**il aurait fallu**
Subjonctif Présent	**qu'il faille**
Subjonctif Passé	**qu'il ait fallu**

Lire *to read*
participe présent:	**lisant**
participe passé:	**lu**

Présent de l'indicatif	**lis, lis, lit, lisons, lisez, lisent**
Passé Composé	**ai lu, as lu, a lu, avons lu, avez lu, ont lu**
Imparfait	**lisais, lisais, lisait, lisions, lisiez, lisaient**
Plus-que-parfait	**avais lu, avais lu, avait lu, avions lu, aviez lu, avaient lu**
Passé Simple	**lus, lus, lut, lûmes, lûtes, lurent**
Futur Simple	**lirai, liras, lira, lirons, lirez, liront**
Futur Antérieur	**aurai lu, auras lu, aura lu, aurons lu, aurez lu, auront lu**
Conditionnel Présent	**lirais, lirais, lirait, lirions, liriez, liraient**
Conditionnel Passé	**aurais lu, aurais lu, aurait lu, aurions lu, auriez lu, auraient lu**
Subjonctif Présent	**lise, lises, lise, lisions, lisiez, lisent**
Subjonctif Passé	**aie lu, aies lu, ait lu, ayons lu, ayez lu, aient lu**
Infinitif Passé	**avoir lu**
Impératif	**lis, lisons, lisez**

Mettre *to put*
participe présent:	**mettant**
participe passé:	**mis**

Présent de l'indicatif	**mets, mets, met, mettons, mettez, mettent**
Passé Composé	**ai mis, as mis, a mis, avons mis, avez mis, ont mis**
Imparfait	**mettais, mettais, mettait, mettions, mettiez, mettaient**
Plus-que-parfait	**avais mis, avais mis, avait mis, avions mis, aviez mis, avaient mis**
Passé Simple	**mis, mis, mit, mîmes, mîtes, mirent**
Futur Simple	**mettrai, mettras, mettra, mettrons, mettrez, mettront**
Futur Antérieur	**aurai mis, auras mis, aura mis, aurons mis, aurez mis, auront mis**
Conditionnel Présent	**mettrais, mettrais, mettrait, mettrions, mettriez, mettraient**
Conditionnel Passé	**aurais mis, aurais mis, aurait mis, aurions mis, auriez mis, auraient mis**
Subjonctif Présent	**mette, mettes, mette, mettions, mettiez, mettent**
Subjonctif Passé	**aie mis, aies mis, ait mis, ayons mis, ayez mis, aient mis**
Infinitif Passé	**avoir mis**
Impératif	**mets, mettons, mettez**

Mourir *to die*
participe présent:	**mourant**
participe passé:	**mort**

Présent de l'indicatif	**meurs, meurs, meurt, mourons, mourez, meurent**
Passé Composé	**suis mort(e), es mort(e), est mort(e), sommes morts(es), êtes morts(es), sont morts(es)**
Imparfait	**mourais, mourais, mourait, mourions, mouriez, mouraient**

Plus-que-parfait	**étais mort(e), étais mort(e), était mort(e), étions morts(es), étiez morts(es), étaient morts(es)**
Passé Simple	**mourus, mourus, mourut, mourûmes, mourûtes, moururent**
Futur Simple	**mourrai, mourras, mourra, mourrons, mourrez, mourront**
Futur Antérieur	**serai mort(e), seras mort(e), sera mort(e), serons morts(es), serez morts(es), seront morts(es)**
Conditionnel Présent	**mourrais, mourrais, mourrait, mourrions, mourriez, mourraient**
Conditionnel Passé	**serais mort(e), serais mort(e), serait mort(e), serions morts(es), seriez morts(es), seraient morts(es)**
Subjonctif Présent	**meure, meures, meure, mourions, mouriez, meurent**
Subjonctif Passé	**sois mort(e), sois mort(e), soit mort(e), soyons morts(es), soyez morts(es), soient morts(es)**
Infinitif Passé	**être mort(e) (s) (es)**
Impératif	**meurs, mourons, mourez**

Naître *to be born*

participe présent:	**naissant**
participe passé:	**né(e)(s)**
Présent de l'indicatif	**nais, nais, naît, naissons, naissez, naissent**
Passé Composé	**suis né(e), es né(e), est né(e), sommes nés(es), êtes nés(es), sont nés(es)**
Imparfait	**naissais, naissais, naissait, naissions, naissiez, naissaient**
Plus-que-parfait	**étais né(e), étais né(e), était né(e), étions nés(es), étiez nés(es), étaient nés(es)**
Passé Simple	**naquis, naquis, naquit, naquîmes, naquîtes, naquirent**
Futur Simple	**naîtrai, naîtras, naîtra, naîtrons, naîtrez, naîtront**
Futur Antérieur	**serai né(e), seras né(e), sera né(e), serons nés(es), serez nés(es), seraient nés(es)**
Conditionnel Présent	**naîtrais, naîtrais, naîtrait, naîtrions, naîtriez, naîtraient**
Conditionnel Passé	**serais né(e), seras né(e), sera né(e), serons nés(es), serez nés(es), seraient nés(es)**
Subjonctif Présent	**naisse, naisses, naisse, naissions, naissiez, naissent**
Subjonctif Passé	**sois né(e), sois né(e), soit né(e), soyons nés(es), soyez nés(es), soient nés(es)**
Infinitif Passé	**être né(e) (s)**
Impératif	**nais, naissons, naissez**

Ouvrir *to open*

participe présent:	**ouvrant**
participe passé:	**ouvert**
Présent de l'indicatif	**ouvre, ouvres, ouvre, ouvrons, ouvrez, ouvrent**
Passé Composé	**ai ouvert, as ouvert, a ouvert, avons ouvert, avez ouvert, ont ouvert**
Imparfait	**ouvrais, ouvrais, ouvrait, ouvrions, ouvriez, ouvraient**

Plus-que-parfait	**avais ouvert, avais ouvert, avait ouvert, avions ouvert, aviez ouvert, avaient ouvert**
Passé Simple	**ouvris, ouvris, ouvrit, ouvrîmes, ouvrîtes, ouvrirent**
Futur Simple	**ouvrirai, ouvriras, ouvrira, ouvrirons, ouvrirez, ouvriront**
Futur Antérieur	**aurai ouvert, auras ouvert, aura ouvert, aurons ouvert, aurez ouvert, auront ouvert**
Conditionnel Présent	**ouvrirais, ouvrirais, ouvrirait, ouvririons, ouvririez, ouvriraient**
Conditionnel Passé	**aurais ouvert, aurais ouvert, aurait ouvert, aurions ouvert, auriez ouvert, auraient ouvert**
Subjonctif Présent	**ouvre, ouvres, ouvre, ouvrions, ouvriez, ouvrent**
Subjonctif Passé	**aie ouvert, aies ouvert, ait ouvert, ayons ouvert, ayez ouvert, aient ouvert**
Infinitif Passé	**avoir ouvert**
Impératif	**ouvre, ouvrons, ouvrez**

Partir *to leave, to depart*

participe présent:	**partant**
participe passé:	**parti(e)(s)**

Présent de l'indicatif	**pars, pars, part, partons, partez, partent**
Passé Composé	**suis parti(e), es parti(e), est parti(e), sommes partis(es), êtes partis(es), sont partis(es)**
Imparfait	**partais, partais, partait, partions, partiez, partaient**
Plus-que-parfait	**étais parti(e), étais parti(e), était parti(e), étions partis(es), étiez partis(es), étaient partis(es)**
Passé Simple	**partis, partis, partit, partîmes, partîtes, partirent**
Futur Simple	**partirai, partiras, partira, partirons, partirez, partiront**
Futur Antérieur	**serai parti(e), seras parti(e), sera parti(e), serons partis(es), serez partis(es), seront partis(es)**
Conditionnel Présent	**partirais, partirais, partirait, partirions, partiriez, partiraient**
Conditionnel Passé	**serais parti(e), seras parti(e), sera parti(e), serons partis(es), serez partis(es), seraient partis(es)**
Subjonctif Présent	**parte, partes, parte, partions, partiez, partent**
Subjonctif Passé	**sois parti(e), sois parti(e), soit parti(e), soyons partis(es), soyez partis(es), soient partis(es)**
Infinitif Passé	**être parti(e)(s)**
Impératif	**pars, partons, partez**

Peindre *to paint*

participe présent:	**peignant**
participe passé:	**peint**

Présent de l'indicatif	**peins, peins, peint, peignons, peignez, peignent**
Passé Composé	**ai peint, as peint, a peint, avons peint, avez peint, ont peint**

Imparfait	**peignais, peignais, peignait, peignions, peigniez, peignaient**
Plus-que-parfait	**avais peint, avais peint, avait peint, avions peint, aviez peint, avaient peint**
Passé Simple	**peignis, peignis, peignit, peignîmes, peignîtes, peignirent**
Futur Simple	**peindrai, peindras, peindra, peindrons, peindrez, peindront**
Futur Antérieur	**aurai peint, auras peint, aura peint, aurons peint, aurez peint, auront peint**
Conditionnel Présent	**peindrais, peindrais, peindrait, peindrions, peindriez, pendraient**
Conditionnel Passé	**aurais peint, aurais peint, aurait peint, aurions peint, auriez peint, auraient peint**
Subjonctif Présent	**peigne, peignes, peigne, peignions, peigniez, peignent**
Subjonctif Passé	**aie peint, aies peint, ait peint, ayons peint, ayez peint, aient peint**
Infinitif Passé	**avoir peint**
Impératif	**peins, peignons, peignez**

Plaire *to appeal, to be liked*

participe présent:	**plaisant**
participe passé:	**plu**

Présent de l'indicatif	**plais, plais, plaît, plaisons, plaisez, plaisent**
Passé Composé	**ai plu, as plu, a plu, avons plu, avez plu, ont plu**
Imparfait	**plaisais, plaisais, plaisait, plaisions, plaisiez, plaisaient**
Plus-que-parfait	**avais plu, avais plu, avait plu, avions plu, aviez plu, avaient plu**
Passé Simple	**plus, plus, plut, plûmes, plûtes, plurent**
Futur Simple	**plairai, plairas, plaira, plairons, plairez, plairont**
Futur Antérieur	**aurai plu, auras plu, aura plus, aurons plu, aurez plu, auront plu**
Conditionnel Présent	**plairais, plairais, plairait, plairions, plairiez, plairaient**
Conditionnel Passé	**aurais plu, aurais plu, aurait plu, aurions plu, auriez plu, auraient plu**
Subjonctif Présent	**plaise, plaises, plaise, plaisions, plaisiez, plaisent**
Subjonctif Passé	**aie plu, aies plu, ait plu, ayons plu, ayez plu, aient plu**
Infinitif Passé	**avoir plu**
Impératif	**plais, plaisons, plaisez**

Pleuvoir *to rain*

participe présent:	**pleuvant**
participe passé:	**plu**

Présent de l'indicatif	**il pleut**
Passé Composé	**il a plu**
Imparfait	**il pleuvait**

Plus-que-parfait	**il avait plu**
Passé Simple	**il plut**
Futur Simple	**il pleuvra**
Futur Antérieur	**il aura plu**
Conditionnel Présent	**il pleuvrait**
Conditionnel Passé	**il aurait plu**
Subjonctif Présent	**qu'il pleuve**
Subjonctif Passé	**qu'il ait plu**
Infinitif Passé	**avoir plu**

Pouvoir *to be able to (can)*

participe présent:	**pouvant**
participe passé:	**pu**

Présent de l'indicatif	**peux (*ou* puis) peux, peut, pouvons, pouvez, peuvent**
Passé Composé	**ai pu, as pu, a pu, avons pu, avez pu, ont pu**
Imparfait	**pouvais, pouvais, pouvait, pouvions, pouviez, pouvaient**
Plus-que-parfait	**avais pu, avais pu, avait pu, avions pu, aviez pu, avaient pu**
Passé Simple	**pus, pus, put, pûmes, pûtes, purent**
Futur Simple	**pourrai, pourras, pourra, pourrons, pourrez, pourront**
Futur Antérieur	**aurai pu, auras pu, aura pu, aurons pu, aurez pu, auront pu**
Conditionnel Présent	**pourrais, pourrais, pourrait, pourrions, pourriez, pourraient**
Conditionnel Passé	**aurais pu, aurais pu, aurait pu, aurions pu, auriez pu, auraient pu**
Subjonctif Présent	**puisse, puisses, puisse, puissions, puissiez, puissent**
Subjonctif Passé	**aie pu, aies pu, ait pu, ayons pu, ayez pu, aient pu**
Infinitif Passé	**avoir pu**

Prendre *to take*

participe présent:	**prenant**
participe passé:	**pris**

Présent de l'indicatif	**prends, prends, prend, prenons, prenez, prennent**
Passé Composé	**ai pris, as pris, a pris, avons pris, avez pris, ont pris**
Imparfait	**prenais, prenais, prenait, prenions, preniez, prenaient**
Plus-que-parfait	**avais pris, avais pris, avait pris, avions pris, aviez pris, avaient pris**
Passé Simple	**pris, pris, prit, prîmes, prîtes, prirent**
Futur Simple	**prendrai, prendras, prendra, prendrons, prendrez, prendront**
Futur Antérieur	**aurai pris, auras pris, aura pris, aurons pris, aurez pris, auront pris**
Conditionnel Présent	**prendrais, prendrais, prendrait, prendrions, prendriez, prendraient**

Conditionnel Passé	aurais pris, aurais pris, aurait pris, aurions pris, auriez pris, auraient pris
Subjonctif Présent	prenne, prennes, prenne, prenions, preniez, prennent
Subjonctif Passé	aie pris, aies pris, ait pris, ayons pris, ayez pris, aient pris
Infinitif Passé	avoir pris
Impératif	prends, prenons, prenez

Recevoir to receive

participe présent:	recevant
participe passé:	reçu

Présent de l'indicatif	reçois, reçois, reçoit, recevons, recevez, reçoivent
Passé Composé	ai reçu, as reçu, a reçu, avons reçu, avez reçu, ont reçu
Imparfait	recevais, recevais, recevait, recevions, receviez, recevaient
Plus-que-parfait	avais reçu, avais reçu, avait reçu, avions reçu, aviez reçu, avaient reçu
Passé Simple	reçus, reçus, reçut, reçûmes, reçûtes, reçurent
Futur Simple	recevrai, recevras, recevra, recevrons, recevrez, recevront
Futur Antérieur	aurai reçu, auras reçu, aura reçu, aurons reçu, aurez reçu, auront reçu
Conditionnel Présent	recevrais, recevrais, recevrait, recevrions, recevriez, recevraient
Conditionnel Passé	aurais reçu, aurais reçu, aurait reçu, aurions reçu, auriez reçu, auraient reçu
Subjonctif Présent	reçoive, reçoives, reçoive, recevions, receviez, reçoivent
Subjonctif Passé	aie reçu, aies reçu, ait reçu, ayons reçu, ayez reçu, aient reçu
Infinitif Passé	avoir reçu
Impératif	reçois, recevons, recevez

Rire to laugh

participe présent:	riant
participe passé:	ri

Présent de l'indicatif	ris, ris, rit, rions, riez, rient
Passé Composé	ai ri, as ri, a ri, avons ri, avez ri, ont ri
Imparfait	riais, riais, riait, riions, riiez, riaient
Plus-que-parfait	avais ri, avais ri, avait ri, avions ri, aviez ri, avaient ri
Passé Simple	ris, ris, rit, rîmes, rîtes, riren
Futur Simple	rirai, riras, rira, rirons, rirez, riront
Futur Antérieur	aurai ri, auras ri, aura ri, aurons ri, aurez ri, auront ri
Conditionnel Présent	rirais, rirais, rirait, ririons, ririez, riraient
Conditionnel Passé	aurais ri, aurais ri, aurait ri, aurions ri, auriez ri, auraient ri
Subjonctif Présent	rie, ries, rie, riions, riiez, rient
Subjonctif Passé	aie ri, aies ri, ait ri, ayons ri, ayez ri, aient ri
Infinitif Passé	avoir ri
Impératif	ris, rions, riez

Savoir *to know*
participe présent: **sachant**
participe passé: **su**

Présent de l'indicatif	**sais, sais, sait, savons, savez, savent**
Passé Composé	**ai su, as su, a su, avons su, avez su, ont su**
Imparfait	**savais, savais, savait, savions, saviez, savaient**
Plus-que-parfait	**avais su, avais su, avait su, avions su, aviez su, avaient su**
Passé Simple	**sus, sus, sut, sûmes, sûtes, surent**
Futur Simple	**saurai, sauras, saura, saurons, saurez, sauront**
Futur Antérieur	**aurai su, auras su, aura su, aurons su, aurez su, auront su**
Conditionnel Présent	**saurais, saurais, saurait, saurions, sauriez, sauraient**
Conditionnel Passé	**aurais su, aurais su, aurait su, aurions su, auriez su, auraient su**
Subjonctif Présent	**sache, saches, sache, sachions, sachiez, sachent**
Subjonctif Passé	**aie su, aies su, ait su, ayons su, ayez su, aient su**
Infinitif Passé	**avoir su**
Impératif	**sache, sachons, sachez**

Suivre *to follow*
participe présent: **suivant**
participe passé: **suivi**

Présent de l'indicatif	**suis, suis, suit, suivons, suivez, suivent**
Passé Composé	**ai suivi, as suivi, a suivi, avons suivi, avez suivi, ont suivi**
Imparfait	**suivais, suivais, suivait, suivions, suiviez, suivaient**
Plus-que-parfait	**avais suivi, avais suivi, avait suivi, avions suivi, aviez suivi, avaient suivi**
Passé Simple	**suivis, suivis, suivit, suivîmes, suivîtes, suivirent**
Futur Simple	**suivrai, suivras, suivra, suivrons, suivrez, suivront**
Futur Antérieur	**aurai suivi, auras suivi, aura suivi, aurons suivi, aurez suivi, auront suivi**
Conditionnel Présent	**suivrais, suivrais, suivrait, suivrions, suivriez, suivraient**
Conditionnel Passé	**aurais suivi, aurais suivi, aurait suivi, aurions suivi, auriez suivi, auraient suivi**
Subjonctif Présent	**suive, suives, suive, suivions, suiviez, suivent**
Subjonctif Passé	**aie suivi, aies suivi, ait suivi, ayons suivi, ayez suivi, aient suivi**
Infinitif Passé	**avoir suivi**
Impératif	**suis, suivons, suivez**

Tenir *to hold*

participe présent:	**tenant**
participe passé:	**tenu**

Présent de l'indicatif	**tiens, tiens, tient, tenons, tenez, tiennent**
Passé Composé	**ai tenu, as tenu, a tenu, avons tenu, avez tenu, ont tenu**
Imparfait	**tenais, tenais, tenait, tenions, teniez, tenaient**
Plus-que-parfait	**avais tenu, avais tenu, avait tenu, avions tenu, aviez tenu, avaient tenu**
Passé Simple	**tins, tins, tint, tînmes, tîntes, tinrent**
Futur Simple	**tiendrai, tiendras, tiendra, tiendrons, tiendrez, tiendront**
Futur Antérieur	**aurai tenu, auras tenu, aura tenu, aurons tenu, aurez tenu, auront tenu**
Conditionnel Présent	**tiendrais, tiendrais, tiendrait, tiendrions, tiendriez, tiendraient**
Conditionnel Passé	**aurais tenu, aurais tenu, aurait tenu, aurions tenu, auriez tenu, auraient tenu**
Subjonctif Présent	**tienne, tiennes, tienne, tenions, teniez, tiennent**
Subjonctif Passé	**aie tenu, aies tenu, ait tenu, ayons tenu, ayez tenu, aient tenu**
Infinitif Passé	**avoir tenu**
Impératif	**tiens, tenons, tenez**

Vaincre *to vanquish, to conquer*

participe présent:	**vainquant**
participe passé:	**vaincu**

Présent de l'indicatif	**vaincs, vaincs, vainc, vainquons, vainquez, vainquent**
Passé Composé	**ai vaincu, as vaincu, a vaincu, avons vaincu, avez vaincu, ont vaincu**
Imparfait	**vainquais, vainquais, vainquait, vainquions, vainquiez, vainquaient**
Plus-que-parfait	**avais vaincu, avais vaincu, avait vaincu, avions vaincu, aviez vaincu, avaient vaincu**
Passé Simple	**vainquis, vainquis, vainquit, vainquîmes, vainquîtes, vainquirent**
Futur Simple	**vaincrai, vaincras, vaincra, vaincrons, vaincrez, vaincront**
Futur Antérieur	**aurai vaincu, auras vaincu, aura vaincu, aurons vaincu, aurez vaincu, auront vaincu**
Conditionnel Présent	**vaincrais, vaincrais, vaincrait, vaincrions, vaincriez, vaincraient**
Conditionnel Passé	**aurais vaincu, aurais vaincu, aurait vaincu, aurions vaincu, auriez vaincu, auraient vaincu**
Subjonctif Présent	**vainque, vainques, vainque, vainquions, vainquiez, vainquent**
Subjonctif Passé	**aie vaincu, aies vaincu, ait vaincu, ayons vaincu, ayez vaincu, aient vaincu**
Infinitif Passé	**avoir vaincu**
Impératif	**vaincs, vainquons, vainquez**

Valoir *to be worth*
participe présent: **valant**
participe passé: **valu**

Présent de l'indicatif	**vaux, vaux, vaut, valons, valez, valent**
Passé Composé	**ai valu, as valu, a valu, avons valu, avez valu, ont valu**
Imparfait	**valais, valais, valait, valions, valiez, valaient**
Plus-que-parfait	**avais valu, avais valu, avait valu, avions valu, aviez valu, avaient valu**
Passé Simple	**valus, valus, valut, valûmes, valûtes, valurent**
Futur Simple	**vaudrai, vaudras, vaudra, vaudrons, vaudrez, vaudront**
Futur Antérieur	**aurai valu, auras valu, aura valu, aurons valu, aurez valu, auront valu**
Conditionnel Présent	**vaudrais, vaudrais, vaudrait, vaudrions, vaudriez, vaudraient**
Conditionnel Passé	**aurais valu, aurais valu, aurait valu, aurions valu, auriez valu, auraient valu**
Subjonctif Présent	**vaille, vailles, vaille, valions, valiez, vaillent**
Subjonctif Passé	**aie valu, aies valu, ait valu, ayons valu, ayez valu, aient valu**
Infinitif Passé	**avoir valu**
Impératif	**vaux, valons, valez**

Venir *to come*
participe présent: **venant**
participe passé: **venu(e)(s)**

Présent de l'indicatif	**viens, viens, vient, venons, venez, viennent**
Passé Composé	**suis venu(e), es venu(e), est venu(e), sommes venus(es), êtes venus(es), sont venus(es)**
Imparfait	**venais, venais, venait, venions, veniez, venaient**
Plus-que-parfait	**étais venu(e), étais venu(e), était venu(e), étions venus(es), étiez venus(es) étions venus(es)**
Passé Simple	**vins, vins, vint, vînmes, vîntes, vinrent**
Futur Simple	**viendrai, viendras, viendra, viendrons, viendrez, viendront**
Futur Antérieur	**serai venu(e), seras venu(e), sera venu(e), serons venus(es), serez venus(es), seront venus(es)**
Conditionnel Présent	**viendrais, viendrais, viendrait, viendrions, viendriez, viendraient**
Conditionnel Passé	**serais venu(e), serais venu(e), serait venu(e), serions venus(es), seriez venus(es), seraient venus(es)**
Subjonctif Présent	**vienne, viennes, vienne, venions, veniez, viennent**
Subjonctif Passé	**sois venu(e), sois venu(e), soit venu(e), soyons venus(es), soyez venus(es), soient venus(es)**
Infinitif Passé	**être venu(e)(s)**
Impératif	**viens, venons, venez**

Vivre *to live*
participe présent: **vivant**
participe passé: **vécu**

Présent de l'indicatif	**vis, vis, vit, vivons, vivez, vivent**
Passé Composé	**ai vécu, as vécu, a vécu, avons vécu, avez vécu, ont vécu**
Imparfait	**vivais, vivais, vivait, vivions, viviez, vivaient**
Plus-que-parfait	**avais vécu, avais vécu, avait vécu, avions vécu, aviez vécu, avaient vécu**
Passé Simple	**vécus, vécus, vécut, vécûmes, vécûtes, vécurent**
Futur Simple	**vivrai, vivras, vivra, vivront, vivrez, vivront**
Futur Antérieur	**aurai vécu, auras vécu, aura vécu, aurons vécu, aurez vécu, auront vécu**
Conditionnel Présent	**vivrais, vivrais, vivrait, vivrions, vivriez, vivraient**
Conditionnel Passé	**aurais vécu, aurais vécu, aurait vécu, aurions vécu, auriez vécu, auraient vécu**
Subjonctif Présent	**vive, vives, vive, vivions, viviez, vivent**
Subjonctif Passé	**aie vécu, aies vécu, ait vécu, ayons vécu, ayez vécu, aient vécu**
Infinitif Passé	**avoir vécu**
Impératif	**vis, vivons, vivez**

Voir *to see*
participe présent: **voyant**
participe passé: **vu**

Présent de l'indicatif	**vois, vois, voit, voyons, voyez, voient**
Passé Composé	**ai vu, as vu, a vu, avons vu, avez vu, ont vu**
Imparfait	**voyais, voyais, voyait, voyions, voyiez, voyaient**
Plus-que-parfait	**avais vu, avais vu, avait vu, avions vu, aviez vu, avaient vu**
Passé Simple	**vis, vis, vit, vîmes, vîtes, virent**
Futur Simple	**verrai, verras, verra, verrons, verrez, verront**
Futur Antérieur	**aurai vu, auras vu, aura vu, aurons vu, aurez vu, auront vu**
Conditionnel Présent	**verrais, verrais, verrait, verrions, verriez, verraient**
Conditionnel Passé	**aurais vu, aurais vu, aurait vu, aurions vu, auriez vu, auraient vu**
Subjonctif Présent	**voie, voies, voie, voyions, voyiez, voient**
Subjonctif Passé	**aie vu, aies vu, ait vu, ayons vu, ayez vu, aient vu**
Infinitif Passé	**avoir vu**
Impératif	**vois, voyons, voyez**

Vouloir *to want*
participe présent: **voulant**
participe passé: **voulu**

Présent de l'indicatif	**veux, veux, veut, voulons, voulez, veulent**
Passé Composé	**ai voulu, as voulu, a voulu, avons voulu, avez voulu, ont voulu**
Imparfait	**voulais, voulais, voulait, voulions, vouliez, voulaient**
Plus-que-parfait	**avais voulu, avais voulu, avait voulu, avions voulu, aviez voulu, avaient voulu**
Passé Simple	**voulus, voulus, voulut, voulûmes, voulûtes, voulurent**
Futur Simple	**voudrai, voudras, voudra, voudrons, voudrez, voudront**
Futur Antérieur	**aurai voulu, auras voulu, aura voulu, aurons voulu, aurez voulu, auront voulu**
Conditionnel Présent	**voudrais, voudrais, voudrait, voudrions, voudriez, voudraient**
Conditionnel Passé	**aurais voulu, aurais voulu, aurait voulu, aurions voulu, auriez voulu, auraient voulu**
Subjonctif Présent	**veuille, veuilles, veuille, voulions, vouliez, veuillent**
Subjonctif Passé	**aie voulu, aies voulu, ayons voulu, ayez voulu, aient voulu**
Infinitif Passé	**avoir voulu**
Impératif	**veuille, veuillons, veuillez**

Answers to the Exercises

CHAPTER 1

What Do You Know Already?

1. a	4. b	7. a
2. b	5. b	8. a
3. a	6. a	9. b

Quick Practice

I.
1. seau = "so"
2. parle = "parl"
3. peau = "poe"
4. fou = "foo"
5. hôte = "howt"
6. note = "not"
7. mai = "meh"
8. poli = "polee"
9. bureau = "buro"
10. carré = "kah ray"

II.
1. hybride = "ibrid"
2. brun = "bruh"
3. quantité = "kanteeteh"
4. compagnon = "companyioh"
5. theater = "teh atr"
6. maison = "meh zoh"
7. gagner = "ganyeh"
8. psychologue = "pssee ko log"

III.
1. liaison between **les** and **amis (z)** and **vont** and **aller**.
2. liaison between **des** and **achats (z)**.
3. liaison between **vont** and **ils**.
4. no liaison.
5. no liaison.
6. liaison between **des** and **arbres (z)**.
7. no liaison.
8. no liaison.
9. liaison between **est** and **en**.
10. liaison between **ils** and **ont (z)** and **dix** and **ans (z)**.

IV.   1. c
          2. e
          3. a
          4. d
          5. b

Les homophones

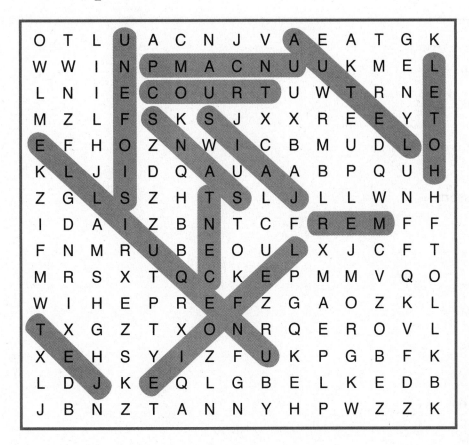

CHAPTER 2
What Do You Know Already?

1. vous
2. tu
3. nous
4. ils/elles
5. il/elle/on
6. ils/elles
7. tu
8. tu
9. il/elle
10. vous

Quick Practice

I.
1. réfléchissons
2. chantez
3. paie
4. nageons
5. fond
6. punit
7. achète
8. espérons
9. rejettent
10. appelles

II.
1. mangeons
2. laisse
3. entrent
4. quittent
5. défie
6. applaudissons
7. rougit
8. descends
9. maigrit
10. essaie
11. hésitez
12. commençons

III.
1. préparons
2. aimons
3. achetons
4. choisissons
5. réussissons
6. entendons
7. mangeons
8. appelons
9. espérons
10. rougissons

IV.
1. Il y a (voici) deux ans que Catherine et André travaillent en Europe.
2. Ils préparent le dîner depuis midi.
3. Il y a (voici) trois mois que Claude projette un voyage aux Etats-Unis.
4. Paul oublie ses devoirs depuis lundi.
5. Il y a (voici) dix ans que Monsieur Berthier espère passer ses vacances à Hawaii.

V.
1. D'habitude j'emporte le parapluie.
2. Il y a une heure que j'étudie.
3. Elle cherche le livre.
4. Il voyage chaque année.
5. Elles ont l'habitude de sortir chaque jour.

VI.
1. choisis, choisissez
2. attends, attendez
3. réussis, réussissez
4. réponds, répondez
5. ne parle pas, ne parlez pas
6. n'hésite pas, n'hésitez pas
7. ne copie pas, ne copies pas
8. ne montre pas, ne montrez pas
9. commence, commencez
10. finis, finissez

Le present des verbes reguliers

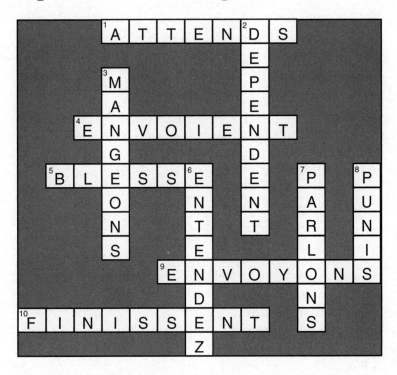

CHAPTER 3

What Do You Know Already?

1. FALSE: **Il pleut** means *it rains*. *He cries* is **il pleure**.
2. FALSE: **Dois** is used for the first and the second persons singular of **devoir**.
3. TRUE
4. TRUE
5. FALSE: **Ne** and **pas** surround the verb.
6. TRUE
7. FALSE: The third person plural of **avoir** is **ont**.
8. TRUE
9. TRUE
10. FALSE: The second person singular of **dire** is **dis**.

Quick Practice

I.
1. faisons
2. va
3. ne voient pas
4. connais
5. sont
6. peignons
7. suivez
8. n'allons pas
9. recevez
10. croyons
11. prennent
12. ennuit
13. faites
14. ne sais pas
15. dors

II.
1. nous pouvons
2. ils font
3. vous recevez
4. nous croyons
5. vous peignez
6. vous partez
7. nous tenons
8. ils prennent
9. nous rions
10. nous écrivons

III.
1. Stéphanie fait-elle ses devoirs maintenant?
2. Ses parents voyagent-ils beaucoup en hiver?
3. Parle-t-il trois langues?
4. Etes-vous fatigué?
5. Jacques veut-il lire ce livre cette semaine?
6. Croient-ils la météo?
7. Ma soeur va-t-elle à la plage?
8. Suivent-ils un cours de maths?
9. Vaut-il mieux finir les devoirs avant d'aller au cinema?
10. Peux-tu sortir maintenant?

IV.
1. N'est-il pas en classe?
2. Ne voyez-vous pas les enfants tous les jours?
3. Ne sort-elle pas souvent?
4. Ne vas-tu pas sortir ce soir?
5. Ne donne-t-il pas ce cadeau à sa femme?
6. Ne partent-ils pas pour New York?
7. Ne vient-elle pas d'arriver?
8. N'avez-vous pas faim?
9. Ne font-ils pas un chateau de sable?
10. Ne reçois-tu pas beaucoup de lettres?

V. 1. Oui je peux…/non, je ne peux pas…
2. Oui, j'écris…/non, je n'écris pas…
3. Oui, je dors…/non, je ne dors pas…
4. Oui, nous commençons…/non, nous ne commençons pas…
5. Oui, j'emploie…/non, je n'emploie pas…

VI. 1. ouvrez
2. lisez
3. sortez
4. soyez
5. ne soyez pas

VII. 1. ne sois pas
2. va chercher
3. ne quitte pas
4. conduis lentement
5. ne mets pas

Le present des verbes irrreguliers

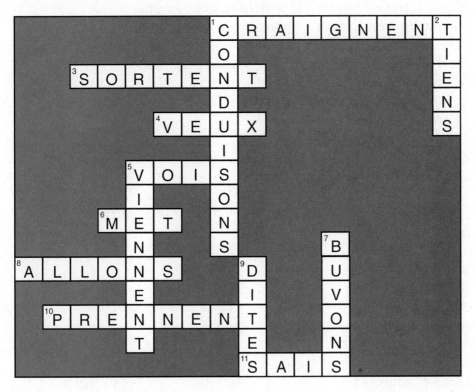

CHAPTER 4
What Do You Know Already?
1. parlaient
2. écrivions
3. allait
4. était
5. écoutiez

6. mangeais
7. avais
8. aimaient
9. riiez
10. buvais

Quick Practice

I. faisait/pleuvait/empêchait/allions/était/c'était/voulait/mangions/essayions/ n'avait pas.

II. 1. était/avait
2. nageait
3. allait/fallait
4. pleurait/permettait
5. s'approchait/aboyait
6. pleuvait

III. 1. Elle n'écoutait jamais ses parents.
2. Nous étudiions ensemble.
3. Il dansait avec Caroline tandis que je dansais avec Josette.
4. Nous commencions toujours à 8 heures.
5. Quand j'avais le temps, j'écrivais des lettres.
6. Elle venait d'acheter une voiture mais elle était trop grande.
7. Si on allait au restaurant?
8. Je lisais pendant qu'elle écrivait une lettre.
9. Nous savions qu'ils venaient à 5 heures.
10. Je ne voulais pas sortir.
11. Depuis quand conduisait-il?
12. Il conduisait depuis janvier.

IV. *(The tense is the imperfect, but the forms—affirmative or negative— are optional.)*
1. lisais/ne lisais pas
2. regardais/ne regardais pas
3. faisais/ne faisais pas
4. faisais/ne faisais pas
5. faisais/ne faisais pas
6. voyageais/ne voyageais pas
7. allais/n'allais pas
8. pratiquais/ne pratiquais pas
9. jouais/ne jouais pas
10. allais/n'allais pas

V. • Depuis combien de temps étiez-vous à la porte du magasin?
• Vous attendiez quelqu'un?
• Depuis quand attendiez vous?
• Quelle heure était-il?
• Comment saviez vous cela?

L'imparfait

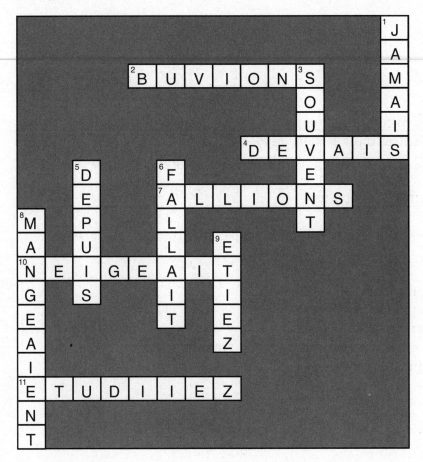

CHAPTER 5
What Do You Know Already?
1. est tombée
2. avons vu
3. ont fini
4. j'ai mangé
5. a dit
6. ont acheté
7. a fermé
8. avez su
9. sont venues
10. as compris

Quick Practice

I.
1. Je suis allée
2. J'ai déjeuné
3. J'ai répondu
4. J'ai mis
5. Je suis rentrée

II.
1. Josette a sorti la voiture du garage.
2. Les élèves sont entrés dans la salle de classe.
3. Le mois dernier, nous avons passé une semaine au bord de la mer.
4. La robe qu'elle a achetée a coûté cher.
5. Elles ont rencontré des copains.

III. a plu/ont décidé/a fallu/sont entrés/n'ont pas trouvé/a dû/n'a pas pu/retrouvés.

IV.
1. Nous n'avons pas bien compris ce passage.
2. Ils sont sortis rapidement.
3. Elle a toujours travaillé dans cette école.
4. Le professeur a encore expliqué cette règle grammaticale.
5. Ils ont conduit prudemment.

V.
1. as laissé
2. a quitté
3. sont partis
4. a quitté
5. a laissés
6. laissez
7. sort
8. quitte
9. laisse
10. quitter

VI.
1. me trouvais
2. étais
3. étais/ne les connassait pas
4. s'agissait
5. savais/étaient/jouions/est arrivé/était/portait
6. avait/brandissait
7. m'a regardée/a jeté/étais/ne pouvais pas
8. était
9. m'as offerte
10. m'a dit/allais
11. étais
12. j'ai rencontré/m'a donné
13. était

Le passé composé

1 (down) DESCENDUS
2 (down) AVONS
3 (down) SOUVI
4 (down) REPONDU
5 (down) LAISSE
6 (across) SORTIES
7 (down) AVANTHIER
8 (across) EU — **8 (down)** ESTALLE
9 (across) PASSES
10 (across) QUITTER
11 B
12 (across) DEVENUS
13 (across) RECEMMENT

CHAPTER 6

What Do You Know Already?

1. a		5. a	
2. b		6. b	
3. a		7. b	
4. b		8. a	

Quick Practice

I.
1. avait plu
2. avait eu
3. n'avait pas été
4. s'était cassée
5. avions dit/n'avait pas voulu

II. Optional responses

III.
1. Le repas avait toujours été préparé par papa.
2. Je n'avais pas reconnu Marie quand je l'ai vue au congrès.
3. Les Lemaître étaient déjà rentrés de voyage quand je les ai vus.
4. J'ai vu Carole le jour de Noël. La veille, elle s'était fiancée.
5. Une fois qu'Alain avait fini ses devoirs, il sortait toujours avec ses amis.
6. Il voulait aller au restaurant parce qu'il n'avait pas encore mangé.
7. Il y avait une semaine qu'elle était malade.

IV. a eu lieu/faisait/est tombée/ne pouvait pas/a dû/l'a transportée/tenait/avait acheté/s'est pas rendu compte/était resté/causait/a téléphoné/l'avait trouvé/est arrivé/lui a dit/n'avait.

V. Composition

Le plus-que-parfait

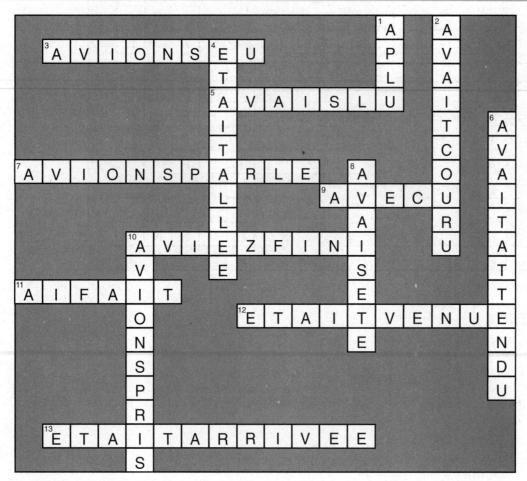

CHAPTER 7

What Do You Know Already?

1. e	6. c
2. h	7. d
3. a	8. f
4. i	9. j
5. b	10. g

Quick Practice

I.
1. se trouve/trouve
2. entendons/s'entendent
3. nous lavons/lavons
4. se trompe
5. achète

II.
1. Hier, Suzanne s'est promenée dans le village.
2. Les élèves que j'ai vus venaient de France.
3. Ils se sont regardés.
4. Elle s'est trouvée dans une rue qu'elle ne connaissait pas.
5. Nous nous sommes trompés d'adresse hier.
6. L'actrice s'est évanouie à la fin de la pièce.
7. Nous nous sommes amusés à la fête.
8. Elle s'est brossé les cheveux avant de sortir.
9. Vous vous êtes rencontrés quand vous étiez à l'université.
10. Elle s'est réveillée de très bonne heure.

III.
1. réveille-toi/réveillez-vous
2. lave-toi/lavez-vous
3. habille-toi/habillez-vous
4. dépêche-toi/dépêchez-vous
5. souviens-toi d'appeler grand-mère/souvenez-vous...

IV.
1. Nous allons nous amuser.
2. Maman va se reposer.
3. Vous pouvez vous baigner tous les jours.
4. Vous allez vous coucher tard.
5. Vous pouvez vous réveiller quand vous voulez.

V.
1. Non, je ne me lave jamais les mains avant le dîner.
2. Non, je ne me brosse pas les dents.
3. Non, je ne me couche jamais à dix heures.
4. Non, je ne me réveille jamais à six heures.
5. Non, je ne vais pas m'acheter un nouveau livre d'anglais.

VI.
1. Ne vous cachez pas tout le temps!
2. Ne t'achète pas un anorak très cher!
3. Ne nous téléphonons pas tous les jours!
4. Ne nous embrassons pas devant tout le monde!
5. Ne te moque pas de mes amis!

VII.
1. s'agit
2. se sont rencontrés/se sont regardés/ne se sont pas parlé
3. se sont-ils vus
4. s'est trompée
5. s'est passé/se sont-ils aperçus
6. se sont rendu compte
7. se sont-ils aimés
8. ils ne se sont pas aimés

VIII. Conversation

IX.
1. s'est maquillée
2. s'est reposée
3. s'est mis
4. se trouvait
5. s'est caché
6. nous amusons
7. s'est salie
8. me suis disputé(e)
9. nous détendons
10. s'embrassent

X. a trébuché/est tombé/s'est tordu/se trouvait/s'est précipité/l'a remercié/ s'est levé/s'est dirigé/a remarqué/a essayé/était/a pu/a été/était.

Les verbes pronominaux

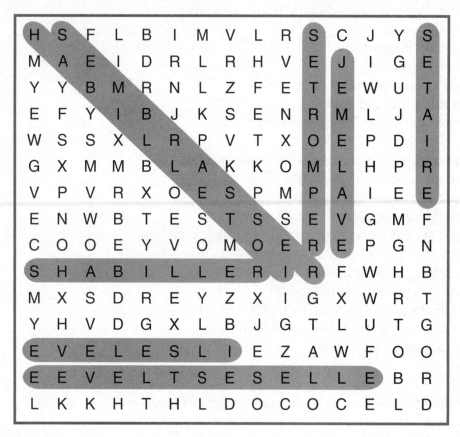

CHAPTER 8
What Do You Know Already?
1. a   5. a
2. b   6. b
3. b   7. a
4. a   8. b

Quick Practice

I.
1. Nager beaucoup, c'est bon pour la forme.
2. Voyager souvent, ça forme la jeunesse.
3. Réfléchir avant de parler, c'est sage.
4. Savoir quand il faut répondre, c'est une bonne idée.
5. Chercher la bonne réponse, ce n'est pas facile.

II.
1. sans
2. avant de
3. afin de /pour
4. avant d'
5. afin de/pour

III.
1. Écouter
2. Lire
3. fermer
4. ne pas sortir
4. regarder

IV.
1. J'entends jouer les enfants/J'entends les enfants jouer.
2. Ils voient arriver le train/Ils voient le train arriver.
3. Nous regardons courir les chevaux/Nous regardons les chevaux courir.
4. Je sens venir un mal de tête/Je sens un mal de tête venir.
5. Elle laisse dormir les enfants/Elle laisse les enfants dormir.

V.
1. L'actrice s'est fait faire un costume original.
2. Le film a fait rire les enfants.
3. Les gâteaux ont fait grossir la jeune fille.
4. Je me suis fait faire (j'ai fait faire) une autre clé pour le bureau.
5. Elle n'a pas fait manger la purée au bébé.

VI.
1. Nous espérons le voir demain.
2. Elle les a fait chanter.
3. Elle leur a fait chanter la chanson.
4. Ne les faites pas sortir.
5. Je les ai laissé tomber.

VII.
1. Après avoir ouvert la fenêtre.
2. Après s'être dépêchés.
3. Avant d'acheter une bicyclette.
4. Avant de sortir.
5. Après avoir fini l'examen.

VIII.
1. Il est important de les écouter.
2. Elle a un travail à faire.
3. La pensée de perdre est terrible.
4. J'ai trois livres à lire ce semestre.
5. Il est facile de parler avec elle.

L'infinitif

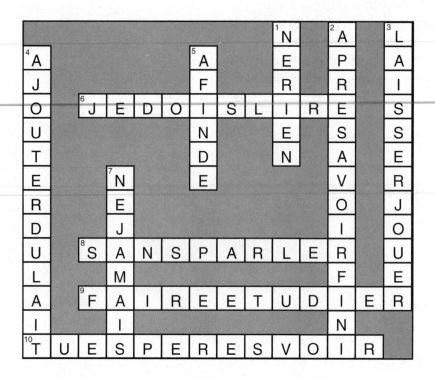

CHAPTER 9

What Do You Know Already?
1. parlâmes
2. naquit
3. ouvrirent
4. allâtes
5. finit
6. oubliai
7. attendis
8. dis

Quick Practice

I. était/était/savaient/annonça/allait/essayèrent/avait/vivait/connaissait/ apprit/était/appela/dit/fit/voulait/prit/commença/fit/prit/mit/dit/alla/ donna/se rendit/dormait/réveilla/donna/se leva/demanda/voulut/dormit/ se réveilla/voulut/avait/fit/fut/était/célébra.

II.
1. La Bastille a été attaquée par le peuple de Paris le 14 juillet 1789.
2. L'ordre de tirer sur la foule a été donné par le gouverneur de la Bastille.
3. Le pont-levis de la forteresse a été baissé.
4. Le gouverneur a été exécuté par la foule.
5. Le 14 juillet a été choisi comme fête nationale par la France en 1880.

III. 1. Christophe était toujours entouré d'amis.
2. On a demandé à Colette de conduire pour aller à l'école.
3. La maison a été détruite par la tornade.
4. On n'a pas trouvé la réponse à ce problème.
5. Le chateau fut (a été) construit en 1600.

IV. 1. Les étudiants ont fermé la porte.
2. On a peint le tableau en 1850.
3. Le professeur a résolu le problème.
4. Plusieurs hommes ont construit la tour.
5. Les élèves aiment le professeur.

Le passe simple

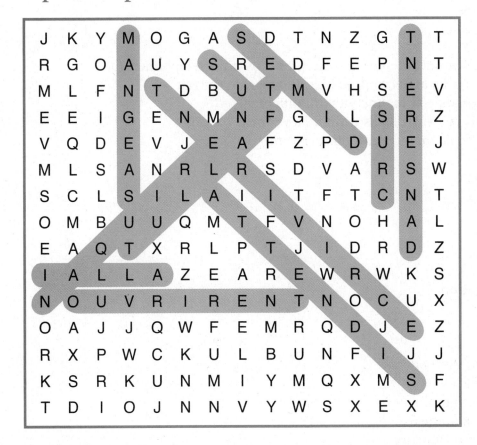

CHAPTER 10

What Do You Know Already?

1. irons
2. finiras
3. commencera
4. viendra
5. prendrai
6. serions
7. pourrions

    8. donnerais
    9. mangerait
   10. aimerais

Quick Practice

I.   1. J'irai
       2. je rendrai visite
       3. je visiterai/que feras-tu
       4. elle voudra aller
       5. il ne pleuvra pas
       6. nous irons
       7. j'irai/je verrai
       8. iras-tu
       9. je passerai
      10. tu aimeras

II.   1. Quand ils voudront aller au restaurant, ils nous téléphoneront.
       2. Aussitôt qu'ils arriveront, je leur donnerai le cadeau.
       3. Je me demande si Jeanne viendra dimanche.
       4. Je ne suis pas sûr(e) s'ils iront à New York.
       5. Il ira à l'école quand l'autobus arrivera.

III.   1. arriveront
       2. fera beau
       3. pleut
       4. était
       5. j'ai faim

IV.   Conversation

V.   Rédaction

VI.   1. aura compris/pourra
       2. traversera
       3. verrai/donnerai
       4. J'aurai économisé
       5. auras reçus/pourras

VII.   1. J'aimerais
       2. J'épouserais
       3. Je vivrais
       4. J'aurais
       5. J'achèterais
       6. Je verrais
       7. Je porterais
       8. Je pourrais
       9. Je dormirais
      10. Je recevrais

VIII.
1. ne sortiront pas
2. aurait été difficile
3. êtes
4. finira
5. pourrais
6. auriez su
7. viendra
8. aurait dévasté
9. je quitte
10. pourriez-vous?

IX. Rédaction

X.
1. Elle a dû abréger son voyage
2. je devais lire
3. tu devrais
4. J'aurais dû
5. il a dû

Le futur et le conditionnel

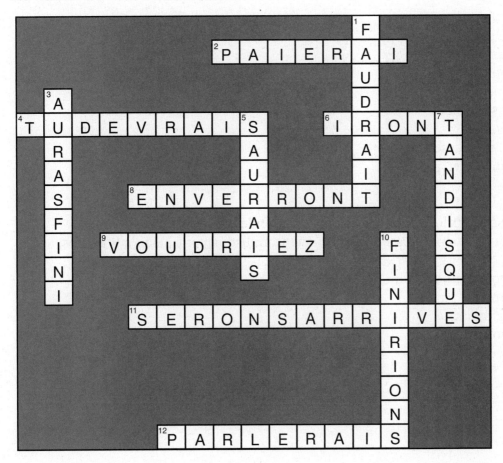

CHAPTER 11

What Do You Know Already?

1. sois
2. mangions
3. fasse
4. sente
5. finissiez
6. lisent
7. aies
8. entende
9. parlent
10. nagions

Quick Practice

I.
1. tu nettoies
2. vous rangiez
3. tu écoutes
4. vous jetiez
5. vous téléphoniez

II.
1. tu viennes
2. elle soit
3. vous preniez
4. il ne comprend pas
5. je fasse
6. vous ouvriez
7. ils savent
8. elle ne puisse pas
9. il ne pleuve pas
10. ils sont

III.
1. fasse attention/finisse le chapitre/réponde aux questions.
2. aient le temps/puissent arriver avant midi/dormant jusqu'à 9 heures.

IV.
1. Il nous faut acheter
2. Il lui faut partir
3. Il te faut dire
4. Il vous faut
5. Il me faut

V.
1. aillent voir
2. boive
3. sache
4. fassent
5. voie

VI.
1. Ma soeur espère que nous allons jouer au tennis.
2. Monique s'étonne qu'ils soient en retard.
3. Papa exige que nous fassions nos devoirs.
4. Maman veut que je prenne mon imper.
5. Marie-Christine est triste de ne pas pouvoir aller voir cette pièce.
6. Je souhaite qu'elle fasse attention.
7. Nous pensons qu'elle est chez elle.
8. Pierre ne croit pas que Suzanne soit fâchée.
9. J'insiste qu'il vienne à l'heure en classe.
10. Elle s'étonne que je ne comprenne pas.

VII. Conversation

VIII.
1. Bien qu'elle soit malade, elle fait ses devoirs.
2. J'explique encore une fois pour que vous compreniez.
3. Ils iront à la plage à condition qu'il fasse beau.
4. Connaissez-vous quelqu'un qui sache le chinois?
5. Elle s'occupe du chien des voisins jusqu'à ce qu'ils reviennent.
6. Je répondrai à ses lettres pourvu qu'il m'écrive.
7. Michel range ses affaires de peur que sa mère soit furieuse.
8. J'ai lu le livre en attendant que le film sorte.

IX.
1. C'est dommage que vous ne soyez pas allé les voir.
2. J'ai peur qu'il ait oublié le rendez-vous.
3. Je suis heureuse qu'ils soient ici.
4. Mon professeur veut que nous soyons toujours à l'heure.
5. Il est possible que Patrick ait déjà visité ce musée.
6. Elle est contente que nous soyons allés la voir.
7. Je suis désolé que vous n'ayez pas pu rester plus longtemps.
8. Fabienne est heureuse que sa fille ait eu une bonne note.
9. Il faut qu'il fasse attention.
10. Elle doute que Pierre soit en Europe.

Le subjonctif

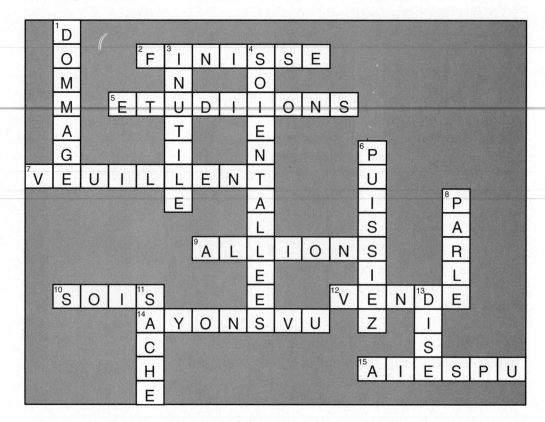

CHAPTER 12

What Do You Know Already?

1. connaissant
2. parlant
3. disant
4. ayant
5. finissant
6. allant
7. attendant
8. écrivant
9. venant
10. partant

Quick Practice

I.
1. courant
2. aimant
3. sortant
4. ne sachant pas
5. sortant

II.
1. Cette histoire est intéressante.
2. La course est un sport excellent.
3. Mon frère aime lire.
4. Les enfants jouent.
5. Sachant qu'il pleuvait, elle a pris son parapluie.

III.
1. en apprenant
2. en vendant
3. courant
4. souriante
5. en grandissant
6. pensant
7. en mangeant
8. récitant
9. en bavardant
10. étant

IV.
1. Ayant étudié jusqu'à minuit.
2. Étant arrivé(e)(s) tôt.
3. Ayant quitté à minuit.
4. Ayant été malade.
5. Ayant ouvert la fenêtre.

V.
1. Il demande avec qui nous sortons.
2. Elle dit qu'elle est fatiguée.
3. Nous demandons s'ils sont occupés.
4. Elle nous dit d'aller au parc.
5. Je me demande s'ils vont à la plage.
6. Elle demande qui vient avec nous.
7. Son père ordonne qu'il se taise.
8. Il me conseille de lire ce livre.
9. Elle me demande quel film je veux voir.
10. Il me dit de ne pas oublier mon sac.

VI.
1. Le professeur a dit qu'il expliquerait ce problème.
2. Elle m'a demandé avec qui je viendrais.
3. Il a écrit qu'il aimerait m'inviter (nous inviter).
4. Je me demande avec quoi ils vont écrire.
5. Elle m'a expliqué qu'elle n'avait pas compris.
6. Il suggère que je finisse avant le dîner.
7. Elle a demandé si j'avais oublié la réponse.
8. Elle m'a dit qu'elle avait vu Pierre la veille.
9. Mon père exige que je fasse mes devoirs.
10. Maman a dit que la lettre était arrivée ce matin-là.

Le participe présent

```
V T M L D W F V G X F O H T Q
X I N U W X J Z V C Y T Z N E
F O V A E W S A L B A X T A D
H X J D V O L T F E W G F Y O
Q H H B G U N J I J B V H O X
U W N H P A B T N A L I I V J
N Z U Z E A U V I V X H C C G
W R M G Y M D J S R N Q J H A
H H N G F T C K S C F J T Y P
M A T N A S I D A W M N J R E
M A K W Z Q P G N H A X S P I
P N P B I Q R B T Y D E K H N
A C P O G R D J A T R C X Z O
V V I L X T E T A N T H R X P
H F E N S A C H A N T X O T D
```

CHAPTER 13

What Do You Know Already?

1. les	6. une
2. l'	7. des
3. la	8. un
4. le	9. des
5. les	10. une

Quick Practice

I. le discours/une jeune femme/un homme/le bras/des histoires/Le Premier
    Ministre/au peuple/l'argent/aux arts/la vérité/le théâtre/le cinéma/
    la musique/pianiste/un budget.

II. 1. la
     2. des
     3. les
     4. des
     5. de
     6. de

7. –
8. la/l'
9. –
10. une/de

III.

—Pierre, où sont les pommes?
—Il n'y avait pas de pommes, j'ai acheté des oranges.
—Est-ce que, tu as acheté du lait?
—Oui, j'ai acheté deux bouteilles de lait.
—As-tu trouvé les haricots verts?
—Oui, mais je n'aime pas les haricots verts.
—Je sais, mais as-tu acheté les haricots verts?
—Oui, j'ai acheté les haricots verts et aussi les pommes de terre.
—Et les fromages?
—Oui, voici les fromages.
—Mais tu as seulement acheté deux fromages!
—Je n'avais pas assez d'argent.

IV.

1. Angélique est allée au Sénégal, à Dakar.
2. Patrick est allé au Canada, à Montréal.
3. Geneviève est allée en Norvège, à Oslo.
4. Jean-Pierre et Paulette sont allés en Angleterre, à Londres.
5. David est allé en Egypte, au Caire.

V.

1. Salwa vient de Beyrouth au Liban.
2. Holger vient de Stockholm en Suède.
3. Mona vient du Caire, en Egypte.
4. Anna vient de Milan en Italie.
5. Hiroshi vient de Tokyo au Japon.

VI.

Traduction:
They slowly went down the Bréda quarter; because it was Sunday, the streets were deserted, and faces of bourgeois appeared (could be seen) behind windows. The carriage began to go faster; the sound of the wheels made the passers-by turn around; the leather of the open top was shining, the servant braced his chest, and the two dogs sitting near each other looked like ermine muffs on the pillows.

VII.

1. au Havre
2. à Paris
3. de Floride
4. à Sydney
5. au Maroc.

VIII.

Rédaction

Les articles

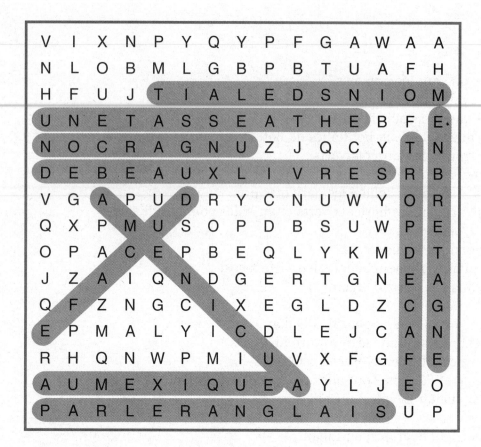

```
V I X N P Y Q Y P F G A W A A
N L O B M L G B P B T U A F H
H F U J T I A L E D S N I O M
U N E T A S S E A T H E B F E
N O C R A G N U Z J Q C Y T N
D E B E A U X L I V R E S R B
V G A P U D R Y C N U W Y O R
Q X P M U S O P D B S U W P E
O P A C E P B E Q L Y K M D T
J Z A I Q N D G E R T G N E A
Q F Z N G C I X E G L D Z C G
E P M A L Y I C D L E J C A N
R H Q N W P M I U V X F G F E
A U M E X I Q U E A Y L J E O
P A R L E R A N G L A I S U P
```

CHAPTER 14
What Do You Know Already?
1. TRUE
2. FALSE: **Amis** is the plural of **ami**.
3. TRUE
4. TRUE
5. FALSE: The noun **médecin** is always masculine.
6. TRUE
7. TRUE
8. FALSE: The feminine of **fou** is **folle**.
9. TRUE
10. TRUE

Quick Practice

I.
1. le
2. le
3. la
4. le
5. la
6. le
7. le
8. le
9. l'
10. l'

II.
1. la
2. une
3. la
4. un
5. un
6. le
7. un
8. le
9. le
10. la

III.
1. J'ai vu un cheval./Et moi, j'ai vu trois chevaux.
2. J'ai rencontre un jeune homme./Et moi j'ai rencontré trois jeunes gens.
3. J'ai eu un pneu crevé./Et moi j'ai eu trois pneus crevés.
4. J'ai jeté un caillou./Et moi, j'ai jeté trois cailloux.
5. J'ai lu un journal./Et moi j'ai lu trois journaux.
6. Je suis allé à un bal./Et mois je suis allé à trois bals.
7. J'ai vu un hibou./Et moi j'ai vu trois hiboux.
8. J'ai offert un cadeau./Et moi j'ai offert trois cadeaux.
9. J'ai visité un château./Et moi j'ai visité trois châteaux.
10. J'ai peint un tableau./Et moi j'ai peint trois tableaux.

IV.
1. C'est
2. Il est
3. Elle est
4. C'est
5. C'est
6. Il est
7. C'est
8. C'est
9. Elle est
10. C'est

Les noms

Crossword puzzle:

- 1 (down): LACREPE
- 2 (down): LADANSEUSE
- 3 (across): UNE IMAGE
- 4 (down): LATOUR
- 5 (down): LEPOMMIER
- 6 (across): UN AUTEUR
- 7 (across): LE COURAGE
- 8 (down): LENTEMMENTOININ — L E C O U R A G E / LE (down): LE
- 9 (across): UNE VICTIME
- 10 (across): LE COMMUNISME

CHAPTER 15

What Do You Know Already?

1. g	6. c
2. a	7. d
3. h	8. e
4. b	9. j
5. i	10. f

Quick Practice

I.
1. publique
2. ennuyeuse
3. méchante
4. gentille
5. chère
6. bête
7. favorite
8. douce
9. noire
10. finale

II. magnifique/bel/pluvieux/petite/gentille/jolie/rouge/grandes/merveilleux/
adorables.

III.
1. le jour même
2. ta propre voiture
3. un soldat brave
4. un garçon pauvre
5. la seule femme

IV.
1. The very day of his(her) arrival, it began to rain.
2. Take your own car, not your father's.
3. He is a brave soldier; he is not afraid to fight.
4. He's a poor boy; he cannot afford a car.
5. The only woman I love is you, my darling.

V.
1. Oui, il parle méchamment.
2. Oui, elle a répondu impatiemment.
3. Oui, il explique patiemment.
4. Oui, il parle nerveusement.
5. Oui, il a répondu honnêtement.

VI.
1. Je suis fatiguée parce que hier soir j'ai mal dormi.
2. Ils voyageaient beaucoup autrefois, mais plus maintenant.
3. Mes deux frères se disputent constamment.
4. Ils s'aiment profondément.
5. Il faut absolument voir ce film; il est merveilleux.
6. Elle ne parle pas bien anglais.
7. Tu m'aimes? Et bien, moi je t'aime davantage.
8. Elle conduit toujours prudemment.
9. Je ne sais pas pourquoi il parle toujours d'un ton brusque.
10. Il a essayé de comprendre sans succès.

VII.
1. toute
2. tous
3. toute
4. tous
5. tout
6. toutes
7. tout
8. tout
9. tout
10. toutes

Adjectifs et adverbes

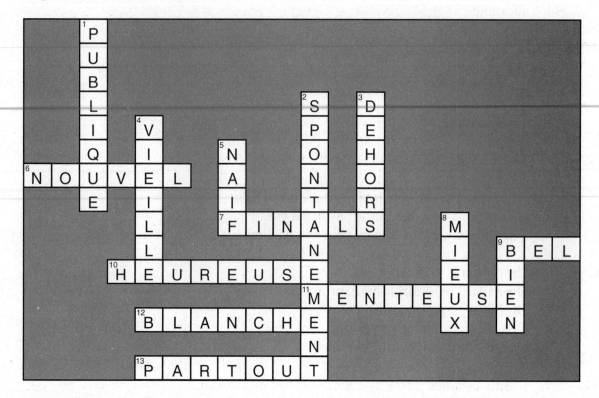

CHAPTER 16

What Do You Know Already?

1. b	5. b
2. b	6. a
3. a	7. a
4. b	8. b

Quick Practice

I.
1. Elle lui a dit bonjour.
2. Je l'ai achetée.
3. Marc les a oubliés.
4. Il me la dit.
5. Il le leur a offert.
6. Louis et Colette me l'ont demandée.
7. Nous le lui montrons.
8. Tu lui as parlé.
9. Nous les étudions.
10. Il me l'a montrée.

II.
1. Ce livre m'appartient.
2. Les fleurs? Il les lui a données.
3. Ils l'ont reçue hier.
4. Ils leur ont obéi.
5. Henriette lui a téléphoné.

III.
1. Oui, j'en ai acheté deux.
2. Oui, j'en ai pris.
3. Oui, j'y vais.
4. Oui, j'ai peur de ne pas y réussir.
5. Oui, j'en ai étudié plusieurs.
6. Oui, j'y ai passé la journée.
7. Oui, je m'en suis occupé.
8. Oui, je lui en ai envoyé une.
9. Oui, j'en ai mangé.
10. Oui, ils en ont chanté beaucoup.

IV.
1. Je les y ai vus.
2. Je vais la lui prêter.
3. Nous la lui avons racontée.
4. Il la lui donne.
5. Elle en a étudié.

V.
1. Ils viennent chez moi et ensuite ils vont chez toi.
2. Elle a préparé un repas spécial pour lui.
3. Il lui écrit pou lui demander si elle aimerait sortir avec lui.
4. Asseyez-vous derrière moi.
5. Je lui parle parce que je me fie à elle.
6. Nous pensons à lui.
7. Je me suis habituée à eux car je les connais depuis longtemps.
8. Cette voiture ne leur appartient pas, elle m'appartient.
9. Je ne m'y intéresse pas.
10. C'est toi qu'il aime.

VI.
1. C'est toi (vous) que j'ai vu hier.
2. Je ne peux pas vivre sans toi (vous).
3. Ni lui ni moi.
4. Je pense à eux.
5. Je n'y suis pas habitué(e).
6. Je ne suis pas habitué(e) à elle.
7. Envoie-le(la) lui.
8. Il travaille avec moi.
9. Viens chez moi.
10. Je ne veux pas sortir! Moi non plus.

Le pronoms personnels

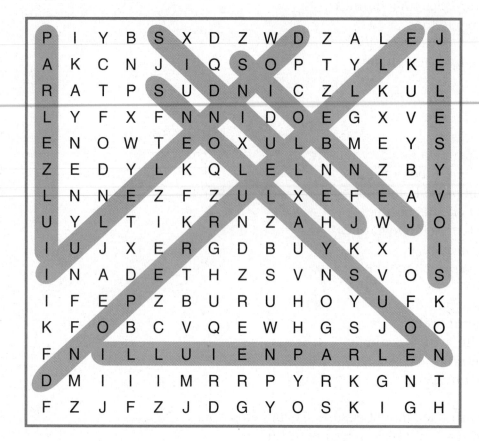

P	I	Y	B	S	X	D	Z	W	D	Z	A	L	E	J
A	K	C	N	J	I	Q	S	O	P	T	Y	L	K	E
R	A	T	P	S	U	D	N	I	C	Z	L	K	U	L
L	Y	F	X	F	N	N	I	D	O	E	G	X	V	E
E	N	O	W	T	E	O	X	U	L	B	M	E	Y	S
Z	E	D	Y	L	K	Q	L	E	L	N	N	Z	B	Y
L	N	N	E	Z	F	Z	U	L	X	E	F	E	A	V
U	Y	L	T	I	K	R	N	Z	A	H	J	W	J	O
I	U	J	X	E	R	G	D	B	U	Y	K	X	I	I
I	N	A	D	E	T	H	Z	S	V	N	S	V	O	S
I	F	E	P	Z	B	U	R	U	H	O	Y	U	F	K
K	F	O	B	C	V	Q	E	W	H	G	S	J	O	O
F	N	I	L	L	U	I	E	N	P	A	R	L	E	N
D	M	I	I	I	M	R	R	P	Y	R	K	G	N	T
F	Z	J	F	Z	J	D	G	Y	O	S	K	I	G	H

CHAPTER 17

What Do You Know Already?

1. mon
2. tes
3. leur
4. notre
5. vos
6. cet
7. cette
8. ces
9. ces
10. ce

Quick Practice

I.
1. Sa maison.
2. Son amie Marie.
3. Vos professeurs.
4. Notre famille.
5. Leurs livres.
6. Les vacances de Laure.
7. Le parapluie est à Laure.
8. Mon ami Alain.
9. Le livre est à moi.
10. Je n'ai pas vu vos amis (tes amis).

II.
1. les miens
2. la tienne
3. les leurs
4. du mien
5. la vôtre
6. au leur
7. aux siens
8. le mien
9. le vôtre
10. les tiennes

III.
1. ce/cette
2. ce
3. cette
4. ces
5. cette
6. ce/ce
7. cet
8. cet

IV.
1. celle
2. celui-ci
3. celle-ci/celle-là
4. celui-ci/celui-là
5. celui
6. ceux
7. ceux
8. cela

V. Rédaction

VI. Message

Possessifs et demonstratifs

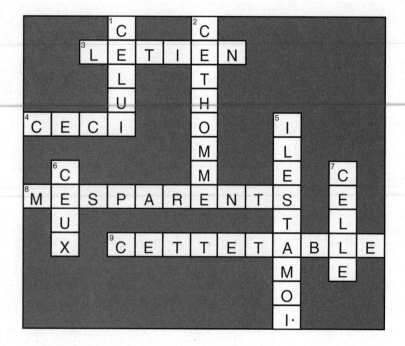

CHAPTER 18
What Do You Know Already?

1.	b	5.	b
2.	b	6.	a
3.	a	7.	b
4.	b	8.	a

Quick Practice

I.
1. qui
2. qui
3. qui
4. que
5. que
6. qu'
7. qui
8. qu'
9. qui
10. qu'

II.
1. dont
2. dont
3. qui
4. que
5. dont
6. dont

7. dont
8. qui
9. que
10. qu'

III. 1. qui/laquelle
      2. auquel
      3. auxquels
      4. duquel
      5. auquel
      6. lesquels
      7. laquelle
      8. lequel
      9. qui/lequel
      10. qui/laquelle

IV.   1. La jeune fille avec qui (laquelle) il va se marier.
      2. La maison autour de laquelle il y a un grand jardin.
      3. Le spectacle auquel nous avons assisté était excellent.
      4. La femme à qui j'ai parlé était très gentille.
      5. Le film auquel je pense est très long.

V.   1. qu'
      2. que
      3. d'où
      4. où
      5. que
      6. où
      7. où
      8. où
      9. d'où
      10. que

VI.   1. ce qu'
      2. Ce dont
      3. Ce qui
      4. ce qui
      5. ce qui
      6. ce à quoi
      7. ce que
      8. Ce qui

VII. 1. celle que
      2. ceux que
      3. Celui dont
      4. celles que
      5. Celui dont

Les pronoms relatifs

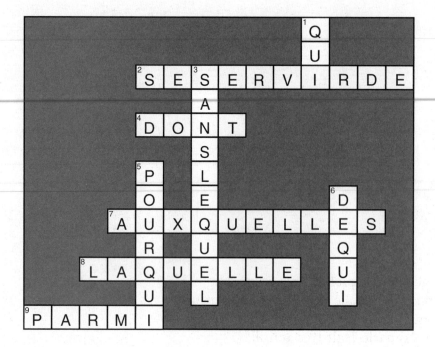

CHAPTER 19

What Do You Know Already?

1. Elle cherche son livre.
2. Je vais à la boulangerie.
3. Tu finis de faire tes devoirs.
4. Ils vont à l'école en voiture.
5. Nous faisons nos devoirs pendant que nous écoutons la radio.
6. Ils entrent dans la salle de classe.
7. Je téléphone à mes parents.
8. Elle a fait ses devoirs en une heure.

Quick Practice

I.
1. envers
2. après
3. au
4. à
5. à
6. à
7. de
8. de
9. de
10. à

II.
1. As-tu (avez-vous) fini de faire tes(vos) devoirs?
2. J'ai écrit cette rédaction (cet essai) en quatre heures.
3. Tu me manques beaucoup (vous me manquez)
4. Il a dit à ses élèves (étudiants) d'écrire un poème.
5. Je suis allé(e) chez le dentiste.

III.
1. depuis
2. pour
3. pendant
4. pendant
5. depuis

IV.
1. dans
2. au
3. de
4. d'
5. aux
6. en
7. en
8. de
9. du
10. à

V.
1. Je cherche une voiture.
2. Ces tasses à thé sont jolies.
3. Il parle à voix haute (à haute voix).
4. Je voyage depuis hier.
5. Le professeur d'anglais n'est pas ici aujourd'hui.

VI.
1. Delphine va au cinéma tandis que Paulette va chez ses amis.
2. Après que j'ai vu le film, maman m'a offert le livre.
3. Lorsque Patrick vient, il apporte un dessert.
4. Elle mange puisqu'elle a faim.
5. Quand le train arrive, l'horloge sonne.

Les prepositions

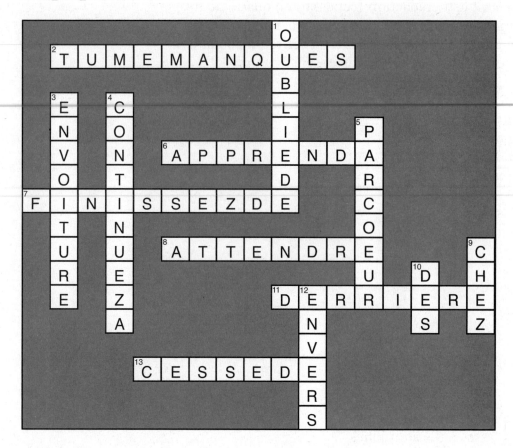

The crossword puzzle contains the following answers:

Across:
- 2. TUMEMANQUES
- 6. APPRENDA
- 7. FINISSEZDE
- 8. ATTENDRE
- 11. DERRIERE
- 13. CESSEDE

Down:
- 1. OBLIDED
- 2. TUTURE (FUTURE)
- 3. ENVOYOTURE
- 4. CONTINUEZA
- 5. PARCOUREUS
- 9. CHEZ
- 10. DES
- 12. ENVERS

CHAPTER 20

What Do You Know Already?

1. plus intelligente que
2. plus de temps que
3. moins d'argent que
4. aussi grand (grande) que
5. moins fatigué que
6. moins que
7. plus de devoirs que
8. aussi bon (bonne) que

Quick Practice

I.
1. mieux que
2. aussi élégante
3. a autant de patience que
4. moins fatiguée
5. autant que

II.   Conversation

III.
1. autant
2. aussi
3. aussi

4. autant
5. autant

IV.
1. la meilleure agence
2. le pire
3. la plus belle
4. l'hôtel le plus élégant
5. la plage la plus calme

V.
1. le meilleur
2. le moins sportif
3. le plus intéressant
4. la plus célèbre
5. le moins long

VI. plus, comme, de plus, comme, davantage, plus, plus, plus, plus, plus, plus.

VII.
1. Nicole parle comme un enfant.
2. Comme j'étais fatigué(e), je ne suis pas sorti(e).
3. Je voyage beaucoup, mais tu voyages davantage.
4. J'ai plus de patience que toi (vous).
5. Il ne joue pas au tennis. Moi non plus.

La comparaison

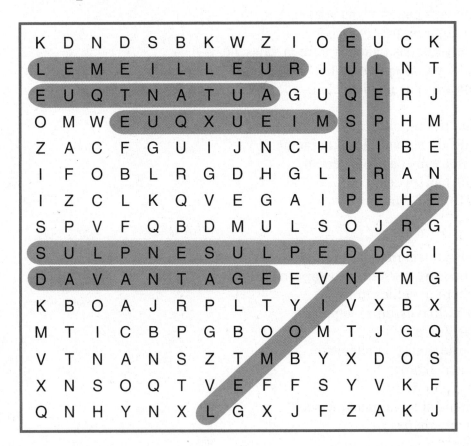

CHAPTER 21
What Do You Know Already?
1. Elle n'a pas étudié.
2. Nous ne nous réveillons pas avant dix heures.
3. Ne courez pas; c'est dangereux.
4. Je ne vais pas finir avant six heures.
5. Ils n'ont pas de devoirs.
6. Tu n'écoutes jamais le professeur.
7. Il ne fait rien!
8. Personne n'est arrivé en retard.

Quick Practice
I.
1. Elle n'a pas acheté de bijoux.
2. Il n'a pas écrit de lettre à sa fiancée.
3. N'as-tu pas vu les voisins?
4. N'étaient-ils pas fatigués après le voyage?
5. Elle ne veut pas voyager en été.
6. Nous n'aimons pa la salade.
7. Je n'ai pas rencotré Maurice au café.
8. Il ne travaille pas dans un supermarché.
9. N'ont-ils pas passé un examen hier?
10. Je ne peux pas conduire.

II.
1. Non, je ne vais pas finir ma soupe.
2. Non, je n'ai pas appris ma leçon.
3. Non, je ne veux pas t'aider à faire la vaisselle.
4. Non, je n'ai pas téléphoné à tant Lucie pour la remercier.
5. Non, je ne vais pas me dépêcher.

III.
1. Il dit de ne pas répondre.
2. Elle m'a dit de ne pas aller au cinéma.
3. Nous ne pouvons pas voir l'écran.
4. Ne sont-ils pas sortis?
5. Ne viens-tu pas? Oui!

IV.   Moi,
1. je ne perds jamais rien.
2. je n'ai rencontré personne au supermarché.
3. je n'ai acheté ni cahier ni livre.
4. je n'aime ni le poisson ni le poulet.
5. je n'étudie guère.
6. je ne regarde jamais la télévision.
7. je n'ai plus d'argent.
8. rien ne me plaît ici.
9. je n'ai jamais aimé la musique rock.
10. je n'ai aucun chapeau.

V.
1. Rien n'est intéressant dans ce livre.
2. Es-tu (êtes-vous) jamais allé en Alaska?
3. Je n'ai pas acheté une nouvelle voiture. Moi non plus.
4. Ils n'ont rencontré que Sara.
5. Personne n'a vu Jean-Claude hier.
6. Elle ne comprend rien.
7. Nous n'avons acheté ni crayons ni stylos.
8. Je ne vois guère le directeur.
9. Je ne suis allé(e) nulle part hier.
10. Je n'ai pas encore reçu les fleurs.

VI.
1. Elle n'offre jamais de café à personne.
2. Nous ne voyons jamais personne chez les voisins.
3. Il n'y a jamais rien d'intéressant à la télé.
4. Paul ne fait jamais rien en classe.
5. Personne n'est jamais absent.

VII.
1. quelqu'un de
2. quelqu'un d'
3. rien d'
4. personne de
5. quelqu'un de

La negation

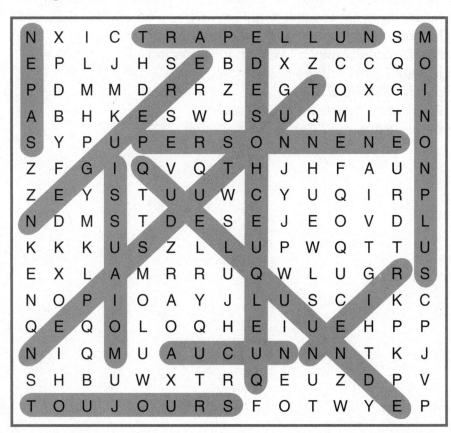

CHAPTER 22

What Do You Know Already?

1. (a) Est-ce qu'ils travaillent beaucoup?
   (b) Travaillent-ils beaucoup?
2. (a) Est-ce que nous avons faim?
   (b) Avons-nous faim?
3. (a) Est-ce que tu es allé au cinéma?
   (b) Es-tu allé au cinéma?
4. (a) Est-ce qu'il a vendu sa voiture?
   (b) A-t-il vendu sa voiture?
5. (a) Est-ce qu'elle parle à ses amis?
   (b) Parle-t-elle à ses amis?

Quick Practice

I.
1. As-tu étudié hier soir?
2. As-tu compris la troisième partie?
3. Ta mère est-elle professeur?
4. Enseigne-t-elle la trigonométrie?
5. T'a-t-elle aidé?
6. Veux-tu que je te l'explique?

II.
1. Est-ce que vous aimez…? Aimez-vous…?
2. Est-ce qu'ils se sont réveillés…? Se sont-ils réveillés…?
3. Est-ce qu'Alain a oublié…? Alain a-t-il oublié…?
4. Est-ce que Jacqueline s'est couchée tard? Jacqueline s'est-elle couchée tard?
5. Est-ce que les enfants….? Les enfants se sont-ils…?
6. Est-ce qu'elles veulent écouter…? Veulent-elles écouter…?
7. Est-ce que je peux sortir…? Puis-je sortir…?
8. Est-ce qu'il a fait…? A-t-il fait…?
9. Est-ce qu'elle achète…? Achète-t-elle…?
10. Est-ce que Caroline a fait …? Caroline a-t-elle fait…?

III.
1. Quelle
2. Quel
3. quels
4. Quel
5. Quels

IV.
1. Qu'est-ce que
2. Qui
3. Qu'est-ce que
4. Que
5. Qui est-ce que
6. qui
7. Qu'est-ce que
8. quoi
9. Qui (Qui est-ce qui)
10. Que

V.
1. Qu'est-ce que vous mangez?
2. Qui a posé la question?
3. Qu'est-ce qu'elle t'a offert/Que t'a-t-elle offert?
4. Qui as-tu rencontré au café/Qui est-ce que tu as rencontré au café?
5. Qu'est-ce que c'est que le Sahara?

VI.
1. lequel
2. lequel
3. lesquels
4. lesquelles
5. lesquelles

VII.
1. A laquelle
2. Auquel
3. Duquel
4. Auquel
5. Desquels

VIII.
1. Quand
2. Où
3. Comment
4. qui
5. Combien
6. Pourquoi
7. Qui
8. Quel
9. Quand
10. Qui

Les interrogatifs

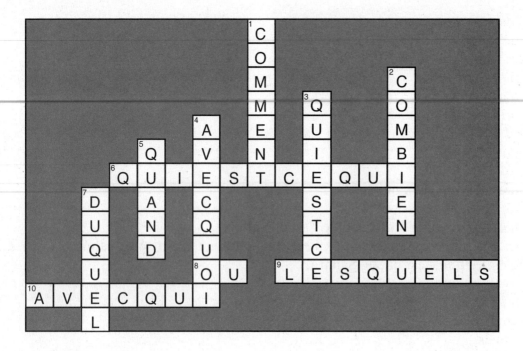

CHAPTER 23

What Do You Know Already?

1. i	6. c
2. f	7. e
3. a	8. f
4. g	9. d
5. b	10. h

Quick Practice

I.
1. onze
2. quarante cinq
3. soixante-douze
4. quatre-vingt-dix-sept
5. cent deux
6. cent soixante-cinq
7. trois cent quatre-vingt-dix
8. quatre cent soixante-quinze
9. neuf cent dix-huit
10. neuf cent soixante-dix
11. mille cent cinquante et un
12. douze mille cinq
13. cent cinquante-neuf mille
14. un million cent quarante mille
15. quatre millions cent mille

II.   Conversation

III.   1. premier
           2. premiers
           3. quarante et unième
           4. deuxième
           5. vingt-septième
           6. dixième
           7. cinquième
           8. cent unième
           9. mille et une
          10. trentième

IV.   1. Une quinzaine de roses
           2. Le cinquantième jour
           3. Une trentaine d'étudiants (élèves)
           4. Des centaines de jouets
           5. Henri Huit

V.   1. Le dix-huit avril mille neuf cent quatre-vingt-onze
           2. Le vingt août mille neuf cent quatre-vingt-quatorze
           3. Le vingt-deux août mille neuf cent quatre-vingt-seize
           4. Le cinq juillet deux mille quatre
           5. Le dix juillet deux mille quatre
           6. Le quatorze juillet deux mille quatre
           7. Le dix-huit juillet deux mille quatre
           8. Le cinq août deux mille quatre
           9. Le six septembre deux mille cinq
          10. Le vingt-cinq décembre deux mille cinq

VI.   1. b   5. a
           2. a   6. b
           3. b   7. b
           4. a   8. a

VII.   Rédaction

VIII. 1. Deux heures et quart
           2. Sept heures dix
           3. Six heures trente-cinq *ou* sept heures moins vingt-cinq
           4. Onze heures vingt
           5. Midi
           6. Treize heures quarante-cinq *ou* quatorze heures moins le quart
           7. Dix-sept heures trente
           8. Dix-neuf heures sept
           9. Vingt-trois heures dix-huit
          10. Minuit

IX.
1. Nous sommes en retard.
2. Il est cinq heures précises.
3. Ma montre avance de cinq minutes.
4. Elle s'est levée de bonne heure dimanche.
5. Il est minuit.
6. À quelle heure te couches-tu? (vous couches-vous)
7. Ta montre retarde.
8. Le train est à l'heure.

Le nombres, les dates et les heures

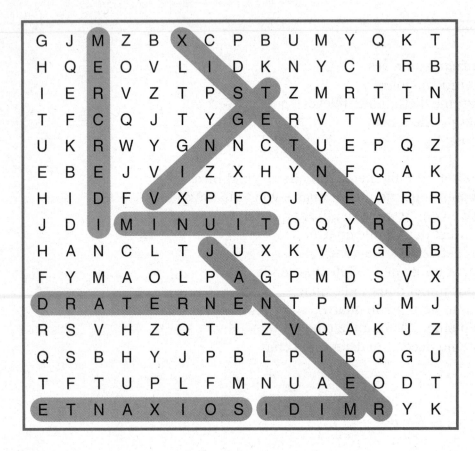

Index

charts of, 325–345
de after, 237–239
direct object pronoun placement before, 200
-er, 104, 325
followed by subjunctive, 134–135
infinitive followed by, 207–208
-ir. See -ir verbs
irregular. *See* Irregular verbs
in past conditional, 121–123
in present conditional, 120–121
pronominal. *See* Pronominal verbs
-re. See -re verbs
reflexive. *See* Reflexive verbs
regular. *See* Regular verbs
superlative placement after, 252–253
vivre, 344

Vocabulary, 303–318
Voici . . . que, 26
Voilà . . . que, 26
voir, 344
vouloir, 84, 345
Vowels, 3–5

W

Weights, 160
When, 116–118
Where, 231–232
Which, 225–226
Which and whom, 225–226
Who, 225–226
Whose, 227–228

Y

y, 204–206

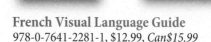